words of life

COLUMBIA UNION CONFERENCE

YEAR OF THE BIBLE DEVOTIONAL BOOK

Featuring Favorite Bible Verses From Members

Ricardo Bacchus, Editor

Words of Life
Columbia Union Conference
2021 Year of the Bible Devotional Book

Editor: Ricardo Bacchus
Publisher and Project Manager: Celeste Ryan Blyden
Art Director and Production Manager: Kelly Butler Coe
Promotions Manager: V. Michelle Bernard
Copyeditors and Proofreaders: Beth Thomas, Lisa Krueger and Sandra Jones
Translator: Domitila Rosette
Project Assistant: Shirley Rowley
Design: TM Design, Inc.

Published by Columbia Union Conference of Seventh-day Adventists
5427 Twin Knolls Road, Columbia, MD 21045 • columbiaunion.org

Devotionals included in this book were submitted in 2020 with the written consent of each author. Views and opinions are those of each author and do not necessarily represent the Columbia Union Conference, the Seventh-day Adventist Church, or the editors.

Additional copies available, while supplies last. To order, call Pacific Press® Publishing Association at (800) 447-7377, and ask for "Columbia Union Devotional."

Scripture quotations in this devotional book quote the following Bible versions:

Scriptures quoted from CEV are from the Contemporary English Version®. Copyright © 1995 American Bible Society. All rights reserved.

Scripture quotations marked ESV are from *The Holy Bible*, English Standard Version® (ESV®), copyright © 2001 by Crossway, a publishing ministry of Good News Publishers. Used by permission. All rights reserved.

Scriptures quoted from ICB are from the International Children's Bible®, copyright © 1986, 1988, 1999, 2015 by Tommy Nelson. Used by permission. All rights reserved.

Scripture quotations marked KJV are from the King James Version.

Scripture quotations marked TLB are from *The Living Bible* copyright © 1971 by Tyndale House Foundation. Used by permission of Tyndale House Publishers Inc., Carol Stream, Illinois 60188. All rights reserved.

Scripture quotations marked *The Message* are taken from *The Message*. Copyright © 1993, 2002, 2018 by Eugene H. Peterson. Used by permission of NavPress Publishing Group.

Scripture quotations marked NASB are taken from the NEW AMERICAN STANDARD BIBLE®, Copyright © 1960, 1962, 1963, 1968, 1971, 1972, 1973, 1975, 1977, 1995 by The Lockman Foundation. Used by permission. lockman.org

Scripture taken from the New Century Version®. Copyright © 2005 by Thomas Nelson. Used by permission. All rights reserved.

Scripture quotations marked NIV are from THE HOLY BIBLE, NEW INTERNATIONAL VERSION®. Copyright © 1973, 1978, 1984, 2011 by Biblica, Inc.® and International Bible Society. Used by permission of Zondervan. All rights reserved worldwide.

Scripture marked NKJV is taken from the New King James Version®. Copyright © 1982 by Thomas Nelson. Used by permission. All rights reserved.

Scripture quotations marked NLT are taken from the Holy Bible, New Living Translation, copyright © 1996, 2004, 2007, 2013, 2015 by Tyndale House Foundation. Used by permission of Tyndale House Publishers Inc., Carol Stream, Illinois 60188. All rights reserved.

Scriptures quoted from RSV are from the Revised Standard Version of the Bible, copyright © 1946, 1952, 1971 by the Division of Christian Education of the National Council of the Churches of Christ in the U.S.A. Used by permission. All rights reserved.

Dear Columbia Union Conference Family:

Welcome to the Year of the Bible devotional book. Throughout 2021, we will place a special emphasis on the Bible—God's Love Letter to us. The Bible explains God's message of hope and reveals His great plan of salvation. This timeless treasure provides guidance for our lives, answers to our questions, inspiration for our worship and is the only test of discipleship. The Bible paints a picture of who God is, draws us to Him and transforms our character.

We'd like to thank every Columbia Union member—student, educator, pastor, ministry leader, employee, administrator—who contributed to this endeavor. We are so proud and thankful to those who sacrificed their time and energy to write from their heart—allowing God to use their powerful and uplifting stories and testimonies for His glory.

As we embark on this new year together, may the words you read renew your hearts and minds as you spend time in God's presence. Let us hold fast to Jesus, for His return is imminent. Until then, may the "Words of Life" God gives to each of us deepen our walk with Him. And may we be inspired, strengthened and empowered to *experience the mission*.

In His Service,

Dave Weigley, President

Rick Remmers, Executive Secretary

Emmanuel Asiedu, Treasurer

"Be kind and compassionate to one another, forgiving each other, just as in Christ God forgave you." EPH. 4:32, NIV

Put God First

But seek ye first the kingdom of God, and his righteousness; and all these things shall be added unto you. Matt. 6:33, KJV

JANUARY

Put God First

"But seek ye first the kingdom of God, and His righteousness; and all these things shall be added unto you" (Matt. 6:33, KJV).

During my early teenage years, this verse became very special to me. Shortly after my baptism at age 13, my father died, and I was left to navigate life virtually on my own. The local Seventh-day Adventist church became a central part of my life, and I decided to live to please God in all things.

What does it mean to seek first the kingdom of God and His righteousness? For me it means to make God's priorities mine and to incorporate the principles of His Word in every aspect of my life.

After completing high school in Guyana, I received a scholarship from the ministry of education to attend a two-year college. At the conclusion of the first term, I was confronted with the challenge of writing exams on Sabbath. I informed the dean that I could not do this because of my religious convictions. Initially, the dean told me that the school had always held exams on Saturday and that it would be difficult to change the schedule.

But God honored my decision, and for the duration of my time at that college, exams were no longer scheduled on Sabbath.

I have faced similar challenges here in the United States, but God has kept His promise in every situation as I have honored His Word.

Dear God, thank You for the gift of your Son, Jesus, for the presence of Your Holy Spirit and for the treasure of the Bible, Your holy Word. Please help me to live by every word that proceeds out of the mouth of God. Amen.

David Richmond is a member of the West End Simple Home church in Pennsylvania.

Light in the Darkness

"Your word is a lamp to my feet and a light to my path"
(Ps. 119:105, NKJV).

Friday was almost over. Our Pathfinder club had settled in a beautiful open field close to a stream with just a few feet of forest between our camp and the creek.

My friend and I volunteered to get water for the evening's activities. But soon the sun started to set, and the forest got dark fast. By the time we filled our buckets, the forest was pitch black.

Without flashlights, the darkness felt like a wall. We started our walk to camp, taking small, timid steps together. The sound of the creek diminished, but, after walking for a couple of minutes, we heard a waterfall. With each step we took, the waterfall got louder and louder.

In the distance, we saw a little flicker and started walking toward the little light. More lights joined, and, as the sound of the waterfall faded away, we heard the Pathfinders' voices screaming out our names. Once we had light, we could see the way.

Without God's Word, we are in darkness, hopeless and in danger. We look for safety, but darkness impedes us from finding the way to Life. But, when we use God's Word, light shines on our path, and we find the safety that only Jesus can give.

As Jesus says, "I am the way, the truth, and the life. No one comes to the Father except through Me" (John 14:6, NKJV).

Lord, please fill our hearts and minds with God's Word, and may Your light shine on our path each day. Amen.

Eli Rojas is the ministerial secretary for the Chesapeake Conference.

Live by Faith

"For we live by faith, not by sight"
(2 Cor. 5:7, NIV).

This short verse contains guidance on how to live our lives. Will the current pandemic pass? When? How much longer will it last? Will my life ever calm down again? In the midst of this storm, time is not standing still; it is not waiting for me to catch up. It will not go back to redeem days. I am not getting any younger. In fact, to the contrary, every joint in my body is starting to hurt.

But I believe in and live by faith. I know that nothing in the future, whether I succeed or fail or am in good health or not, will stunt my growth in God, because I believe in Him and His Word.

We are in this storm together, and must have faith that better days are ahead, "for God has not given us a spirit of fear, but of power and of love and of a sound mind" (2 Tim. 1:7, NKJV). We are sons and daughters of a King who already defeated evil.

Our King, Jesus Christ, please give us the strength to walk through the stormy paths of life. May we see the light at the end of the tunnel. By placing faith in You, may You assure us of this promise. Amen.

Laura Ottati-Romero is the director of Children's Ministries and the executive assistant of Multicultural Ministries for the Allegheny West Conference.

Prisoners of Praise

"About midnight Paul and Silas were praying and singing songs to God as the other prisoners listened" (Acts 16:25, NCV).

Remember this frequent directive from your teenage years? "Make sure you're home before midnight!" Midnight—that darkest part of the night when, in the absence of light, vulnerabilities to one's very existence emerge.

Paul and Silas understood these vulnerabilities. Just "about midnight," Roman soldiers unjustly hurled them into prison. This moment was made more daunting because they were chained in the dark innermost part of the prison. We know what that feels like, right? When we experience those dark "midnight seasons" in our lives from which we would like to escape but can't. It is here that I have discovered a powerful principle from Paul and Silas through which my midnight moments have been infused with clarity, light and deliverance.

I imagine Paul saying to Silas, straining his eyes to discern his face through the desperate midnight darkness: "Silas, we're in a tough situation. There is no way of escape, so let's just start singing praises." The Scriptures confirm that, because they chose to be prisoners of praise, they were delivered from the prison of their circumstances. And not only were they delivered, but so were the other prisoners. Additionally significant is that these heroes of faith were content to stay in prison— living "above their circumstances"—where they experienced the presence of Christ—the One who inhabits praise.

Dear Lord, thank You for the wonder-working power of praise that transforms our midnight moments into powerful testimonies of Your presence and deliverance. Amen.

Cheryl H. Kisunzu is the provost of Washington Adventist University in Maryland.

Pushing Back Against Spiritual Distancing

"I pray for them. ... that You should keep them from the evil one. ... that they may be made perfect in one, and that the world may know that You have sent Me, and have loved them as You have loved Me. ... And I have declared to them Your name, and will declare it, that the love with which You loved Me may be in them, and I in them (John 17:9–26, NKJV).

Jesus came that we may have life and have it more abundantly. It is the enemy that comes to steal, kill and destroy (John 10:10).

From the beginning, one of the enemy's most effective strategies has been to divide and separate—to distance us from God and each other. Since our first wandering apart in the Garden of Eden, keeping us in the age-old conflict between good and evil has depended on our remaining separate. From each other and from God.

Often, the lure is to get us to choose between polar opposites—be it politics, ideologies, religion, race. The deceiver doesn't care which end of the pole we run to, as long as it keeps us at odds with one another. He knows we can't be in conflict and peace at the same time.

As candles next to each other cast a brighter light, the Spirit quickens believers who come together. We receive power when we draw near to God. If we understood how very life-threatening separation is to us spiritually, we would push back. Our togetherness with God and each other is so vital to our recovery and victory that it was the single most important thing on Jesus' mind the night before He died on the cross.

Heavenly Father, may Jesus' plea for us be our reality! Amen.

Rick Aldridge is a chaplain at Fort Hamilton Hospital for Kettering Adventist HealthCare in Ohio.

The Phone Call

**"Before they call I will answer; while they are still
speaking I will hear" (Isa. 65:24, NIV).**

"I don't know what to do, Lord! I want you both in my life!" I cried out to God.

I was teaching at the local church school when I met him. He was a single father. Most mornings he drove his daughter, niece and nephew to school. He did not, however, attend our church and came up with many excuses. Our relationship was getting serious, and I was at a crossroads. So I decided to have yet another heart-to-heart with the Lord.

"Lord, I have prayed to you so often for a Christian man to share my life with. I love You and him! However, if I cannot have you both, I choose you, Lord!" My resolve was firm. I had to break up with him.

So I made the dreaded phone call: "Hello, is Rodney there?"

The person on the other line responded, "You will never believe what Rodney is doing right now! He's having a Bible study with Uncle Oscar!"

My mind began to whirl with questions! Who was Uncle Oscar, and how did he get Rodney to study the Bible? At that moment, God's promise crossed my mind and filled my heart: "Before they call I will answer; while they are still speaking I will hear."

My eyes filled with tears of joy as I realized God had worked out my request even before I asked Him. As I remained faithful to Him, I was able to share the life I longed for with a Christian man. God is indeed faithful to those who call upon His name!

Thank You, Father, for answering my prayers before I even ask, and for honoring Your daughter's faith in such a mighty way! Amen.

Amy Cromer is an elder at the West Wilmington church in Delaware.

Just Ask

"For with God, nothing shall be impossible" (Luke 1:37, NIV).

When I was younger, I had the privilege of staying with my grandmother, a woman with no formal education. Although she couldn't read or write, she memorized several Bible verses relating to God's promises. Anytime she faced challenges, she would recite verses to strengthen her faith. I remember my grandma's favorite saying: "God is so powerful and bigger than anything, whether challenges or situations." Needless to say, I grew up loving Bible stories and God's promises.

When I arrived to the United States in 2004 to study at La Sierra University (Calif.), two main obstacles stood in my way: How would I pay for my tuition, and how would I adjust to American culture? For the first time in my life, I was truly on my own. So I asked my grandma how I would be able to cope in this new country. And how would I afford my tuition and fees?

Without hesitation, my grandma replied, "With God all things are possible. I don't know how we can pay your fees, but God has a plan and knows exactly how He will take care of you. Just ask Him."

She directed me to Luke 1:37: "For with God, nothing shall be impossible." From that day forward, I decided to rely solely on God. And He came through! I was able to graduate debt-free and without any loans.

In our moments of discouragement, when facing our fiercest battles and uphill challenges, let us recall the promises of God and rely on Him. You may not know how to deal with a current situation in your life, but God does. Just ask Him.

Lord, may You be our first point of contact, not our last resort. Amen.

Emmanuel Asiedu is the treasurer and CFO of the Columbia Union Conference.

Finding Home

"Come unto Me, all ye that labour and are heavy laden, and I will give you rest" (Matt. 11:28, KJV).

The eastern box turtle is one of the most widely known turtles in West Virginia. When my kids were growing up, they caught them year after year. We have found turtles on woodland trails and even rescued them from the middle of the road countless times, bringing them home to be the family pet for a few days before releasing them again.

Two winters ago, we attended an indoor wildlife camp, sponsored by our local state park, and we learned a lot of fascinating things about our little turtle friends. One thing was that these turtles will live in the same area their entire lives. They are also born with a type of internal homing device that, if they are moved, helps them to find their way back home. These turtles will spend the rest of their lives searching restlessly for the place they were born until they either find it or die of exhaustion.

I relate this to a person's life before they find Christ. They are always searching for something, knowing something in their lives is lacking or missing. They are tired and burdened with the world's cares until they find their home in Christ. It is then they can take off their shoes, lean back, relax and enjoy the rest only the Savior can provide.

Dear God, let us find our rest in You. Allow Your lovingkindness to wash over us like a flood, so that we may rest in the peace only You can give. Amen.

Rebecca Trent is a member of the Grace Outreach church in West Virginia.

Joy Is a Promise

"Most assuredly, I say to you that you will weep and lament, but the world will rejoice; and you will be sorrowful, but your sorrow will be turned into joy. ... And in that day you will ask Me nothing" (John 16:20, 23, NKJV).

I witnessed my parents' tears under the oppression of the communist regime in Romania, as the secret police escorted them for interrogations. They persecuted me—a student at the time—for not attending school on the Sabbath. I cried and prayed for deliverance like the Israelites did in Egypt.

My fellow church members and I were faithful to God during these times. Putting spiritual matters first, after being interrogated, we would go directly to church. At night, we held baptisms and remodeled the interior of the church. At home, we hid our Bibles so the police wouldn't find them. And God showed me that His promises are true.

My parents wanted a better future for my two brothers and me, so based on the family's decision, my father escaped through the former Yugoslavia to a refugee camp in Austria, and, about a year later, came to the United States.

Our sorrow turned into joy when my family reunited with him, free from the communist oppression. As a result of God's unconditional love, our anguish vanished.

In the States, God led me into ministry, and now I joyfully tell others about my faithful Lord who keeps His promises.

God, I praise You for Your providence. My heart goes out to all who are under similar oppression around the world. May they feel God's presence, and may their sorrow turn into joy one day soon. Amen.

Marius E. Marton is the pastor of the Elyria district in Ohio.

Just the Boost I Needed

"God is my strength and power: and He maketh my way perfect"
(2 Sam. 22:33, KJV).

Growing up, I was a relatively shy child. I gravitated to the background, and, in most situations, chose to be an observer rather than a participant. In school, I answered questions or read aloud, but only if the teacher asked. I was active in church, but only when it involved groups. I'd sing in the choir, but never considered solos.

So, when I was about 12 and received a request to be a speaker at a church event, I couldn't understand why. My parents encouraged me to accept the invitation, and my father, a church elder and speaker, offered to help me prepare.

Selecting a topic and writing the message was the easy part because it was something I could do on my own. It was the thought of having to deliver the message in front of a congregation that terrified me.

Somehow I was introduced to 2 Samuel 22:33. At that moment, I felt as if God was speaking directly to me, reassuring me that, though I felt weak and uncomfortable, He would be my strength and power. It was just the boost I needed to complete my assignment without completely falling apart.

Ever since that experience, this verse has been my favorite. It is the one I rely on for any daunting task. In my occupation as a communicator, where I'm often required to publicly speak, I cannot help but look back and give credit to that verse—customized just for me. It has pushed me out of my fears and insecurities and encouraged me to follow God's perfect path with confidence.

God, I praise You for all the promises found in Your Word. Amen.

LaTasha Hewitt is the director of communication and Church Ministries coordinator for the Allegheny East Conference.

Never Alone

"Be strong and courageous. Do not be afraid or terrified because of them, for the Lord your God goes with you; He will never leave you nor forsake you" (Deut. 31:6, NIV).

When I read this verse, I feel safe and protected. Many times in my life, I've been scared to do things, but then I sit back and remember that God is always by my side. When I was about 7 years old, I remember biking around my neighborhood. I was coming to a hill, when suddenly my bike slid. I hit my face on the concrete and busted my chin open. I screamed in agony to my brother to go get our mom.

When we got inside, my parents called one of their friends, and he suggested we go to a clinic. At the clinic, they immediately told us to go to the ER. When we got there, they gave me some medicine and told me I needed stitches. While I was waiting, I was nervous, but my dad was there to keep my spirits up. As I walked fearfully into the operating room, I felt alone, but realized my dad was there holding my hand.

The operation went smoothly, and I recovered within two weeks. Just like my dad, God is with me when I am scared or in any situation. There is no room for fear when God is there. From this experience, I learned that I do not have to fear when taking a test, doing something new or when I feel alone.

Dear God, please help me to remember that when I am scared, I do not have to be, because I know that You are always with me. Amen.

Lia Watson is a freshman at Takoma Academy in Maryland.

Boldly I Come

"For I am not ashamed of the gospel of Christ, for it is the power of God to salvation for everyone who believes" (Rom. 1:16, NKJV).

The fledgling Christian church grew out of the fertile soil of the early believers' bold faith in a loving God who sent His Son to die for our sins. Ten of the original disciples died martyrs.

Paul boldly declared, with the temple of Diana mere yards away, "God ... does not dwell in temples made with hands" (Acts 17:24, NKJV). Paul understood how dangerous this was. A little more than 400 years earlier, the philosopher Socrates was executed for similar offenses.

Paul's "heathen opponents called his attention to the fate of Socrates, who, because he was a setter forth of strange gods, had been condemned to death, and they counseled Paul not to endanger his life in the same way [But Paul] was determined to accomplish his errand among them, and, at all hazards, to tell his story" (Ellen White, *The Acts of the Apostles*, p. 236).

We are Christians today because of the bold faith of previous generations who left homes and families, lost jobs, laid their precious children in graves, gave their last money to support God's work, were ridiculed, ostracized, tortured and killed. If even a single generation of these nameless Christians had said, "It costs too much to follow Jesus," the entire Christian church would have died at that point. Our faith exists because of their faithfulness. The faith of future generations is counting on your faithfulness.

This sacred responsibility inspires me to live boldly for Jesus and to not be ashamed of being a Seventh-day Adventist.

Lord Jesus, empower me to live boldly for You in every way. Amen.

Gary Gibbs is the president of the Pennsylvania Conference.

Only Jesus

"Neither is there salvation in any other: for there is none other name under heaven given among men, whereby we must be saved" (Acts 4:12, KJV).

In academy we were required to take a class on the Bible. One of our ongoing assignments was to read and summarize sections of Ellen White's book, *The Desire of Ages*—something I had never done before.

Later in the year, we came to Chapter 17 where White focused on Nicodemus. My eyes were opened; I was a sinner and in need of Christ. I read so many godly pleas for my soul to surrender to Him, and, in tears, I underlined them feverishly. I could feel Him calling me. But what happens when we don't listen and respond?

Thirty years later, I attended a Bible study via Zoom. As Juan, the presenter, brought the truth to our study, we discussed the story of the disciples' boat that began to sink in the Sea of Galilee. Juan's thoughtful and God-given questions, and our sincere answers, reminded me of the Bible studies in academy, and those heart-tugs returned.

The next day after church, I picked up my 30-year-old copy of *The Desire of Ages* and flipped through it to find and think about the highlighted and underlined statements I chose so long ago. Then I got to Nicodemus' story again.

As I read, I realized that there is nothing in the entire universe that will ultimately save us from hurt, pain, rejection, loneliness, trauma, injustice, fear, nor any other ungodly thing, except for Jesus. As we accept Him by faith, He will save us and give us hope to live through these last days.

Dear God, thank You for not leaving me. Please save me right now. Amen.

Rodney Turner is a member of the First Church of Montclair in New Jersey.

Perspective > Problem

"'For I know the plans I have for you,' declares the Lord, 'plans to prosper you and not to harm you, plans to give you hope and a future'" (Jer. 29:11, NIV).

Life is a matter of perspective, especially when facing a problem.

When things don't go your way, and people seem to conspire against you, remember there are still many blessings in your life. One of the best ways to handle a problem is to try to look at it from God's perspective, because His plans for your life are the best.

Many people respond to sudden difficulties with anger, frustration, bewilderment and a host of other negative emotions. Imagine what would happen if you responded with gratitude instead, not for the problem itself, but for the opportunities the problem can offer.

A few years ago, as I traveled through a country in South America, I was assaulted, robbed and left with nothing, not even money for food. At that moment, I had a decision to make: either sit immobilized and cry about what had just happened to me, or ask for God's plan and help. I chose the latter, and He kept His promise and provided for my needs during the remainder of the trip.

Are you facing a problem or difficulty that seems impossible to solve? Live with gratitude and confidence in God's plan for your life, because, in His hands, the impossible becomes possible.

Lord, thank You that, by abiding in You, we can change our perspective. Amen.

Pablo Cisneros is the pastor of the Luso-Brazilian church in New Jersey.

The Spirit's Doing

"For I am the Lord your God who takes hold of your right hand and says to you, 'Do not fear; I will help you'" (Isa. 41:13, NIV).

One of the very first Bible promises I ever memorized was Isaiah 41:13. What comforting words to know that God's presence and willingness to care for me made fear go away and filled my heart with assurance and peace.

When I was 14 years old and into my years as a student, I sold literature every summer. This ministry allowed me to pay my studies. But most important, it helped me develop skills and attitudes that became essential in my ministry and whole life. One of the blessings I learned was to trust in the Lord. The daily struggle to knock on doors was real. What made me proceed was the confidence in Him, as He provided me with the right words that touched the hearts of people. Every sale was a miracle! Some people said to me, "I don't know how or why I bought these books. You have something special." I know it was not me, but the Spirit's doing.

There were many opportunities to pray with people and share God's blessed words. And God always showed Himself. In fact, when I arrived from Argentina to canvas in Pennsylvania with my friend Julio, a new congregation—Reading Spanish—was planted.

Life becomes an adventure when we place ourselves in the Lord's hands every day and allow Him to guide and work in and through us. We will experience God's mighty acts, and our trust in Him will grow deeper and deeper.

Lord, take my hands, and make me an instrument of Your love. Amen.

Rubén Ramos is the vice president of Multilingual Ministries for the Columbia Union Conference.

My Sole Desire

"Now also when I am old and greyheaded, O God, forsake me not; until I have shewed thy strength unto this generation, and thy power to every one that is to come" (Ps. 71:18, KJV).

I believe that life experiences impact what favorite Bible verse we choose; then, the Bible verse, in turn, impacts our lives going forward.

When I first became my mother's caregiver, it was recommended that I read Psalm 71. I see my life in these verses, particularly verse 18. I see the steps on which God brought me to where I am today—a place where my sole desire is to share Christ with those around me.

Where I am in life is not where I imagined. Previously, having position and possessions, I felt I should be doing more for the Lord. Now, God has given me the responsibility to be the full-time caregiver for my 81-year-old mother who has dementia. I left everything and moved to Florida to live with her. When I could no longer care for her and also work, my mom and I moved in with my sister in Maryland.

It is only in a situation like this that I would find myself without a job; however, it frees me to focus on working for the Lord. He brought me to a church where I am doing Bible work. I count it a huge blessing that my mother's condition does not prevent her from going out with me. She attends Bible studies and even canvasses with me. Often, having her with me is actually an asset!

Father God, please empower me to continue to be used by You. Amen.

Mirlene Andre is a member of the Light Bearers Mission Company in Maryland.

Lessons From a Kayak Fiasco

"The Lord is my shepherd; I shall not want" (Ps. 23:1, KJV).

This morning I had a thought about "a life interrupted"—those times when life just doesn't go as planned. For many years, I have clung to Psalm 23:1, for it reminds me that my wants are important to God.

One of my wants is for my family to take trips together regularly. Some time ago, we traveled to a local state park to kayak. The day was sunny, and the river flowed peacefully. We partnered up and started down the river. I was in the kayak with my youngest son, who was 11 at the time, and he made it known that I was not his first choice of partners. I sensed he lacked confidence in my boating ability. I took offense to this—I had been a Camp Fire girl, a Girl Scout and a Pathfinder, and had even spent two summers at camp.

The adventure started out smoothly, but soon our kayak kept drifting toward the riverbank. My son and I began to argue. We paddled furiously, but decided it was best we changed partners. During the transfer, our kayak overturned, and I watched my flip flops float down the river.

That morning, our plans hadn't included the kayak fiasco. But we came together, turned the kayak back over and retrieved my flip flops. We ended up having a great time and can even laugh about it now.

As a single mother of two sons, I often feel pressured to have all the answers, but have learned to lean more on God and less on me.

Lord, I trust You, even if I don't know what the day holds for me. Amen.

Kimberly Upchurch is a member of the Ephesus church in Ohio.

The Blessing of Community

"Which is Christ in you, the hope of glory" (Col. 1:27, NKJV).

In this text, Apostle Paul speaks about the *mystery of the church*. Only Christ makes the church *holy* and *glorious*, merely through His holy presence. A genuine or real church community is not an idealized human projection. Some members have dreams for their community, but this dreaming sometimes may be an obstacle to the genuine, real, authentic and spiritual sense of the community. Idealized community is a hindrance because members who endorse it have demands and an accusing spirit. They see only failures, sins, shortcomings; finding faults become a sacred task. When their idealized image of the church community is destroyed, they become resentful and accuse everyone, including God Himself. This leads to spiritual despair, and, ultimately, spiritual death.

We should accept the church as a gift from God. Yes, we are all sinners, but the mystery of the church community is His precious gift. Wishful dreaming of a perfect community becomes transformed into the actual conscious participation in the real and authentic community through Christ's gift of the Holy Spirit. Sinners are transformed into a holy sanctuary of saints, not by effort or spiritual fervor, but by His presence alone. Christ in you is the only hope of glory, says Paul. Frail and weak community is transformed into a safe haven and refuge—a fellowship of love that continues to grow in eternity. Giving up on the idealized dream of the perfect community opens the door for authentic involvement in the given community, receiving the gift of God's fellowship of saints.

Dear Lord, let us receive the real community fellowship as your precious gift, and experience Christ's presence in our midst as the only hope of glory. Amen.

Alex Santrac is the pastor of the Middletown Valley and Catoctin View churches in Maryland.

'Do Not Urge Me to Leave You'

**"But Ruth replied, 'Don't urge me to leave you. ...'
When Naomi realized that Ruth was determined to go
with her, she stopped urging her" (Ruth 1:16, 18, NKJV).**

I have experienced a bitter spirit like Naomi. As an African-American woman, I have experienced many losses through racism, sexism, classism and misogynoir. Of those losses, it has been the ones I have suffered within my faith community that have been the most devastating because they resulted in misperceptions of God. Like Naomi, my misperception of God evoked anger, disappointment and bitterness. But unlike Naomi, my misperception also led to loss of identity with God.

In my grief, bitterness of spirit and state of separation from God, I could not perceive Him as the source of my comfort and restoration. Therefore, I urged the Holy Spirit—God's appointed Source of comfort and restoration—to abandon me, as Naomi entreated Ruth. In pain, I urged the Holy Spirit to abandon me, by turning away from prayer and God's Word.

Fortunately, as Ruth did not give in to Naomi, the Holy Spirit did not give in to me. Those times that I turned away, the Holy Spirit pleaded with me, "Do not urge me to leave you!" When I perceived the Holy Spirit's determination to remain, I submitted and allowed the Spirit to journey with me, abide with me, and, eventually, take care of me by entreating me to pray and study God's Word. In time, through submitting to the Holy Spirit's care, I experienced the restoration of my perception of God and my identity in Him.

Lord, may we perceive that You can restore us through the Holy Spirit, who is determined to go with us wherever we go. Amen.

Barbara Washington is a chaplain fellow at Soin Medical Center for Kettering Adventist HealthCare in Ohio.

'How Are You?'

"Jesus wept" (John 11:35, NLT).

This verse is the shortest verse in the Bible, but it is packed with a powerful punch. It shows that feeling negative emotions is part of the human experience. To me, it signifies that it's OK to not be OK.

We are accustomed to saying "I'm fine" whenever we are asked how we are doing, when, in reality, we could be feeling angry, sad, confused and helpless—the complete opposite of fine.

As I write, a pandemic is sweeping over the world. I know that I am not fine, even though I may say I am to those who ask. I may even say it with a smile. But deep down, I know the uncertainty of the future is anxiety-provoking. Not being able to control certain aspects of my life or even plan for the upcoming month makes me want to cry.

Am I feeling sad or angry? Or both? I'm not even sure I know. That is why this verse, how Jesus portrayed His humanity, great sadness and anger as a result of what sin had done to the world, really speaks to me during this time.

The story doesn't end here though. A few verses later, Jesus says, "Didn't I tell you that you would see God's glory if you believe?" (John 11:40, NLT). Jesus is reminding us that He is still in control of the world, and, if we believe in Him, we will see His glory.

Dear God, may the madness that is happening all around us eventually end, and may we see Your mercy and love shine through the darkness and uncertainty. Amen.

Crystal Lubis is a member of the Capital Chinese church in Maryland.

The Hand of God

"But His hand is stretched out still" (Isa. 9:12, NKJV).

This verse in the Bible caught my attention. I wondered if I was reading it correctly. I looked at it in several versions, each showing a different picture than the New King James Version. I decided to see what Ellen White wrote about it:

"In different ways God works to attain one purpose—the saving of souls. By different methods the gracious Redeemer deals with different minds. The change of heart is as truly wrought out by one process as by another. ... Yet who dare say that God does not still love and regard as His child the one so sorely beset, and that His hand is not still stretched out to save? The heavenly Shepherd knows where to find the lambs that are straying from the fold. He will gather them in. ... In such places as these there are those who will bloom more sweetly for the Lord than many who live in more favored places. All around them they will shed the fragrance of His grace as they bloom in most unpromising places" (*This Day With God*, p. 67).

This describes the picture I envisioned hearing these words over and over. What an amazing God we have! He sees those whom we may have given up on and think are hopeless, and, in His discipline, He stretches out His hand to them.

Do you see His hand in your life? Do you feel Him picking you up? You can bloom and be a fragrance of His grace! Will you grasp His life-giving hand? He will hold onto you and keep you.

God, take me into Your loving hands always. Amen.

Peggy Curtis Harris is a member of the Beltsville church in Maryland.

If God Is With Us, Who Can Be Against Us?

"The Lord your God is with you, the Mighty Warrior who saves. He will take great delight in you; in His love He will no longer rebuke you, but will rejoice over you with singing" (Zeph. 3:17, NIV).

During the quarantine, God is with us and He is mighty to save us from COVID-19 by protecting us from evil. We can take great delight in God by reading His Word and by praying every night. We have to pray from our hearts, and we have to pray for everyone not to get COVID-19 and for the sick ones to get better from it.

We should not be afraid during this time, because, if we listen to God, then we will have the same faith that Daniel had when he was thrown into the lion's den. We can trust in Him during good and bad times. We can be thankful that we have the freedom to study our Bibles during this difficult time. This is a wonderful time to let our lights shine for Jesus and to share the wonderful news about His soon coming.

We are experiencing God's love every day as He gives us life, strength, health, faith, self-control and wisdom. Even though we are in quarantine, we still can rejoice in God by communicating with our family members that are far away and with our friends. When we talk to our friends every week, we can encourage them to study God's Word, eat healthy food and drink lots of water.

Dear Father in Heaven, thank You for taking care of us in hard times. Help us to be witnesses for You. Amen.

Iulia Folscher is a second-grader at Richmond Academy in Virginia.

Hope in Him

"This I call to mind and therefore I have hope. The steadfast love of the Lord never ceases. His mercies never come to an end. They are new every morning. Great is Your faithfulness. The Lord is my portion ... therefore I have hope in Him" (Lam. 3:22–24, RSV, adapted).

My first recollection of Jeremiah's words came as a 19-year-old. It opened my eyes to the many mercies God brings into my life on a daily basis. That was true when I studied abroad as a college sophomore, and true four years later when my father died at 59. It's been true throughout my life.

Jeremiah's words were born during a time of national and personal crisis, when all hope seemed to have disappeared. His words mean even more to me now during my own personal health crisis. God has had a way to help me see His faithfulness every day.

Sometimes I wonder if my ministry has had any lasting impact. And then, at just the right moment, I receive a phone call, a card, an email or a text from an old friend or former church member who shares how God worked through me to lead them to Christ, nurture their relationship with Him or give leadership to their congregation.

God is good, loving and faithful. That is why I have hope in Him. Many of us go through our own times of crises, whether it be health, financial or family issues. That's when we most need to recall God's faithfulness to us.

Dear God, may Jeremiah's words, which gave birth to a well-loved hymn, inspire us to have hope in Your faithfulness by opening our hearts and eyes to see Your daily mercies. Amen.

Rob Vandeman recently announced plans to retire from the Columbia Union Conference after nearly 50 years as a pastor and administrator.

Who Am I?

**"I sought the Lord, and He heard me, and delivered
me from all my fears" (Ps. 34:4, KJV).**

On Sunday, March 29, 2020, I received a call from my daughter Andrea,
a nurse, telling me that she had a temperature of over 101 degrees, was
being sent home from work and was going to be tested for COVID-19. I
prayed with my daughter and claimed God's promises over her.

As the days went on, Andrea started getting better, and I proclaimed
to family, "Praise the Lord, our prayers have been answered." But on
April 9, when she finally got the results back showing she was positive
for COVID-19, my faith started to waiver. I had heard on the news
that doctors were reporting that sometimes patients diagnosed with
COVID-19 would get better, and then, within a few hours, would be placed
on a ventilator.

While these thoughts ran through my mind, the Holy Spirit spoke to me
and said, "Who am I to you?" I immediately picked up my Bible and turned
to Exodus 3:14 where God told Moses who He was: "I AM THAT I AM."

My prayer quickly changed from, "Lord, heal my daughter" to "Lord,
forgive me for doubting You. Help me to have faith in You."

Before turning to the Bible, I thought I had to pray more, fast more; I had
to do something reasonable to help God as I waited for Him to heal my
daughter. I was trying to force God to be what I wanted Him to be instead
of allowing Him to be who He is.

*God, if we find ourselves wavering in our faith, may we turn to Your Word, and
may You remind us that You are a faithful, loving God, and the great "I AM."
Amen.*

Kelly Strickland is an elder at the Rehoboth church in Pennsylvania.

Built in Him

"And now, just as you accepted Christ Jesus as your Lord, you must continue to follow Him. Let your roots grow down into Him, and let your lives be built on Him. Then your faith will grow strong in the truth you were taught, and you will overflow with thankfulness"
(Col. 2:6–7, NLT).

I find that my favorite text can shift depending on where I am in my spiritual journey. At times, I have found over the years that it seems easier to whine about issues than change my attitude to "overflow with thankfulness." The text states that as I grow in Christ and my life is built on Him, then the natural overflow will be thankfulness, for the fruit of a mature Christian is thankfulness.

Some months back, I received a really negative email from someone who seemed to have inside information on my life—stuff in which I wasn't even aware. My initial reaction wasn't good, but then I realized that, since I am built on Christ, my Savior, that this fact, in and of itself, is reason enough to be thankful. My worth is built in Him!

God, when things goes awry, may we choose to change our outlook from grim to thankfulness, because our hope is built on You and nothing less. Amen.

Bill Miller is the president of the Potomac Conference.

One Day Soon

"And God will wipe away every tear from their eyes; there shall be no more death, nor sorrow, nor crying. There shall be no more pain, for the former things have passed away" (Rev. 21:4, NKJV).

You never expect it will happen to you. On May 23, 2016, at around 11 a.m., my (seemingly) perfectly healthy 13-year-old son collapsed at school from a sudden cardiac arrest (SCA). Providentially, my husband and I, teachers at the small Adventist school, had recently been trained in CPR. But we never expected to use it beyond CPR class, let alone on our own son.

Approximately 90 percent of those who suffer an SCA die, yet despite all odds, our son survived and suffered no ill effects. Our family has been blessed, for not everyone has a happy ending to their story. That is why Revelation 21:4 means so much to me. I cannot wait for the day when there will be "no more death, nor sorrow, nor crying." What a glorious day that will be!

God, I praise You for saving my son's life and that Your Son will soon return to take us home, where pain will be a thing of the past. Amen.

Clare Hoover is the principal and a teacher at the Zanesville Adventist School in Ohio.

Thank You for Loving Me

"Then a voice came from heaven, 'You are My beloved Son, in whom I am well pleased'" (Mark 1:11, NKJV).

When I was a child, praise had to be earned, and success seemed just out of reach. I was born with misshaped hips and legs, resulting in my needing to wear braces on my legs. This delayed my ability to walk, and completely canceled any ability to run or ride tricycles until the braces could be removed.

In school, I discovered that reading and math skills were hard to learn, and I was almost always behind my classmates. Ashamed of this, it didn't seem to matter how hard I worked, I just couldn't keep up. Poor depth perception, particularly when it came to small moving objects, meant that I wasn't very good at sports. At recess I was usually one of the last kids picked.

As an adult, success isn't as hard to find as it used to be. I've learned to compensate for my mild dyslexia, and I've overcome most of my learning challenges. Fitness is now more important than athletics, and I don't find myself comparing my abilities with others quite so much. Still, there's a little boy inside me that's desperately yearning to be able to do what his brothers and classmates seem to find so easy: to get an "A" on my homework; to be good at things; to do something someone will be proud of.

That's why I treasure these words spoken by the Father to His Son: "You are My beloved Son, in whom I am well pleased." It's good to know that my Heavenly Father doesn't make it too difficult for me to earn those words from Him.

God, thank You for loving me and being proud of me. Amen.

Jon K. Clayburn is the pastor of the Meridian Road, New Castle and Shenango Valley churches in Pennsylvania.

Bearing Fruit

"But the fruit of the Spirit is love, joy, peace, forbearance, kindness, goodness, faithfulness, gentleness and self-control. Against such things there is no law" (Gal. 5:22–23, NIV).

When I think about the fruit of the Spirit, I think about our pastor's Week of Prayer. Each day he focused on one "Fruit of the Spirit" and brought a different fruit to represent that particular "fruit." He told us how the fruit was good for our bodies, and then related it to our spiritual lives. At the end of each talk, we got to taste the yummy fruit.

When I think about the fruit of the Spirit, some fruits stick out more than others. They are all important, but love, patience, faithfulness and self-control are the ones that mean the most to me.

We need love because God loves us and wants us to love our neighbors as we love ourselves. We need to love everyone because God first loved us. We need patience because, when people are sometimes slow or drive us crazy, we need to practice patience with them. We need faithfulness because when life gets tough and you don't know what to do, you need to have faith in God. He will get you through everything, even when life is at its hardest. Lastly, we need self-control. When we feel angry, we need to remember to have self-control and know that God will help us.

I have to use these fruits every day when I watch my brother. I have to be patient with him and understand why he may get angry at times. I also have to use self-control and close my mouth when I feel like saying bad things back to him.

Dear God, please help me to be faithful and remember that You will give me self-control. Amen.

Sara Clow is a sixth-grader at Tappahannock Junior Academy in Virginia.

No Need to Operate

"Have you not known? Have you not heard? The everlasting God, the Lord, the Creator of the ends of the earth, neither faints nor is weary. His understanding is unsearchable. He gives power to the weak, and to those who have no might He increases strength. Even the youths shall faint and be weary, and the young men shall utterly fall, but those who wait on the Lord shall renew their strength; they shall mount up with wings like eagles, they shall run and not be weary, they shall walk and not faint" (Isa. 40:28–31, NKJV).

In my 35 years of ministry, these verses have carried me through many storms and blessings. This passage became even more relevant when I got into a terrible car accident.

One day, as I traveled to Belize City, Belize, to pick up materials for the last baptism of an evangelism crusade, I came across two big trucks, both trying to overtake the other on a steep curve. I tried to pull away, but one truck did the same and hit me head on, completely crushing me. The ER doctors explained that my broken ribs had punctured my lungs, causing them to collapse.

Prior to the emergency operation, I claimed the promise in this verse before falling into unconsciousness. But, right before they started the operation, I suddenly regained consciousness. To everyone's amazement, I was able to breathe, and there was no need to operate. God had completely healed me!

Nowadays, when I preach the gospel, there are times I raise my voice in worship. And I tell the brethren, "I am exercising my new lungs!" Still today, I see the power of God in my life.

My Savior, renew my strength as I wait on You. Amen.

Ramon Escalante is the Hispanic Ministries coordinator for the Allegheny East Conference.

One Unforgettable Sabbath

**"Not giving up meeting together... but encouraging one another—
and all the more as you see the day approaching" (Heb. 10:25, NIV).**

In my 22 years of ministry, I have had many unforgettable Sabbaths, but
none more so than in Delta Junction, Alaska. My wife and I were settling
into our new subarctic district during the coldest part of the year. Delta
Junction is located 90 miles southeast of Fairbanks and 250 miles south
of the Arctic Circle. When we arrived, it was a "balmy" 16 degrees; by
Thanksgiving, it had fallen to negative 38 degrees. My body adjusted
quickly to these sub-zero temperatures, but nothing prepared me for
what awaited that Sabbath morning in January.

The church was three miles from our parsonage. That Sabbath morning, our
outdoor thermometer read -51 degrees! Surely no one would think of holding
church at that unheard-of temperature. As the new guy in town, I thought I
would drive over to the church to see if anyone was crazy enough to show up.

Sure enough, lights were on and members were having Sabbath School!
I sheepishly entered and saw our head elder playing his accordion while
leading 15 to 20 people in song. Seeing the new pastor entering slowly, a
twinkle came to his eye, and he gave me a slight nod that seemed to say,
"Happy Sabbath, Pastor, so glad you decided to join us!"

I don't remember what I preached on that memorable Sabbath, but I
do recall about 35 people attended worship. The importance of church
fellowship, particularly in worshipping together on His Sabbath, was
reinforced that day.

*Lord, thank You for brothers and sisters who so faithfully worship You in spirit
and in truth. Amen.*

*Fred C. Shoemaker is the pastor of the Hillsboro, Middletown and Wilmington churches
in Ohio.*

Keep On Praying

"Ask, and you will be given what you ask for. Seek, and you will find. Knock, and the door will be opened" (Matt. 7:7, TLB).

In the Sermon on the Mount, Jesus explained to His disciples that prayer is a lifestyle, not just a group of moments in life. Jesus used a continuous tense for the three verbs here: "ask," "seek" and "knock." These verbs translate to "keep on asking," "keep on seeking" and "keep on knocking." These actions show us the different prayers we need in different situations in our lives.

"Keep on asking" refers to our needs, wants and wishes that reflect the Lord's will in our lives. It is not pushing buttons to get what we want.

"Keep on seeking" tells us that we always have new things to learn. A life with Jesus is a continuous search for deeper knowledge of Him and what He is doing in each moment of our lives.

"Keep on knocking" demonstrates the power of our Lord Jesus to make all things possible. I may pray for an entire night to God like Daniel, or maybe a few days like Esther, or maybe more than 30 years like Joseph. If I keep on praying for His will to be done, I believe He will make the way to victory.

At the end of the three, we have an assurance of His response. "Keep on praying, and you will receive, find and the door will be opened." Every time our lives are in constant communion with God, we will experience a deeper relationship with Him.

Dear God, help us to make prayer a lifestyle. Amen.

Ignacio Goya is the director for Chesapeake Conference's Adventist Community Services.

"Do everything in love." 1 COR. 16:14, NIV

FEBRUARY

The Patient

**"By this shall all men know that ye are my disciples,
if ye have love one to another" (John 13:35, KJV).**

Love is a word easily tossed around without much thought. In many ways, love is acceptance, compassion, even tolerance. As a nurse in an inpatient mental health unit, I was assigned a patient no one else wanted. I typically didn't read my assigned patients' charts before personally meeting and speaking with them. All I knew was that he was depressed and that he was at one time the grand dragon of the Ku Klux Klan.

Because I met him prior to reading his chart, I came in without bias, and established a tentative relationship with him. My first impression was that he was a kind, sad, old man. As he told me about his son who was in jail, I listened to, comforted and prayed with him. Though he regretted and took ownership of his past, I assured him that God loved and forgave him.

One day, as he clung to his Bible, he said, "The people I have been the meanest to have been the kindest to me." For me to hate or despise him would have been useless; I could not have hated him more than he hated himself. I sensed he had genuine regret for his past actions, and my duty was to accept—not judge—him as he was now and show him forgiveness and acceptance in my kindness. After all, has not Christ forgiven me?

Lord, thank You for giving us Your love for others. Amen.

Dorothy L. Brown is a member of the Centerville church in Ohio.

Trust God

"Therefore, I say to you, do not worry about your life, what you will eat or what you will drink; nor about your body, what you will put on. Is not life more than food and the body more than clothing?"
(Matt. 6:25, NKJV).

My mom and I were driving home from Washington, D.C. We were in Virginia when our brakes stopped working. Thankfully, my mom managed to pull over into someone's driveway and stop the car. She didn't have a phone at the time, and there wasn't anyone at the property—Just two big dogs guarding the place.

Mom said, "Let's pray!" We prayed for someone to come and help us, but no one did.

I said, "Mom, I don't think God is listening."

My mom answered, "God always listens, we just have to trust Him." So we prayed some more.

A little later, a car pulled up next to us. The man asked if it was OK for him to park there while he checked his car. It had been running fine until he reached that property, and now something was wrong. My mom told him she knew God had sent him there to help us.

Mom used his phone to call my dad. My dad said his phone had just started working again. She would not have been able to reach him if she had called earlier. The man tried to start his car, but it wouldn't start. It wasn't until my dad arrived and fixed our car that the man's car started, and he was able to leave. I think God caused the man's car to stop working so he could help us.

Dear God, please help us to focus on what's happening now, not the future. Help us to trust You! Amen.

Chloe Juncal is a seventh-grader at the Manassas Adventist Preparatory School in Virginia.

What Does It Take to Be a Hero?

"They were stoned, they were sawn in two, were tempted, were slain with the sword. They wandered about in sheepskins and goatskins, being destitute, afflicted, tormented—of whom the world was not worthy. They wandered in deserts and mountains, in dens and caves of the earth" (Heb. 11:37–38, NKJV).

I look at the wonderful heroes of the Bible and think of how great it would be to be used by God like they were. After all, Hebrews 11 is about the greatest heroes the world has ever seen.

Then I think of what it *really* meant to be a hero. Those people suffered more things than any of us would want to. If only we could be a hero without the suffering that accompanies it. I also believe that if you asked them if they considered themselves heroes, they would probably think you're crazy. In fact, they probably would have preferred to escape their situations. These circumstances were marked with extreme trials. What makes them heroes is their faith and their complete dependence on God.

My favorite part of this passage is, "of whom the world was not worthy." Do you ever feel like you do not fit here on earth? Like you are always going against the grain because you want to follow God, but it seems like the world is determined to walk away from Him? That's because we don't belong here. Instead, we long for Jesus' return—the greatest Hero the world will ever see.

Dear God, let me be the hero that will take a stand for You and lead a precious soul to the real Hero. Amen.

Brandon Senior is the district pastor of the Washington, Uniontown Hilltop, Mon Valley, Greensburg and East Suburban churches in Pennsylvania.

A Lame Man Is Healed

"Silver and gold I do not have, but what I do have I give you: In the name of Jesus Christ of Nazareth, rise up and walk" (Acts 3:6, NKJV).

Has something amazing ever happened to you that filled you with joy? According to the dictionary, joy means "a source or cause of delight." God wants us to have joy because He wants us to be happy. God is happy when we are happy. Let me tell you a story of how God used two people to make one man's life joyful.

It all started when two of Jesus' disciples, Peter and John, were walking into the temple to pray. A lame man was lying next to the temple begging for money, and when he saw the disciples, he held out his hands and asked for money. Peter told him, "Silver and gold I do not have, but what I do have I give you: In the name of Jesus Christ of Nazareth, rise up and walk."

Peter then took the man's arm and pulled him up. The man's feet suddenly grew stronger. He stood up and went into the temple with the disciples, walking and leaping while praising God who had healed him. All the people saw the man and remembered that he was the one who had been begging for money at the temple gate. The people were filled with wonder and amazement.

It's so cool that a man who didn't experience joy in his life ended up with so much!

God, thank You for loving us and giving us joy, just like the lame man. Amen.

Connor Walls is a fifth-grader at Vienna Adventist Academy in Virginia.

When Silence Speaks Louder Than Words

"If only you could be silent! That's the wisest thing you could do"
(Job 13:5, NLT).

A few years ago, I ran across this scripture verse as I was studying the story of Job, and I taped it to the bottom lefthand corner of my computer screen at work. I purposely placed this text there so that, as soon as I got to work each day, I would be reminded about the integral role silence can play as I maneuvered throughout the workday.

Job's friends came to visit him at the lowest, darkest moment of his life. Their visit sought to bring comfort and companionship to their friend, but their conversation did the opposite, stirring up confusion and blame. When Job could take no more, out of frustration he told his friends to shut up! Even though Job may have appeared abrupt in his response to his friends, he did not leave them without a compelling caveat, as he extolled the wisdom and virtue of silence.

In a world that embraces the intricate nuanced dance of verbalism, silence is often shunned. Words can be weaponized, and, at times, cause more harm than good. This verse reminds me about the importance of being judicious in what is communicated, and that not everything that comes to mind needs to be shared. Therefore, the sage application of silence can serve as a beneficial and wise tool in navigating the complexities of life. Every time I look at this scripture verse posted on my desktop, the Lord reminds me of Job's desperate cry for silence, and I vow to make it my choice to use my voice wisely.

Lord, help me to embrace the wisdom that can be found in the depths of silence. Amen.

Cheryl Osbourne Chavers is an elder at the Calvary church in Virginia.

Plans That Included Me

"'For I know the plans I have for you,' declares the LORD,
"plans to prosper you and not to harm you, plans to give you
hope and a future'" (Jer. 29:11, NIV).

God has plans for me! And if He has plans for me, that must mean that I'm on His mind. God thinks about me! This text has grounded and encouraged me at different stages of my life, and I'm shocked every time I ponder that the Creator of the universe has time to think about me.

When I was a child, my brothers and I lived many years with extended family waiting for my immigrant parents to take us to live in the United States with them. During those years, my father died and my mother remarried and started a new family.

One day my dreams came true! My mother came with her new husband and my new baby sister to take us to our new home. I was utterly disappointed to find myself in a broken and dysfunctional home that was in many ways worse than what I had before. As I faced the defining years of adolescence, I thought about my future. How was life going to turn out for me? What did I want to be? How could I ever afford college? I felt that no one else was thinking about my future or had any expectations of me.

As I reflect back on those turbulent years, I now know that God was indeed thinking about me; He was making plans. His plans included university, graduate school, a loving husband and three beautiful children of my own.

God thinks about you, too, and He is making plans for you.

Thank You, God, for the plans that You have for us. Amen.

Denny Rengifo is a chaplain at Adventist HealthCare in Maryland.

From Test to Testimony

"But He knoweth the way that I take: when He hath tried me I shall come forth as gold" (Job 23:10, KJV).

No matter how turbulent the tests God sends or allows in my life, this scripture gives me an assurance of His abiding presence. In my experience, God's tests help to grow my patience, faith and trust in Him. The following test took me to a new level of trust in God's faithfulness, and became my testimony:

In November 2017, I relocated to Baltimore from Columbia, Md. Despite uncertainty about this untimely move, I was grateful for God's goodness: I was closer to my church, met new friends and was able to witness in the community. Nonetheless, the daily commute to my job in Columbia became wearisome and caused anxiety. I started to pray earnestly about moving back to Columbia to be near my family and job, but could not find affordable housing.

One day, I drove by an apartment community in an ideal location. "Lord, I want to live here," I said. Every day, I drove by, until, in December 2019, the Holy Spirit impressed me to submit an application. Unfortunately, there were no vacancies, but the very kind woman in the office added me to their waiting list. Months went by and winter road conditions made my 30-minute commute even more challenging. "How much longer, Lord?" I asked.

In January 2020, the Holy Spirit impressed me to go back to the community. Finally, there was a vacancy! On February 7, 2020, God moved me back to Columbia, closer to my family and my job, just where I had prayed to live— and just before the coronavirus pandemic escalated.

Regardless of the duration and size of the test, God always knows what is best.

Father, thank You for bringing me forth as gold. Amen.

Pamela Pinder is a member of the Liberty church in Maryland.

'I Will Give You Rest'

**"Come to Me, all who are weary and heavy-laden,
and I will give you rest" (Matt. 11:28, NASB).**

When our adult sons were young boys, I remember telling my mother, "This mother thing is not that hard."

I still remember her answer: "The bigger the boys get, the bigger the problems get."

My mother was right. We love our boys and are blessed to be their parents. But the truth is, at times, being a parent can be hard and stressful. As a family, we've had both amazing and troubled times. Over the years, my husband and I learned that prayer is crucial not only to marriage, but parenting as well.

Initially, the reason I claimed that Matthew 11.28 was my favorite Bible verse was because both of our boys were "embedded" in the text: *Matthew*, the name of our eldest son, and 11:28, the birthday of our younger son, Andrew. But as time passed, my Bible study deepened, and I soon realized there was a much stronger reason this verse should be my favorite.

In this verse, I found one of the most amazing promises from Jesus that I so desperately needed. The invitation to bring Him my worries, anxieties and troubles in exchange for His rest—true rest that can only be found in Him—was unbelievable. After many years of silently carrying my burdens, I made the decision to take Jesus up on His offer. What a verse and what a promise. I have learned that I need this rest daily. Maybe you do too.

Dear God, we are tired and heavy-laden for many different reasons. Thank You for being willing and able to take on our burdens daily and for gifting us with Your rest. Amen.

Hazel R. Marroquin is the pastor for Children and Family Ministries at the Sligo church in Maryland.

A Foggy Start

"From the ends of the earth … You are My servant, I have chosen you and have not cast you away: Fear not, for I am with you; Be not dismayed, for I am your God. I will strengthen you" (Isa. 41:9–10, NKJV).

Loneliness settled among my thoughts like a heavy winter fog. I had recently moved across the continent to begin graduate studies at the University of British Columbia in Vancouver, Canada. While excited about the research opportunities ahead, I missed my family and community back home in the United States. I had no relatives or friends in this new city along the Pacific coast. I remember thinking, *What have I done? I just moved across an entire continent to the end of North America!* Anxiety always exaggerates trouble, doesn't it?

Hoping to hear a message of comfort, I opened my Bible to revisit passages of God's guidance, presence and promise of a brighter future. In my season of loneliness, God spoke a message of hope in the prophetic blessing recorded in Isaiah 41:9–10.

While the loneliness still remained, my spirits were lifted. I wasn't afraid, and I was not alone. He who tends the grand universe, treasures a university grad. There would be new friendships, adventures and a valued educational experience ahead. More importantly, I faced the unknown comforted, strengthened and chosen by God.

In a small, student apartment, the light of a heard prayer pierced my darkness, and the fog started to lift.

God, in our season of loneliness, come through, as You always do. Amen.

Kylynda C. Bauer is a member of the Middletown Valley church in Maryland.

No More Sea

**"And I saw a new heaven and a new earth: for the first heaven
and the first earth were passed away; and there was no more sea"
(Rev. 21:1, KJV).**

The apostle John's description of the new earth says there will be "no
more sea." The seashore is one of my favorite places. For me it has been
a place of recreation and relaxation. I have many fond memories of
family vacations at the ocean when I was a child and later with my own
children—collecting seashells, watching dolphins play, riding waves with
my boogie board. Now, as an adult, I still enjoy the sea whenever I can; I
especially like snorkeling and sailing. So, this foreboding forecast of "no
more sea" is a bit disappointing.

However, the book of Revelation is filled with colorful imagery and symbols,
and "the sea" is one of them. It is not the literal sea in which John here
speaks. Revelation 17:15 tells us that "the sea" is a symbol for people,
multitudes, nations and tongues that are contrary to the kingdom of God.
John is speaking of wicked humanity, evil power and corrupt governments.
When John says there will be "no more sea," he wistfully looks forward to a
new world where evil, wickedness and sin are forever gone.

I love this text because it foretells of a world to come without sin, sorrow
and suffering. "No more sea" means no more poverty, no more oppression,
no more fear, no more abuse, no more guilt, no more tears, no more
separation, no more cancer and no more death. They will be no more!

I long for such a world, and for riding my boogie board in the river of life.

Heavenly Father, thank You that "no more" is in our future. Amen.

*Frank Bondurant is the vice president of Ministries Development for the
Columbia Union Conference.*

He's Preparing a Place

"And if I go and prepare a place for you, I will come again and will take you to Myself, that where I am you will be also" (John 14:3, ESV).

I have heard this beautiful verse read many times in sermons. Preachers strive to describe what Jesus is preparing in heaven. Apparently, Jesus has a great construction company, and He has been building luxurious houses for the redeemed for more than 2,000 years. But the reality is that the verse just prior says, "In my Father's house there are many dwellings." So what did Jesus go to prepare?

The Bible teaches us that, because of our sins, you and I cannot enter heaven. But, through Jesus' sacrifice on the cross, and through His intercession before His Father with His own blood, He is making us a place.

Between 1900–1950, millions of European immigrants arrived on America's shores by boat. One of these immigrants was my great-grandfather, Vichenso Marincola. He came to prepare a better future for his family. After some time, he got a job and learned English. He later found a place to live and raised enough money for his wife and three daughters to be together with him.

At the immigration department, he explained he had enough money to provide for his family. When they asked him what his wife and daughters had in Italy—their country of origin—he answered: "Nothing. They have nothing, but I have everything necessary here, so they have the right to be with me."

Jesus is doing that exact thing now—appearing before the Father to show that, although we have nothing, He has already paid the price for us!

Lord, may we accept Your free gift so that we can be with You together forever. Amen.

José Daniel Espósito Forciniti is the Hispanic Ministries director for the Potomac Conference.

Hoping for a Future

"For I know the thoughts that I think toward you, says the Lord, thoughts of peace and not of evil, to give you a future and a hope" (Jer. 29:11, NKJV).

All my life, God has called me to trust and obey Him. I had no idea how old I'd be when I got married or if I'd have children or what my career path would be, but He did. Referring to Him giving us a future and hope, Jeremiah goes on to say that we are to seek, find and search for God with all of our hearts. And that's exactly what I did.

One hazy, summer day, as I gazed at the hills of Loma Linda in California, I called upon the Lord, for I had a decision to make. A resident of Maryland, my visit to the West Coast was to celebrate my friend's graduation from medical school. I asked God if I should move to California. My brain said to attend Loma Linda University Medical Center, but the Holy Spirit's presence called me to stay on the East Coast. I just didn't know why.

Looking back, I realize that I made the right decision. I met my husband at a place I'd least expect to find someone—one of the reasons why I had contemplated moving out of the area. Not long after we got married, I had a near-death experience on a rafting trip. In the moment, I knew God would save me from the grip of the river's mighty rapids because of the "future and hope" He had promised. And He miraculously dislodged my foot before I drowned.

I now understand the expression "my life flashed before my eyes," and, as I praise the Lord that I had the opportunity to become a mom the following year, this verse comes full circle. Never lose hope.

Heavenly Father, thank You that You always have my future in mind. May I, in turn, continually place my hope in You. Amen.

Jina Bacchus is a member of the Beltsville church in Maryland.

A Search for Peace

"Blessed are the peacemakers, for they shall be called sons of God"
(Matt. 5:9, NKJV).

As I write this, our world is in turmoil. Nightly protests still rage around our country after the killing of George Floyd at the hands of police officers. In this new reality, I wondered what Google could teach me about peace. A .51-second search revealed 1.34 million hits! People are hungry for peace!

As I glanced over many of the summaries, I learned there are articles about the Peace Corps, peace prizes, peace poles, a peace college, peace endowments, peace gardens, peace institutes and peace protests. There are women for peace, Jews for peace, Buddhists for peace, religions for peace, musicals for peace and children for peace.

Further investigation reveals a plethora of formulas, all designed to deliver peace. I found some of them to be noble and inspirational, while others simplistic and shallow. Most of them were based on human efforts to resolve conflict and get along with others. And, though human efforts have at times achieved temporary peace, human effort alone can't change a heart—where real peace is generated.

The good news for us is that we don't need to sort through 1.3 million pages on the internet to find the path to peace. In the Bible, God gives us the only path to genuine, lasting peace. Colossians 1:19–20 teaches, "For it pleased the Father that in Him all the fullness should dwell, and by Him to reconcile all things to Himself, by Him, whether things on earth or things in heaven, having made peace through the blood of His cross" (NKJV).

Peace—lasting peace—comes through the person, Jesus Christ.

Father, today, give me the peace that passes all understanding. May it lift me above even the most significant difficulties of my life. Amen.

Bob Cundiff is the president of the Ohio Conference.

Now That's Love

"Trust in the Lord with all your heart; do not depend on your own understanding. Seek His will in all you do, and He will show you which path to take" (Prov. 3:5–6, NLT).

Becoming a widow has presented challenges that require my total dependence upon God. It set me on a journey that I never expected to take, nor would I have chosen—but God is in control. I said, "OK, Lord. Take it all, but please don't let my car break down."

One day, I noticed my vehicle inspection was overdue, so I scheduled an appointment to renew my sticker. During the inspection, they also took care of a rattling sound that the car was making and ran a diagnostic test for a "Check Engine" light. When they finished, the repairs were more than $1,000!

I could feel the emotions welling up inside of me, and I managed to suppress them until I got into my car. I was ready to flood into tears, when I was startled from within. *Who do you know that is bigger than all of this?* a voice seemed to say. "You are, Lord!" I exclaimed.

After a moment's pause, I continued, "And since You are and You are accountable for widows, I release this car back to You. I haven't the funds, but all the money in every bank is Yours, and all the cars on a thousand lots are Yours too! I trust You!"

What a weight that flew off of my shoulders! As I was leaving, tears of joy welled up inside me as I realized I was loved so divinely, that I could truly love and trust the One who loved me so. That's love!

Thank You, Lord, that You love us and are bigger than our fears. Amen.

Deb Zuch is the teacher's assistant at the York Adventist Christian School in Pennsylvania.

Perfect Peace

"You will keep him in perfect peace, whose mind is stayed on You, because he trusts in You" (Isa. 26:3, NKJV).

My favorite and most comforting verse in the Bible is Isaiah 26:3. This text brought me peace of mind after I completed writing "love letters" to my husband and children, encouraging them and expounding on how much I loved them and sharing my hopes for their future.

In 2003, I was diagnosed with constrictive pericarditis, an inflammation of the pericardium—the saclike membrane that surrounds the heart. It was a very serious condition, and the doctors had never seen a case like this in someone so young. After a year of medications, it was decided surgery would be my only hope, although the prognosis was still not good. My doctors, however, did not know what a mighty God I served.

As I wrote letters to my family, my fears and anxieties left me, and I knew that God would indeed keep me in perfect peace if I trusted Him completely. I also realized that God had done the same thing for me. He inspired 40 writers to author the Bible—His letters to us of encouragement, promise, hope, and, most of all, love.

By His amazing grace, it's been more than 15 years since my operation, and I still find comfort in this text that gives me perfect peace even today, during this "new normal" and uncertain times in which we find ourselves.

Lord, may we put our trust completely in You, and may the peace that surpasses all understanding be our comfort. Amen.

Denise E. Isaac is a member of the Baltimore-White Marsh church in Maryland.

The Unexpected Prayer

"Therefore confess your sins to each other and pray for each other so that you may be healed. The prayer of a righteous person is powerful and effective" (James 5:16, NIV).

At any time or any place, someone is praying. These are known as "expected prayers"—at church, before meals or during pastors' visits. Such was the case when I visited a member the night before open-heart surgery. We spoke and prayed over his concerns and the comforting hope found in his medical team and his faith.

I returned days later to hear, "Hello, Pastor. Thank you for visiting, but your prayer didn't work! After you left, I fell asleep, but fear awakened me when I realized that in just hours my physician would be holding my heart in his hand as he performed bypass surgery. My door opened, and a lady came in, tidying, mopping and emptying the trash."

She asked, "Are you having surgery today?"

"Yes, how do you know?" he asked.

"Well your eyes are wide open, and you can't sleep. She then told me about the wonderful medical team that prays each morning for the patients, and then she prayed for me. Pastor, when she prayed, it was like an angel whispering in my ear. I slept like a baby."

He reiterated, "Pastor, her prayer worked—your prayer didn't!"

The unexpected prayer—the prayer of a caring person who took a moment to lift someone up to God; who stopped and did what medicine cannot do, and touched another's heart and soul!

Thank You, Lord, that an unexpected prayer can move mountains. Amen.

Peter Bath is the vice president of Mission and Ministry at the Kettering Adventist HealthCare in Ohio.

Peace in Troubled Times

"These things I have spoken to you, that in Me you may have peace. In the world you will have tribulation; but be of good cheer, I have overcome the world" (John 16:33, NKJV).

In February 2020, my husband, Kevin, and I committed to a new adventure. We moved from Dayton, Ohio, to Washington, D.C., as I started my new job as the CEO of Howard University Hospital. This new position, arguably the greatest challenge of my career, required peace and courage to perform the task. And then entered COVID-19.

I needed an extra dose of peace to concentrate on the health and welfare of my staff and patients; to compartmentalize my worries for our five children living in a different region; and for our daughter, a physician, who stated, "Mom, if I get COVID-19, you cannot come and see me."

In the midst of this pandemic, Breonna Taylor, and later George Floyd were killed. It was hard to find peace as I contemplated the unmerited deaths of these precious humans. And I needed serenity as I thought of our youngest son—a new police officer.

Kevin and I were living in temporary housing two blocks from the White House when the protests started. From the early morning to late at night, we witnessed thousands chanting, "No Justice; No Peace" and "Say His Name—George Floyd!"

Finding peace in this life requires trusting blindly in our Higher Power—the One who sees the bigger picture, the One who has a better plan, the One who forms a brighter future. Indeed there will be tribulation in this world, but God has already overcome; therefore, we can too.

Thank You, Lord, for Your peace during troubled times. Amen.

Anita L. A. Jenkins is the CEO for Howard University Hospital in Washington, D.C., operated by Adventist HealthCare.

Like a Deer!

"The Sovereign Lord is my strength; He makes my feet like the feet of a deer, He enables me to tread on the heights" (Hab. 3:19, NIV).

There have been times when my trust in God was in a frequent seesaw. My trust soared high when my circumstances were the way I desired and dipped low when God did not come through for me as I asked Him to. I even questioned whether His promises were real.

My youngest sister was at the height of her nursing career. She was just about to begin her doctoral studies when she was unexpectedly diagnosed with a terminal illness. I bargained with God to spare her life. Not an hour went by that I did not beseech Him earnestly to heal her, but He did not. My faith was deeply tested. I had yet to learn that God's faithfulness was not bound to my particular external circumstance.

This is a truth Habakkuk graphically describes in a situation where all hope of survival appears lost. But in spite of the utter destruction that surrounded him, his trust in God remained firm. He described the strength of his trust like the firm sure-footedness of a deer, an animal with the unique ability to place its back feet exactly where its front feet land, thus capable of leaping over impassable terrain.

Habakkuk uses this analogy to acknowledge the firmness of his trust in his Sovereign Lord from Whom he gains strength. Likewise, when our world appears to be crumbling economically, when health appears to be diminishing, when diseases threaten our very existence, we can trust the God who strengthens us to leap over every mountain of difficulty.

Lord, help us to trust You, even when we do not understand why. Amen.

Violet Cox is the education superintendent for the Allegheny West Conference.

Because of My Mother

"Thou wilt shew me the path of life: in Thy presence is fullness of joy; at Thy right hand there are pleasures for evermore" (Ps. 16:11, KJV).

My mother's passing at the age of 91 was "lost" in the midst of the coronavirus pandemic, but I remember her and her great personal sacrifice when our father returned from the Vietnam War in 1968, only to abandon the family 10 days later.

The text says that God will "shew me the path of life," but for a 15-year-old whose life had just imploded, I could not see my way forward. Thank God for a mother with a deep faith and a desire to follow truth wherever it led.

With only a high school education, she now began the struggle to find adequate employment to support my three younger brothers and me. Days were long and hard, but we always had food and shelter, and we never missed Sunday worship. I cannot recall a moment when our mother did not consider the care and the future of her four boys as the most important task of her hard life.

One day, my brother brought home a Seventh-day Adventist evangelistic handbill he found on the street. My mother attended those meetings faithfully and was baptized at the conclusion.

By now I was the "man of the house" and not enthused with her decision. However, the transformation in my mother's character was a revelation of what Jesus can do to the human heart, and I silently observed her love for Christ. I was baptized three years later, and eventually became a pastor.

God, thank You that our Christian "joy" and "pleasures for evermore" sometimes come by the sacrifice of others. Amen.

Robert W. Snyder is the pastor of the Berwick, Danville and Shamokin churches in Pennsylvania.

A Lesson in Perseverance

"For I know the plans I have for you ... plans to prosper you and not to harm you ... to give you hope and a future" (Jer. 29:11, NIV).

The biochemistry textbook was thick and assignments ominous. My primary question was not *Will I survive this class?* but *Is this even necessary?*

Though I had weathered challenges before, the horror stories about my university's Biochemistry course alarmed me. A graduating senior, I was already swamped by other academic and extracurricular commitments.

Embarking on a detailed, fast-paced journey, I increasingly appreciated how biology and chemistry intertwined. I had a C, however, which terrified me. *God, what is happening?* I began to ask.

Slowly, my grade improved. But my despair did not. The semi-familiar terrain of acid-base properties and protein configurations had become the foreign land of concepts such as enzyme kinetics. I restudied chapters, visited my professor's office constantly and defeatedly noted the course's drop date. *God*, I cried, *show me that I'm not working in vain*.

My pleas continued until one mid-semester morning. Shocked to see my perfect score on a difficult quiz, I also realized that I was enjoying what we were learning. *Wake up*, God told me. *You may not know the entire picture—or how this course will apply to your future, but trust that I know, and rest assured that this experience is worth it.*

That semester, I navigated two difficult courses: Biochemistry and Perseverance in the Face of Uncertainty. With Jeremiah 29:11 as my motto, I emerged victorious from both.

Father, when it's hard to see Your plans, may we claim Your promises and persevere! Amen.

Yasmin Phillip is a member of the New Market church in Virginia.

He Made a Way

**"Nor do we know what to do, but our eyes are upon You"
(2 Chron. 20:12, NKJV).**

Once I "found" this verse, it became a favorite of mine. One Bible that I own is full of verses colored in blue to remind me of God's special promises. This is one of those special verses that has not only helped me handle those tough moments in life, but I believe it has also strengthened those with whom I've shared this verse.

Why do we think we can go through life without leaning on the Lord for His guidance and deliverance? My husband, Dan, and I have faced some pretty tough situations in life—dead-end battles—or so they've seemed. But I've discovered that, as our walk with God continues, we need to keep our eyes on Him and go along for the ride. It's not always easy though.

We have faced enormous debts on our house and car. We have also dealt with decisions, such as quitting a well-paying job in a secular organization to step out in faith into full-time literature evangelism with two children in college. Though we couldn't see how things would turn out, we placed total faith in God, and things worked out beautifully.

Whatever you are going through, do you hear God telling you to look to Him? He is the Source of all answers. He will make a way in the wilderness.

Father, our faith is in You and what You are able to do. You have all power and see the end from the beginning. We have nothing to fear. Looking into Your eyes, we are at peace. Amen.

Valerie Morikone is the communication director for the Mountain View Conference.

You Can Call Me 'The Hallelujah'

"Blessed are you when people insult you, persecute you and falsely say all kinds of evil against you because of me. Rejoice and be glad, because great is your reward in heaven" (Matt. 5:11–12, NIV).

When I was a kid, I used to firmly say I'd be willing to bear persecution—and even die for Jesus. These verses, spoken by Jesus, touch me personally and give me courage to be a witness for Him—no matter the consequence.

At the age of 7, my family lived in a neighborhood where we were the only Seventh-day Adventists. My best friend lived four houses down, and we played almost every day. Her parents even let her go to church with us every Sabbath.

However, one of our neighbors, who called us the "The Hallelujahs," discouraged my friend from going to church by giving her toys and snacks. Suddenly, my friend stopped talking and playing with me; she was now friends with the neighbor's grandkids.

This made me very sad. But what hurt the most was when she and the others mocked me and called me "The Hallelujah." Crying, I told my mom. She hugged me and explained that the word hallelujah means joy and happiness, and, that the next time they called me that, I should thank them because they were calling me something nice.

So I did! And they stopped calling me "The Hallelujah." In fact, a couple of weeks later, my friend and I were playing together again.

Help me, God, to remember that it doesn't matter what I go through in life, because You are my reward in heaven. Amen.

Domitila Rosette is the administrative assistant of the Multilingual Ministries Department for the Columbia Union Conference.

Knock at the Door

"Behold, I stand at the door and knock. If anyone hears My voice and opens the door, I will come in to him and dine with him, and he with Me" (Rev. 3:20, NKJV).

To me, this verse is one of the most personal, heartfelt invitations in the Bible. So often we think of Revelation as the book about the antichrist, the mark of the beast, or the seven last plagues. But first and foremost, it is a book where Jesus patiently waits for us to surrender our hearts to Him so that He can love and lead us.

There have been times in my life when I have been frustrated with God. Times I didn't understand why He was letting certain things happen. Times where I felt He was seemingly ignoring my prayers. Sometimes those frustrations grew to the point where I didn't spend time with Him in daily devotions, and, as a result, experienced the feeling of being separated from Him.

But this verse reminds me that God never leaves me nor forsakes me. He doesn't abandon me to the detours of life, or leave me to drown in my negative thoughts and emotions. He's been patiently and continually knocking on the door—waiting for me to surrender my heart again and let Him in.

I'm thankful He understands our frustrations. I'm thankful He is a faithful Friend. But I'm most thankful that, in His everlasting love, He never stops knocking.

Thank You, God, that we mean too much for You to stop knocking. Amen.

David M. Klinedinst is the evangelism director for the Chesapeake Conference.

Two Are Better Than One

**"Two are better than one, because they have a good
reward for their labor" (Eccl. 4:9, NKJV).**

This verse is one of my favorites because it encourages teamwork. I like working in groups and working with my friends on projects because it's fun! We learn so much from each other.

Have you ever done a group project and the other person won't work with you? How does that make you feel? It probably makes you feel sad because you're the only one working. My teacher assigned a group project in school, and I was excited to work on the project, but my teammate didn't want to do much of the work. I tried to talk to him and encourage him to work with me on the project so that we could finish it and it would not be a lot of work for both of us.

I prayed and asked God to help my teammate focus on the project and help. It's better to help the other person feel better so they will enjoy working with you. Nobody wants to do the work alone, but, if you want the person to do the project, you should help him or her.

We finished the project, and I learned a lot about patience and being a good teammate by praying for the person instead of leaving them alone.

Dear Heavenly Father, please bless everyone today, and let us be good, let us work hard and let us appreciate what others do for us. Help us know that You love us, and that we are better as teammates. Amen.

Anyah Dorsey-Townsend is a fourth-grader at Takoma Academy Preparatory School in Maryland.

Only God Can Do That

"The Lord is my shepherd; I shall not want" (Ps. 23:1, KJV).

My favorite verse in the Bible is Psalm 23:1. I know I am safe if God is my Shepherd. I will always have what I need. Many times, however, when I experience trials, I easily forget this promise and start to distrust and despair. I need to trust God when difficult times occur, and rely on this promise to keep my heart calm.

God saved my life when I was baby. As a premature infant, I weighed only three pounds at birth. The doctors didn't expect me to live. They also thought that, if I did live, I would only have half of my heart and be unable to walk. But God saved me and sustained my life. If it weren't for the Lord, I wouldn't be here today—totally healthy and strong.

During this time of crisis due to the coronavirus, I should not worry but have faith in the Lord, because, at the end of the day, no hand sanitizer can save me—only God can do that.

God has impacted my life by helping me grow spiritually in Him. I enjoy reading His Word and attending church. Accepting Jesus was the best decision I have ever made. He loves me for who I am, no matter what I've done. God always comforts me and uplifts me when I am going through tough times. God is great, all the time. And all the time, God is great!

Dear Heavenly Father, no matter what life brings, You are there for me. You provide for all my needs. You love me unconditionally, and I thank you for saving my life. Amen.

Jennifer Jacobo is an eighth-grader at the Roanoke Adventist Christian School in Virginia.

God Chose Me

"Just as He chose us in Him before the foundation of the world, that we should be holy and without blame before Him in love, having predestined us to adoption as sons by Jesus Christ to Himself, according to the good pleasure of His will" (Eph. 1:4–5, NKJV).

I find it amazing to consider this verse, especially along the lines that I was chosen "before the foundation of the world" by the Almighty God. As I ponder upon this, I am reminded of what was done for me before the foundation of the world. Jesus, the Lamb, was slain! (Revelation 13:8). Jesus and His Father loved me and had a plan for me before I was created (John 3:16).

God has clearly chosen me, and all of us for that matter, but have I chosen God? (Joshua 24:15).

I was adopted when I was 7 years old, and I will never forget when the judge asked me if I would accept my new dad. How could I not? My adopted dad had chosen me, and I needed a dad in my life. Once I came to know the will of my dad, it became easy for me to accept him.

So what is the will of our heavenly Father? The Bible tells me it is to save us from our sins, to deliver us from this evil world and to accept us into His family and loving care (Galatians 1:4). I have discovered the assurance that God has already chosen me. I will never have to fear rejection with God (John 6:37; Romans 8:15). As a result, I have decided to choose God in return (1 John 4:19). How about you?

God, may we choose You, now and forever. Amen.

Joshua Plohocky is the pastor of the Bucks County and Fairview Village churches in Pennsylvania.

Battling the What-Ifs

"Trust in the Lord with all your heart; do not depend on your own understanding. Seek His will in all you do, and He will show you which path to take" (Prov. 3:5–6, NLT).

A few years ago, my husband lost his job. Down to one income with children in private school and bills to pay, I was scared. Late one night, trying to fall asleep with a thousand thoughts racing through my mind, Proverbs 3:5–6 was brought to my mind.

Fast forward to 2020 and living in the "new normal" of COVID-19. With so many unknowns, there were moments of what-ifs; however, as with everything in life, going straight to my Heavenly Father and talking with Him helped to calm my fears. Keeping my favorite Bible verse on a continual loop in my mind also helped.

I learned this verse as a child, but needed a gentle reminder that, even when trials and tribulations come—which they will—we must trust in the Lord with all our heart, and not lean on what we think is best. We must always, without fail, trust in the Lord, because He will certainly show us the correct path.

God, You know the end from the beginning, so why should we be afraid? Amen.

Shannon Kornick is the Human Resources specialist for the Columbia Union Conference.

Go for It!

"I returned, and saw under the sun, that the race is not to the swift, nor the battle to the strong, neither yet bread to the wise, nor yet riches to men of understanding, nor yet favour to men of skill; but time and chance happeneth to them all" (Eccles. 9:11, KJV).

These words hold two very credible sources of endorsement: They were penned by Solomon—the wisest man who ever lived—and, as a part of the canon of Scripture, fall under the category of being inspired by God. The truth of this passage can be viewed in two ways that offer hope to us in our earthly journey and experience.

Life lived long enough will prove that life isn't always fair. Hard work doesn't always lead to success, honesty is not always rewarded and position is not always based on merit. The truth of this verse gives us this pragmatic reality: We are not always where we are based on our merit, nor are we always denied our goals because of our lack.

But there is another way to look at this passage: We should shoot our shot, take our chance and aim for the stars. It's not always the best who win; it's not always the strong who overcome; and it's not always the savvy who get rich. Since time and chance (or providence) happens to everyone, it's our job to be content in His mercy and to be ambitious for His glory!

If you feel like you've been overlooked, remember the person ahead of you isn't necessarily better. And, if you're afraid to go for it, remember it's not always the best person who wins.

Lord, since we don't know how time and chance will turn out, let us go for it! Amen.

Emanuel Baek is a pastor of the West Chester church in Pennsylvania.

"Finally, be strong in the Lord and in His mighty power."
EPH. 6:10, NIV

The Passenger

Seeing other parts of the composition for this, sculptors they were discussed and disarmed the like others without a sleeper or.
(Mark 13:4, NASB)

MARCH

The Passenger

"Seeing the people, He felt compassion for them, because they were distressed and dispirited like sheep without a shepherd" (Matt. 9:36, NASB).

I was pastoring in Denver and my wife had to work almost 2,000 miles away in New York. Lonely, I sometimes looked for new activities to enhance my ministry. Uber driving seemed fascinating. I wanted to know more about inner city culture, so I experimented. In general, we isolate from people in our community, mostly because their lives are so different than ours.

I picked up my first rider very late at night. He was a restaurant worker. As time went on, riders and experiences grew in number. There were young people going to parties, others attending professional sports games. I remember prostitutes, senators, high rollers and so many others. Mental images of hundreds of stoned youth still cause me to weep.

One night, I picked up a passenger and started to his destination. Halfway there, he suddenly turned, looked at me and said, "You're a pastor!"

I was startled. How could he tell from my street clothes?

He continued, "I just beat my wife back there, and I'm so ashamed! Please pull over." I did as he said, thinking he'd get out of the car. Instead, he gave his heart to Christ right in the front seat of my car. Then he instructed me to take him to the local police station, where he turned himself in.

Once we have compassion that moves us from our comfort zone, the Holy Spirit can do amazing things through us. Do we see people as Christ sees them? If not, perhaps that is our starting point in serving others.

Lord, give us compassion to share You through word and deed. Amen.

Roy Weeden is the district pastor of the Williamsport, Milton and Lock Haven churches in Pennsylvania.

The Antidote for Restlessness

**"Come unto me, all ye that labour and are heavy laden,
and I will give you rest" (Matt. 11:28, KJV).**

Jesus' invitation helps me to understand my own story of restlessness. The verse speaks life to me because of the steps I took to experience rest personally, and the rest I invite others in crises to experience in my clinical ministry practice.

When my mother gave birth to me, she abandoned me to my grandmother because she was ashamed to hold a child with a withered left hand in a culture of honor and shame. I grew up not knowing my biological parents until I was about 14 years old. I recall how I was moved around to live with uncles, brothers and church members in my village. When I was around 16 or 17 years old, I met an American Baptist missionary couple who taught me to speak and write English.

Looking back, I see myself as a survivor who did not allow the trauma of my past to determine my future. This is important because, how I interpret my past—including my failures and successes—determines the meaning I make or find in the present and the action I take in the future. Jesus' invitation in Matthew 11:28 helps me to understand my call to be a pastor/chaplain/educator in clinical pastoral care. I believe students enter clinical pastoral education (CPE) with various brokenness and restlessness from conflicts with families, churches and other life events, including struggles from pastoral encounters or case presentations. May we all experience the rest God alone offers from challenges life presents to us.

Lord, when I'm restless, rest my heart and soul. Amen.

Moses Taiwo is the CPE educator and manager for Spiritual Care Services at Kettering Medical Center, part of Kettering Adventist HealthCare in Ohio.

Angel at the Falls

"Are not all angels ministering spirits sent to serve those who will inherit salvation?" (Heb. 1:14, NIV).

In the days when I was young and bold, or as my mother would objectively say, "careless," I ventured out from my hotel room at 2:00 a.m. I thought to myself, *Niagara Falls is a completely safe place. Especially in July! So, why not?* Needless to say, I went on a solo adventure, uninhibited of any possible danger.

Ninety minutes into my city voyage, I realized I may be lost. I reached for the hotel map I had in my pocket, and it was gone! Trying not to panic, I mentally retraced my steps and headed back cautiously. Maybe, in my rush to leave my room, I had left the map on the tabletop.

As I was orienting myself, my thoughts went back to my mother. I remembered her expressing, "We are going to Niagara Falls to have a mother and son time together." She wanted us to have a closer relationship. Shame unexpectedly swept over me. While my mother was sleeping, I was selfishly doing "my own thing." I stopped and asked God for forgiveness.

It was now 4:30 a.m. when I heard a gang of boys from the distance quickly approaching my location. Suddenly, a car appeared in front of me. An elderly lady rolled down her window and said, "Sonny, are you lost?!" Embarrassed, I just smiled. She then gave me the exact directions to get back to the hotel. I thanked her and headed that way. When I glanced back, the car had vanished. It was then that I realized I had met my angel at the Falls.

Lord, when we go astray, bring us back home. Amen.

Carl Rodriguez is the youth director for the Chesapeake Conference.

The Bible in a Nutshell

"For God so loved the world that He gave His one and only Son, that whoever believes in Him shall not perish but have eternal life" (John 3:16, NIV).

I often refer to my favorite Bible verse—John 3:16—as "the Bible in a nutshell" because it explains the main message of the Bible: God loves us so much that He sent His Son, Jesus Christ, to die for our sins so that we can have a chance to be reunited with Him for eternity!

John 3:16 has impacted my life by giving me hope. This verse reminds me that, as a Christ-follower, I have the hope of eternal life when the curtain closes on human history.

Someone once told me that they don't believe in life after death, so they've chosen to enjoy everything in this life. They also said that they didn't believe that Jesus Christ rose from the dead. "How is that possible?" the person asked.

I tried to convince and explain that Jesus is alive and that there is hope of eternal life after death for all who follow Him. It's not my job, however, to convince people that Jesus wants to save their souls. It is my job to live for God and follow Jesus all the way to heaven. My mother says this regarding witnessing: "You do the living and let the Holy Spirit do the convicting."

Knowing that God made a way for me to be saved in His kingdom helps me stay true to the cause of Christ. They say that sometimes you may be the only Bible that people read. I hope that the story of my life will lead people to Jesus Christ.

Dear God, please awaken us to know You, love You and follow Jesus. Amen.

Alexis A. Goring is a member of the Restoration Praise Center in Maryland.

Forgiven

"He has not dealt with us according to our sins, nor punished us according to our iniquities. ... As far as the east is from the west, so far has He removed our transgressions from us"
(Ps. 103:10, 12, NKJV).

God always gives us what we need, not what we deserve. Instead of giving us the punishment we deserve, Jesus Christ has paid for all our sins and all our wrongs. I love what the Bible says about East and West because there is no end to East or West. There is a North Pole and a South Pole, but there is no end from East to West.

When I consider my past sins, I tremble at the thought of what God "might" have justly done to me. When I think of the sufferings He "might" have brought upon me, which would have been no more than I deserved—what pain of body, distress of mind, anguish of bereavement, sorrow, danger, sickness, losses—I "might" have suffered before the point would be reached at which it could be said that I had suffered more than a holy and just God might properly inflict on me.

I can truly say, even when I've blown it big time, that He has not "dealt with me" after my sins. He has never apportioned my punishment to my sins, nor has He regulated the exercise of His mercy by my merits.

Let me make this very clear: God forgives you not because you're good, but because He is good.

Gracious God, thank You for not giving me what I deserved. Thank You for loving me so much that You forgave me instead. Amen.

H. J. Fordham III, is the president of the Allegheny East Conference.

Anthrōpos

"The Sabbath was made for man, not man for the Sabbath. So the Son of Man is Lord even of the Sabbath" (Mark 2:27-28, NIV).

In these verses, Mark could have used the word λαός (*laós*) where we get the word "laity"—a word for mankind or humanity in the New Testament. But most often laity refers to Jews.

Or he could have used the word ἔθνος (*éthnos*) where we get the word "ethnic." It is also a word for mankind or humanity in the New Testament, but most often describes Gentiles.

Instead, Mark uses a different word— ἄνθρωπος (*anthrōpos*)—and repeats it twice. "The Sabbath was made for man (*anthrōpos*), not man (*anthrōpos*) for the Sabbath. So the Son of Man is Lord even of the Sabbath."

The word anthrōpos here does not refer to Jews, Gentiles or any specific category of people. Instead, to this day, anthropology is the scientific study of all humanity. Thus, the Sabbath is a gift for all humanity! Exodus 16:29 says, "They must realize that the Sabbath is the Lord's gift to you" (NLT). Kept right, it is a delight. And Isaiah 58:13-14 adds, "Keep the Sabbath day holy. Don't pursue your own interests on that day, but enjoy the Sabbath and speak of it with delight as the Lord's holy day. Honor the Sabbath in everything you do on that day, and don't follow your own desires or talk idly. Then the Lord will be your delight" (NLT).

So unplug, slow down, and gather your friends and family to connect with Jesus this Sabbath. Invite some guests too. He is waiting for all of you!

God, thank You for the Sabbath rest You set aside for all humankind. Amen.

Mike Fortune is the pastor of the Toledo First church in Ohio.

Learning to Lean on Jesus

"Trust in the Lord with all thine heart; and lean not unto thine own understanding. In all thy ways acknowledge Him, and He shall direct thy paths" (Prov. 3:5–6, KJV).

Genuinely believing in God means to adhere to, trust in, rely on, and, most importantly, have faith in Him. That is scary to me, but I know for certain it is true.

I studied to become a registered nurse, but was unsuccessful in passing my nurse licensing exam. After failing, I gave up and said to myself, "I don't like this feeling," and purposed to only do things I reasonably thought would bring me success.

The fierce desire to pass and overcome my fear never escaped me, so, nearly 20 years after finishing nursing school, I decided to retake the exam once more. This decision caused me grief and consuming anxiety. Every day I woke up to the realization that I may fail. It, however, provided me a daily reminder to earnestly seek the Lord. I humbly prayed and asked God for deliverance from my fear and the strength to withstand the amount of studying I had to accomplish. I also asked Him to help me as a working mom, homeschool teacher, part-time student and wife.

I praise God for His unconditional love, because, throughout the yearlong journey, He faithfully kept me. The few people who knew about my situation heartily prayed for me, and His Word comforted me. I wholly trusted God with my entire being, and He didn't fail me. I passed my exam! But the greatest blessing of all was that I found a closer walk with my best friend, Jesus.

God, may we find a friend in Jesus and sincerely trust in Him. Amen.

Ginelle Edmondson is the Health Ministries director for the Mountain View Conference.

Christ Lives in Me

**"I have been crucified with Christ; it is no longer I who live,
but Christ lives in me; and the life which I now live in the flesh I live
by faith in the Son of God, who loved me and gave Himself for me"
(Gal. 2:20, NKJV).**

I was 17 and the youngest child of a big family growing up on a dairy farm
in Pennsylvania when this verse became special to me. That summer,
I worked alone on the farm, as all my siblings had moved away. This
provided me with a lot of time to think, and I examined the purpose of life
and what I should do with mine. I contemplated a number of avenues, such
as joining the U.S. Marines and volunteering for service in Vietnam, as one
of my older brothers had done.

For some unknown reason, I couldn't find peace of mind except when I
dwelled on Scripture. I also began reading *Steps to Christ* for what seemed
like the first time. Within the pages, I discovered this special verse.

As I look back, I'm certain it was this pivotal time in my life when I sensed
God calling me to the gospel ministry. I committed this verse to memory,
and, as I repeated it to myself, it gave me the peace of mind I sought. I was
so encouraged by its message: I live, but yet, I don't; Christ lives in me.

It is His Spirit that gives my soul peace, comfort and hope, and I live each
day by the power He offers!

*Lord, please live in me today and give me Your peace, presence and power.
Amen.*

Dave Weigley is the president of the Columbia Union Conference.

My Future

"For the Lord Himself will descend from heaven with a shout, with the voice of an archangel, and with the trumpet of God. And the dead in Christ will rise first. Then we who are alive and remain shall be caught up together with them in the clouds to meet the Lord in the air. And thus we shall always be with the Lord" (1 Thess. 4:16–17, NKJV).

As a 4-year-old, I didn't understand the concept of death and that my father would never come home again. For weeks, I stayed up at night waiting for him. By the age of 8, though, I understood that he was not returning and this new unfavorable home where I lived was my only home. I longed for the daddy that I couldn't even remember because I longed for a daddy who cared, provided, listened, held and loved me.

In a small, two-room Seventh-day Adventist school, I learned these verses and immediately claimed them as my own: "And the dead in Christ will rise first." My hope. My promise. My future. I could not wait to see my daddy again!

Years have passed and these verses still remain powerful, but with one growing change: As much as I still long to know my daddy, I have found that I long even more for my heavenly Father. I have a "Daddy" who has taken care of me, provided for me, listened to me, held me and loves me with an eternal love. And I desperately long "to meet the Lord in the air. And thus we shall always be with the Lord!"

Father, I can only imagine what I'll do when I stand before You! Amen.

Debbie Rivera is a pastor at the Ellicott City church in Maryland.

God's Waiting Room

**"Wait patiently for the Lord. Be brave and courageous.
Yes, wait patiently for the Lord" (Ps. 27:14, NLT).**

I feel like the more I serve God, the more encounters I have in His waiting room. This is where I learn to be courageous and wait on Him even when my circumstances say otherwise. In the process of waiting, I have realized that, without faith, it is impossible to wait patiently for the Lord, especially when it seems He is tied up with someone else's emergency.

After my studies, God blessed me with a part-time job, yet it was a struggle to take care of my family's basic expenses. My wife and I presented our scarcity and situation to God while we waited on Him. We kept praying and waiting for me to secure a full-time job, but it didn't happen. In God's great mercy, He provided a job for my wife. Together, our income was just enough to take care of our needs.

Despite God's blessings, I was still arguing with Him for a full-time job. I could not understand what God was doing in my life. And then COVID-19 struck. Many of my co-workers were furloughed, but God kept my part-time job.

Many families were in a dilemma because schools went virtual for the rest of the school year. My part-time job was a blessing in disguise because it created an opportunity for my wife and me to alternate so that our sons could be supervised at home. At the moment, the wait seemed like a curse, but looking back it was a blessing. There are, indeed, blessings in our waiting.

God, may we choose You always. Amen.

Dale Walton is a staff chaplain at the Troy Hospital for Kettering Adventist HealthCare in Ohio.

Nothing Can Separate Us

"For I am convinced that neither death, nor life, nor angels, nor principalities, nor things present, nor things to come, nor powers, nor height, nor depth, nor any other created thing, will be able to separate us from the love of God, which is in Christ Jesus our Lord"
(Rom. 8:38–39, NASB).

Romans 8:32 tells us that God did not spare His own Son, but handed Him over to save us. This act alone is enough to convince us that nothing can ever separate us from His love. This work of love continues as Christ, who died for us all and faced persecution from Satan and his evil angels and from religious and political powers, is able to sympathize with our weaknesses as He intercedes for us (Hebrews 4:15). This is our assurance that no tribulation, trial, burden, temptation or power we experience on earth can separate us from the everlasting love of God.

Heavenly Father, we praise You for the evidences of Your love that we see displayed every day in our lives. We praise You for the ultimate sacrifice You made on our behalf, through Your Son, Jesus Christ. Help us to accept Your love with a grateful heart and to give evidence of our love and devotion to You every day by submitting our lives to You and Your will. Amen.

Kimberly Ondrizek is a member of the Indiana church in Pennsylvania.

Don't Lose Hope

"Cast all your anxiety on Him because He cares for you"
(1 Pet. 5:7, NIV).

When the COVID-19 outbreak happened, we were stuck at home in quarantine. All we could do was stay home and work or watch the news, hoping to hear something good. During that time, I noticed people having anxiety because they did not know what the future held. So many crazy things have happened recently, and as everything looks to be worsening, it feels endless.

However, don't lose hope. We need to continue praying, having faith and keeping our heads up, because we know that God is here with us, and things will be better soon.

Honestly, I have anxiety about the future, especially since I am young. I still don't fully understand all that is going on, but God has really helped me with my personal anxiety during these times. First Peter 5:7 is a great reminder to keep our faith in God because He is in control of the future and will take care of us.

God, please help us not to lose hope and to continue to pray, have faith and move forward when anxiety comes. Amen.

Arria Williams is an eighth-grader at the Mount Vernon Seventh-day Adventist Elementary School in Ohio.

Remember

"Therefore I tell you, do not worry about your life, what you will eat or drink. ... Look at the birds of the air; they do not sow or reap or store away in barns, and yet your heavenly Father feeds them. Are you not much more valuable than they? Can any one of you by worrying add a single hour to your life? (Matt. 6:25–27, NIV).

In spring of 1976, we stood in front of our home, and nothing was left but ashes. We were able to save the orange Ford Pinto wagon and my dad's wallet that contained the only money we had. My parents seemed calm, but I am sure they were worried about the future.

Through God's providence, the five of us ended up in Eatonville, Wash. Day after day, God took care of us with food, jobs and necessities. As a young teen, I remember thinking how dedicated my parents were to prayer, and the answered prayers solidified for me that our God cares.

During the pandemic, like everyone else, I had questions: Will my mom, who lives in a nursing facility, be OK? Will I still have a job? How long will this crisis last? But, once again, the Lord brought to mind Matthew 6:25–34 and the assurance that I don't have to worry. If He cares for the birds and the flowers, how much more does He care for you and me, who have far greater value?

In these uncertain times, we need to remember how God has led us in the past and be reassured that He will lead us now and in the future.

God, even if we can't see the end from the beginning, may we trust You to see us through. Amen.

Lori Farr is the pastor of the Miamisburg church in Ohio.

A Heart for Health

"But Daniel purposed in his heart that he would not defile himself with the portion of the king's delicacies, nor with the wine which he drank; therefore he requested of the chief of the enunchs that he might not defile himself" (Dan. 1:8, NKJV).

The rewards of the Bible-based diet in Daniel's story resonated with me when I became a Seventh-day Adventist. My Christian journey up to that point had been a circuitous one. However, each path led me to be more reconciled to the Scriptures. Daniel's example continues to influence the dietary improvements I make for better health, wisdom and discernment.

For years in social work, I observed how marginalized clients' decision-making, health, finances, and self-worth were impacted by the limitations of fresh produce and wholesome food availability and affordability. High calorie, nutritionally low and convenience food products were easily accessible to them. My journey led me to share recipes, samples and shopping experiences with those in my sphere of influence.

God blessed not only me, but family, friends and clients. Failure to thrive babies gained weight and some adults lost weight. Grocery funds lasted longer. Meal planning increased and fast food consumption decreased.

When I left social work for home-based childcare, I provided plant-based meals to my young clients. The Lord always blessed me with families who welcomed a plant-based diet, regardless of their practice at home. I believed with God's help, these children would be healthy and wise, more able to discern between right and wrong. Indeed, I believe they grew to be more articulate, fit and knowledgeable than their peers. God did it!

Dear Lord, may Your Word create in me an appetite for holiness and healthy living as I also purpose to be wise. Amen.

Gillian Jefferson Chavers is the head deaconess at the Calvary church in Virginia.

Lean Into Jesus

"[The disciples] feared exceedingly, and said to one another, 'Who can this be, that even the wind and the sea obey Him!'" (Mark 4:41, NKJV).

"Your COVID-19 test is positive." This was the spoiled icing on the rancid cake that had been the last three months of our lives.

March 2020 started with 31 days of quarantine because my doctor feared that my asthma could compromise me if I were to catch COVID-19.

At the beginning of April, we learned my father-in-law fell, hit his head and was rushed to the hospital. The day we planned to drive from Maryland to Colorado to be with him, a tree fell on our house. The next day, a deer flew across the highway and smashed into our new car just four hours into our trip. All shops were closed in the area, so we kept driving. Three hours later, we received the call that my father-in-law had passed. It was a tearful drive the rest of the way.

My mother-in-law is a brave cancer survivor, however, her treatments have left her mostly bedridden. We packed her house and moved her back to Maryland to be with us, but our place was not adequate, so we also had to move homes. The day we moved, I started feeling COVID-19 symptoms.

This storm seemed relentless, and the waves were coming so fast. *How will we ever survive?* I thought. But then an overwhelming peace came over me.

The disciples were amazed that Jesus could control the storm. However, an even greater miracle, possibly, is that He can calm us when we are caught in life's raging storms. Thankfully, Jesus is in our boat.

God, how can we fear when You are near? Amen.

Steve Leddy is the director of Evangelism and Church Planting for the Potomac Conference.

God's Word for Perplexed People

**"And because lawlessness will abound, the love
of many will grow cold" (Matt. 24:12, NKJV).**

Our world is in crisis, and it's more than a fast-moving series of disasters and emergencies. Many people are appalled as they see riots, burning and looting of cities, wars and everything once so apparently stable falling apart. Society is being pulled apart by vicious undercurrents, and the filth and slime of immorality are oozing from the seams. Instead of being a refuge, society has become the breeding ground of alcoholism, drug addiction, violence, murder and the destruction of matrimony. All is stark testimony that the Spirit of God is being withdrawn from the earth and that the end is near.

As we live in these perplexing times, every Seventh-day Adventist Christian must ask these questions: Shall I be spared the withdrawal of God's Holy Spirit? Am I seeking God as my only hope and refuge in this fateful hour? Is my soul a leaking vessel? Am I in any way unconsciously absorbing this godless spirit that is spelling the doom of the human race?

Ellen White shares, "There are not many, even among educators and statesmen, who comprehend the causes that underlie the present state of society. Those who hold the reins of government are not able to solve the problem of moral corruption, poverty, pauperism, and increasing crime. ... If men would give more heed to the teachings of God's word, they would find a solution of the problems that perplex them" (*Testimonies for the Church*, vol. 9, p. 13).

Father, thank You for Your Word that is living and powerful, a discerner of the thoughts and intents of the heart, as we read in Hebrews 4:12. Amen.

Ferdi Sastropawiro is the head teacher for The Northern Tier Christian School in Pennsylvania.

Empowered by Love

"And be not conformed to this world: but be ye transformed by the renewing of your mind, that ye may prove what is that good, and acceptable, and perfect, will of God" (Rom. 12:2, KJV).

God loves us, and His care for us helps us bring out the absolute best in us all. When we realize how much He loves us, it empowers us to be loving to those around us. Even though we are in quarantine at the time I am writing this, we, as Christians, should let this tragedy be a time to read the Bible more. We should make a difference in the world around us. We should help others by staying safe indoors, telling ourselves it's OK to be away from friends for a while, and, through a consistent prayer life, everything will be just fine in the end.

God is calling us to rise up as Christians and make a difference in this world. I know how scary it can be finding out if you have the coronavirus because my aunt had a scare herself. She was feeling sick, and she had to get tested. My mother and I were very scared because we heard how the virus can kill people very fast.

We prayed the whole time, hoping the test would come back negative. In the name of Jesus, she was fine—the test was negative. Since that day, I have been telling a lot of people that God can work miracles. He saved my aunt, just as I know He will continue to save many others.

Dear Father in heaven, thank You for being the Miracle Worker. Help me to trust You more. Amen.

Talyah Bailey is an eighth-grader at the Harrisburg Adventist School in Pennsylvania.

Wait on the Lord

"But those who wait on the Lord shall renew their strength; they shall mount up with wings like eagles, they shall run and not be weary, they shall walk and not faint" (Isa. 40:31, NKJV).

Having lived in a fast-paced environment all my life, it's been hard for me to learn to wait on the Lord. After all, isn't it better to get things done before it is too late? I have committed many mistakes in my life due to me moving ahead of the Lord. In fact, to me it seems like He is the one sometimes slowing me down. Oh, but if I, at times, would have just waited for God's leading, how things would have turned out differently.

The COVID-19 pandemic has affected many lives and families. When it hit mine, my family and I were devastated. My dad was in the hospital for almost a month, and we prayed and prayed for God to heal him so he could be together with my mom. There were moments when we wanted the hospital to release him, but something always interfered with him coming home. We know now that the Lord was getting everything in order before allowing my dad to return home.

We patiently waited on the Lord, and our strength was renewed during the waiting trial. If my dad would have been released at the time we wanted, we would have run into many problems. We didn't have the proper nursing equipment and hospital bed, and the home wasn't fully disinfected. The day after we had these things in order, my dad was discharged from the hospital.

Lord, may we learn to wait on You, for Your timing is perfect! May we trust in You and renew our strength as we wait. Amen.

Juan Cabrera is a member of the Spencerville church in Maryland.

Do Not Be Afraid

"This is my command—be strong and courageous! Do not be afraid or discouraged. For the Lord your God is with you wherever you go" (Josh. 1:9, NLT).

This verse brings me hope and courage when I am feeling scared. When I was younger, terrible things happened to me. My family was very unkind, and it was scary living in a home where I experienced constant trauma. I did not know about Jesus, so I had no hope of a better life. I used to hide so my family would not find me. Sometimes when they found me, they hurt me.

Even though I did not know Jesus, He was looking out for me. When I was 8-years-old, He sent the Department of Social Services to take my siblings and me to foster families. My entire life changed that day.

The family I was placed in loves God and teaches me all about Him. They send me to a Christian school so I can learn more about Him. One day, I heard this memory verse and it brought me such comfort. It tells me that I do not need to feel afraid, that He is always with me. God loves me enough to always be with me and protect me, and, even if I was the only one on this earth, He would still come and die for me. He would do the same for you too.

I still deal with fear at times. Satan likes to remind me of my past. But I keep quoting this verse, and it helps me to be strong. One day, my dream is to help others like me and teach them this verse too!

Dear Jesus, please help those who are scared and feel alone to know that You love them so much and You will always be there for them. Amen.

Kensley Roark is a fourth-grader at the Desmond T. Doss Christian Academy in Virginia.

Perfect Timing

"And we know that in all things God works for the good of those who love Him, who have been called according to His purpose" (Rom. 8:28, NIV).

This verse reminds me that God will work out things in my life for good. And if we listen to His leadings, how many times can He use us to work out good in other people's lives?

A few years ago, a friend of mine helped me with several projects. I thanked her but felt that I needed to do more to show my appreciation. After a few weeks, I decided to send her flowers. But I didn't know what type of flower or color she liked.

Little did I know how much my friend needed those flowers. The day she received them, she had been let go from work. Not only were the flowers her favorite type and color, but they were from her favorite florist too. Given this, she didn't read the card but called her mother, thinking the flowers were from her. Her mother refused the thank you and told her to read the card.

Looking back, it is easy to see that, by listening to God's leading, I was able to help brighten a friend's day on the exact day she needed it. And maybe, just maybe, I played a small part in helping things work together for good in her life.

Continue to use me, God, to touch those around me. Amen.

Peggy Jean Lee is an assistant treasurer for the Columbia Union Revolving Fund in Maryland.

Why I Believe Romans 8:28

**"And we know that all things work together for good to those who love God, to those who are the called according to His purpose"
(Rom. 8:28, NKJV).**

In the midst of trouble, it can be very difficult to see anything good. More often than not, the darkness of pain and suffering drowns out any glimpse of light and hope. Faith tends to give way to feelings of despair and discouragement. Have you been there? Maybe you are experiencing that dark place right now.

Remember Joseph in the Bible? His multi-colored coat, dreaming mind and the intense hatred of his older brothers? The ones whom he should have been able to trust for protection instead plotted to kill him. Joseph was stripped, beaten, sold into slavery and sent to a foreign land. He had many years to reflect on what happened to him. I've often thought about his attitude toward his brothers and God during those years in Egypt.

After 20 years, Joseph is reunited with his brothers. The Bible gives a glimpse into his heart as he interacts with them. And after their father dies, the brothers are still afraid Joseph may seek retaliation for their prior wrongs. Yet we see what I call the "original" Romans 8:28 found in Genesis 50:20: "But as for you, you meant evil against me; but God meant it for good, in order to bring it about as it is this day, to save many people alive" (NKJV).

Take hold of the same faith that Joseph had in God. He chose to see his experiences through the lens of faith. His perspective was widened to see a plan bigger and more far-reaching than his own life.

Dear God, thank You for being in control of our circumstances for our good and for Your glory! Amen.

Marquita Klinedinst is a member of the Spencerville church in Maryland.

God Grieves Too

"And God shall wipe away all tears from their eyes; and there shall be no more death, neither sorrow, nor crying, neither shall there be any more pain: for the former things are passed away" (Rev. 21:4, KJV).

On June 6, 2018, my family and I were given the worst news any parent can be given. My 7-year-old daughter, Liana Kathryn, was diagnosed with a rare form of cancer known as diffuse intrinsic pontine glioma. When the head of neurosurgery came to speak to me, I asked him to "give it to me straight." You ask that, hoping that it will make things easier.

His words will forever be etched into my mind: "I am sorry to tell you this, but your daughter is going to die." It was as if someone had punched me in the gut or a ton of weight fell on me. Our life in a comfortable cocoon shattered.

Liana battled bravely and honorably against this dreaded disease for six months before succumbing to it November 10, 2018. She was a real trooper.

Liana had a zest for life. A social butterfly, she was a jokester, a prankster and her smile always lit up a room. She was always laughing and giggling. Liana could be hard-nosed at times, but had the sweetest of hearts. And she loved Jesus.

Since that time, I have started a grieving ministry at my church, for Jesus revealed to me in John 11, that He, too, grieves.

God, please comfort and heal the hearts of all those who have lost loved ones. Amen.

Howard Martin is a member of the Fredericksburg church in Virginia.

God's To-Do List

"I will answer them before they even call to me. While they are still talking about their needs, I will go ahead and answer their prayers!" (Isa. 65:24, NLT).

It wasn't until I became a teaching principal that Isaiah's words took root in my soul. Oftentimes, I found myself conversing with God about school and the myriad of situations I had no idea how to solve. Each time my staff, the school board and I found a solution, we were reminded yet again of how faithful He was (and is) to His children.

As we continued to bring our seemingly endless petitions to God, I began to envision each of our needs as items on an enormous to-do list. None of the requests we made were news to Him. Over time, it became clear to me that every new item we added, and subsequently checked off, He had long ago checked off His own list. As I began to reflect on my life, I saw how He had been working things out long before I knew what to ask for.

That is when I realized this verse had taken root—deep root—within my soul. As He revealed His answers, I started referring to this text without noticing. These words were no longer just letters in an obscure text; they were a living promise. I could look back at the evidence and see it so clearly.

My prayers began to change from, "Lord, how will I ever solve this?" to "Father, thank You for having checked this off Your to-do list long ago. May my eyes be open to see the answer You have already provided." I finally understood that my only job was to trust Him and follow His lead.

God, thank You for solving my problems before I even ask. Amen.

Janet Armstrong is the associate superintendent of education for the Potomac Conference.

Where My Help Comes From

"My help comes from the Lord, who made heaven and earth"
(Ps. 121:2, NKJV).

This Bible text has become my "go-to" spiritual promise. So often I find myself in situations where my soul cries out for help. Whether I am hiking up a strenuous path and falling behind, skiing a challenging slope or facing a technological challenge, my Lord is there. God's powerful spirit brings this verse to my mind at times when I am tempted to say an unkind word, express frustration or behave impulsively to defend myself. I lift my eyes to the Lord, and I'm reminded that my help doesn't come from within, but from my Maker—the Creator of the entire universe.

A friend of mine recently expressed her discouragement because she didn't have the funds to continue supporting our local church since her husband lost his job due to COVID-19. Later that day, I texted her an encouraging message to keep looking up because help comes from the Lord who made the heavens, the earth and everything in them. God financially responded soon after, and the couple faithfully resumed giving back to the church.

My faith is strengthened each time I experience my Lord fulfilling His promises to me and others.

Dear Heavenly Father, thank You for always being right here, right now, ready and willing to help Your children! I give You the honor and glory. Amen.

Celinda Bauer is a member of the Middletown Valley church in Maryland.

The Prayer Group

**"Do not be afraid, Jacob, my servant, Jeshurun, whom I have chosen"
(Isa. 44:2, NIV).**

In 2016, I enrolled in an English class to improve my language skills. Our class of 30 students represented 17 different nationalities and beliefs. Four of us formed a small prayer group. We met after class to pray together, and sometimes arrived early to pray for our classmates. We periodically fasted, too, asking God to help us reach our secular friends for Him.

The results of our prayers revolutionized my ministry. By following Jesus' method, we began to mingle with other students, establishing friendship networks and creating strong bonds.

Every Wednesday before we began English class, we had a study group. Students asked questions, and we provided biblical answers. In our study, I realized that, very few—although they defended their beliefs and outwardly practiced what they had learned—had an experience with God.

When we told the love story of God for humanity and His desire to make humanity happy, it touched the most sensitive fibers of their hearts. God's love is universal. It gives us stability, dignity and belonging.

I began to show by example what the gospel of Jesus means. It was during those unforgettable moments in our Bible studies that our friendship and comprehension of other cultures and beliefs grew. Through this study of questions and interactive dialogues, we found God in a fresh way and started seeing changes in the classroom.

God did amazing things in my life and those of my friends. It was like Pentecost! Attending English class became a family reunion of many nations.

God, may we not be afraid to speak up for You. Amen.

Javier Moreno is the pastor of the Baltimore Spanish church in Maryland.

Bouncing Like a Ping-Pong Ball

"Faith means being sure of the things we hope for. And faith means knowing that something is real even if we do not see it. People who lived in the past became famous because of faith. It is by faith we understand that the whole world was made by God's command. This means that what we see was made by something that cannot be seen" (Heb. 11:1–3, ICB).

Sometimes our hearts are full to overflowing with it; other times it feels entirely illusive. I'm referring to hope. As I write this, the COVID-19 pandemic continues. During this time, we've all observed in ourselves and others the ups and downs that it brings.

We may have a nice conversation, hear a message from a pastor, read a positive news report that makes us feel good, even hopeful. Then, days or even minutes later, we hear, see or take in something that leaves us feeling empty, even lost.

At times like these, let's remind ourselves that feelings will bounce around like a ping-pong ball, but God's Word, love and care for us are consistent and do not waver. While we work through our bouncing around feelings, remember to take time to simply rest and find peace in God's truth. Experience His constant presence and His assurance of an everlasting life that will make this life pale in comparison. This is faith. This is hope.

As shared in Hebrews 11, we are foreigners and nomads here on earth, looking forward to a better place—our heavenly homeland. "Faith shows the reality of what we hope for; it is the evidence of things we cannot see" (Heb. 11:1, NLT).

Lord, thank You that we have something better to look forward to. Amen.

Kevin Krueger is the president and general manager of WGTS 91.9 in Maryland.

God Gave Me Strength

"I can do all things through Christ who strengthens me"
(Phil. 4:13, NKJV).

While visiting me on Christmas Eve 2016, my daughter Becky was diagnosed with neuroendocrine cancer. The prognosis was not good. Devastated, I prayed for God to heal her. But I also prayed that if her healing was not within His will, that He would give me the strength to deal with what lay ahead. Three-and-a-half weeks later, my heart broke as my baby lost her battle with cancer.

My older daughter, Tammi, had taken a leave of absence from work and stayed with us. After her sister's passing, I gave her some Bible studies. Witnessing Becky's last days had affected her, and she took the lessons to heart. A few months later, during a phone conversation, she said, "You know, Mom, God really did give you strength during that time. You broke down a time or two, but never in front of her."

On January 4, 2020, Tammi was baptized at the Pocono Grace church in Pennsylvania. While preparing for the baptism, the pastor asked her which scripture verse was her favorite. She promptly answered, "Philippians 4:13."

I miss Becky so very much, but I know that I will see her again one day when Jesus returns, where there will be no more pain, tears, suffering or death. And, as a dear friend told me, "Think of how happy Becky will be to see her sister there too." God is so good. He can bring something good out of the very worst, most tragic moments in our lives.

Lord, thank You for bringing joy out of sadness. Amen.

Dottie Jones is a member of the Berkeley Springs church in West Virginia.

Assurance of God's Help and Presence

"Fear not, for I am with you; be not dismayed, for I am your God. I will strengthen you, yes, I will help you, I will uphold you with My righteous right hand" (Isa. 41:10, NKJV).

I vividly remember when our office started lockdown in March 2020 and ordered all employees to work remotely from home due to the coronavirus. At first, I thought this would be a temporary two-week period; however, for months the lockdown has been prolonged indefinitely with no sign of a complete return to normalcy.

Before the lockdown, it was a joy to attend social gatherings, potlucks and other forms of activities; now they are either non-existent or stressful. Social distancing and wearing masks is the new norm. The economy has collapsed, jobs have been lost, millions are sick, more than a million are dead and millions mourn the loss of loved ones. People, scared of catching this virus, now live in constant fear and anxiety.

In this time of unprecedented uncertainty, where else can we find our help and strength but in God? The world around us may crumble, but, as God's children, we can find strength and help in Him. He is faithful and has promised to help us. We must cling fully to Him to help us in these uncertain times. And, one day soon, we will see the reward for placing our complete trust in Him.

Father God, help us to trust You fully. You are the mighty God! Help us to remember that, when we are tempted to be fearful or dismayed, Your promises are assured. Amen.

Lanny Pongilatan is a member of the Takoma Park church in Maryland.

Hakuna Matata

"Therefore I tell you, do not worry about your life, what you will eat or drink; or about your body, what you will wear. Is not life more than food, and the body more than clothes?" (Matt. 6:25, NIV).

"Hakuna Matata" is a Swahili saying that means, "Don't worry." For many people, that's easier said than done, but not for me. My approach to life is found in Matthew 6:25–34. I learned this, not by choice, but by circumstance.

I am from Haiti, and when I was 5-years-old, my single mother immigrated to the United States looking for a better life for her children. Ten years later, I joined her. During hard times, I learned to trust God who provided food, clothing and shelter for us. I learned to trust Him when I didn't know how my college tuition would be paid. I learned to trust Him during my pregnancy, when the doctors told my husband and me that our one and only son might not make it. In all of these situations, God always made a way.

And now, as a school principal, I have learned to trust God to bring in students and to provide the funding to pay their bills. Year after year, I continue to take Him at His word, and He has never failed. I know that I can trust Him.

I don't know what your situation may be today. But I invite you to just trust God with childlike faith. God always does what He says He will do. Hakuna Matata! Don't worry. Trust God to take care of you. Your worries cannot change your situation, but God can!

Dear God, help us not to worry but to trust You to be our Provider and Comforter. Amen.

Malou Saint-Ulysse is the principal of Meadow View Junior Academy in New Jersey.

He Takes My Cares

**"Cast all your anxiety on Him because He cares for you"
(1 Pet. 5:7, NIV).**

I have a young friend who has been in jail for 15 years. I went to visit him for the first time 12 years ago. I was anxious, scared, guilty, sad. I taught him about Jesus at church when he was a teenager, and I somehow felt I had failed him because I had not recognized that he needed so much more—someone who would listen to him and someone he could trust to help him make meaningful life choices.

When I saw Mauro, he looked so anxious, nervous and scared. I expressed how sad I was to see him in prison. I promised that I would be by his side, write to him, visit him often and daily pray for him to grow, learn, focus and remain safe while captive.

During my visits through the years, we've talked about God, but mostly I've listened to him as he's told me his struggles. I've encouraged him to participate during therapy, to work hard while trusting in God—the One who is preserving him and will allow him freedom when he is ready to face this outside world.

When I visit him now, he's not anxious anymore. He has a beautiful smile, and his eyes are full of confidence and hope. I don't know how much he prays or how much he trusts in God, but I know that I have given God all my anxieties about Mauro. God cares for him and grants second chances. Soon I will get to see him enjoying life as a free man.

Lord, may I not be anxious about anything because You are a wonderful friend who daily invites me to give You my cares. Amen.

Martha Cecilia Monsalve is a member of the Washington Spanish church in Maryland.

True Friends

"Since they could not get him to Jesus because of the crowd, they made an opening in the roof above Jesus by digging through it and then lowered the mat the man was lying on. When Jesus saw their faith, He said to the paralyzed man, 'Son, your sins are forgiven'" (Mark 2:4–5, NIV).

One time, Jesus was preaching at Peter's house. Four friends were on their way to the house, having faith that Jesus would heal their paralytic friend. But the crowd was so big that they couldn't reach Jesus. So they climbed up to the roof and ripped it open!

Can you imagine how surprised everyone was seeing a bed come down from the ceiling of the house? When Jesus saw the friends' faith, He said, "Son, your sins are forgiven." Because of his friends' faith, the paralytic was forgiven!

Wow! What great friends the paralytic had. The friends brought him to Jesus, but the crowd was a barrier. Are we like the friends or the crowd? Do we have that kind of faith and determination to bring people closer to Jesus? I want to be like the paralytic's friends.

Father God, please help us to bring people to You instead of pushing them away. May we be the kind of friend who encourages others to turn to You for help. Amen.

Jason Kim is a fourth-grader at Vienna Adventist Academy in Virginia.

"Come to me, all you who are weary and burdened, and I will give you rest." MATT. 11:28, NIV

APRIL

Upheld by His Hand

"So do not fear, for I am with you; do not be dismayed, for I am your God. I will strengthen you and help you; I will uphold you with My righteous right hand" (Isa. 41:10, NIV).

This verse shows me that God will help me even if I can't see it. He has already helped me in many times of trouble. This verse reminds me that He helped His people by parting the Red Sea. If God can do that, He can definitely help me with my anxiety and confusion. He died on the cross so that He could be with me always and hold my hand and strengthen me throughout my entire life.

This verse reminds me that I am not alone; He is with me, along with His angels. I can always turn to Him for help, because I know that He has it all under control. All I need to do is to have faith in Him.

Sin is a part of us, but we can ask God to help us when it takes control of us. Step-by-step, He will help us. God is the strength we need to go on in life; the True Power in this world; the Shepherd that supports the weak; the One working hardest for us; and the One who destroys our biggest and smallest fears.

Father in Heaven, thank You for taking care of our fears. Thank You that we are not alone. Amen.

Darcy Koilpillai is a seventh-grader at Frederick Adventist Academy in Maryland.

Praising God in the Midst of Pain

**"Let everything that has breath praise the Lord! Praise the Lord!"
(Ps. 150:6, NKJV).**

This text has always been significant to me, but became even more meaningful during a very difficult time in my life. As a result of a car accident, my body was wracked with constant pain. It was painful to be hugged, drive, write and even sleep. After nine months of therapy, nothing seemed to ease the agony, which left me emotionally down and frustrated. But God!

He brought this Psalm back to my memory at just the right moment, and my spirit was renewed just by reading it again. I realized that God had not left me. I still had breath to praise Him, despite the pain! So from that day forward, I started praising Him in the pain. And that is when my healing began.

When life throws everything at you, and you are feeling low and alone, go to God in praise. He will always show up and carry you through the storm. Take it from me—I've experienced it firsthand.

Father, thank You for promises that renew our strength. May we use our words to glorify and praise You, even in difficult circumstances. Amen.

H. Candace Nurse is the secretary/treasurer for the Columbia Union Revolving Fund in Maryland.

Make Us Clean

"'Take away the filthy garments from him.' And to him He said, 'See, I have removed your iniquity from you, and I will clothe you with rich robes'" (Zech. 3:4, NKJV).

Dressed in very humble clothes, rather ragged, with a tanned complexion and a wrinkled face, the poor, old man approached all those who parked on the church's street, offering to watch their cars for a few coins. His destitute condition and his tired appearance betrayed the difficult life he lived.

After several days visiting the new church that I was to pastor, I realized that this man was always willing to offer up his service. I was surprised to learn that every Sabbath for years this man had been helping members, but no one had ever invited him into the church or to study the Bible. Some leaders and I agreed we would not allow this man to take care of our cars outside of the church one more Sabbath while we worshipped God inside.

The following Sabbath, we invited him into the church. It was exciting to see the gratitude on his face, knowing that we saw him as part of our church family. We offered him Bible studies and tended to his basic needs. Finally, he gave his heart to Christ through baptism.

That Sabbath was a truly joyous one. Transformed internally and externally, he wore a simple but very clean suit, stripped of his vile robes and now wearing nice garments.

I will never forget this kind, old man and the lesson he taught me. Regardless of our condition, how bad, how vile, how dirty we are, the Lord comes and says, "Take off those filthy garments and put on rich robes."

God, we are dirty. Please make us clean. Amen.

Peter M. Simpson is the coordinator of Hispanic Ministries and director of Global Mission for the Ohio Conference.

I Have Prayed for You

"'Simon! Simon! Behold, Satan has demanded permission to sift you like wheat; but I have prayed for you, that your faith may not fail'" (Luke 22:31–32, NASB).

Christ and His disciples had just finished the Passover meal. Several events leading up to His crucifixion were about to unfold. He was to be betrayed by Judas, forsaken by His disciples and falsely accused by the Jewish religious leaders. Yet, Christ's concern was for Peter as He assured him, "I have prayed for you."

Satan once demanded and was given consent to "sift" Job. Severely assaulted, Job cursed the day of his birth but did not recant his faith in God.

A similar battle raged in both Peter and Judas, and rages about us today! Satan desires us to compromise our faith in God and lose hope. He strikes our weakest areas, bringing discouragement, hopelessness, doubt, guilt and confusion, as he did with Peter and Judas.

When the darkness of negative emotions threatens to overwhelm us, but we firmly grasp hold of God's promises instead, Satan seeks to destroy. As he wrapped both Peter and Judas in the darkness of lies, so he attempts to deceive us too.

What Peter discovered is that the very weakest areas of our lives is where God is strongest. We need to accept the same promise of Christ: "I have prayed for you, that your faith may not fail."

It is our faith in God's promises, coupled with the principles of His righteousness, that will take us through the dark hours of temptation and life's hardships, no matter how crushing.

Father, please lead us, and may we have faith to trust and follow You. Amen.

M. Moses Andradé is the district pastor of the Beaumont, Drums, Slocum and Wyoming Valley churches in Pennsylvania.

His Promise of Healing

"And Jesus said to him, 'I will come and heal him'" (Matt. 8:7 NKJV).

"Lord, my servant is lying at home paralyzed, dreadfully tormented" (Matt. 8:6, NKJV), the Roman centurion said to Jesus. "But only speak a word, and my servant will be healed" (verse 8), because he believed. The story ends by saying: "And his servant was healed that same hour" (verse 13).

There are two lessons I receive from this wonderful story: First, Jesus has the power to heal no matter the severity of the illness. And second, Jesus can use anyone to bless another person who needs help.

One of my sisters who grew up in our faith, stopped attending church years ago. She suffered from pulmonary edema, and one night she called me very scared because her hands, arms, legs and face were extremely swollen. For almost two months, she had been receiving medical treatment with diuretics, but the swelling in her body did not respond. So that night I prayed with her.

A few days later, seeing that her body was not responding to medical treatment, I said to her: "Sister, let me anoint you." But she replied, "Let me think about it." That week she went to the cardiologist, and they told her that her heart was working only 29 percent and nothing could be done. Following the appointment, my sister allowed me to anoint her.

Due to the COVID-19 pandemic, I anointed her virtually. The next day, the swelling disappeared! God worked a miracle for my sister—both physically *and* spiritually.

Jesus has the power to heal. Like the centurion, let us go to Him and intercede for others.

Dear God, thank You for Your healing touch and for allowing us to intercede for others. Amen.

Jorge Aguero is the president of the New Jersey Conference.

Delivered Again

"Because he has set his love upon Me, therefore I will deliver him; I will set him on high, because he has known My name" (Ps. 91:14, NKJV).

There is certainly safety when we abide in the presence of God. Psalm 91 speaks of His protective love, and, for me, verse 14 encapsulates the promises of the chapter.

Many, many times I've seen God fulfill this promise of deliverance, lifting me up high—far from the grasp of the enemy's reach.

Even though it ranks as one of the more mundane instances of God's heavenly protection, the time when I saw His deliverance exhibited most clearly was on a trip I took during my time in the seminary.

My two daughters, Michaela and Emily, and I were journeying from Andrews University in Michigan to Las Vegas for a summer visit with family. Eighteen-hundred miles were to be clicked off on my SUV's odometer.

With the Great Plains in the rearview mirror, the towering Rocky Mountains filled the windshield. Up I-70 we pushed, crossing the Continental Divide and descending the Colorado Western Slope and forging across Utah, finally arriving on the north side of Las Vegas.

There on I-15, just past the Spaghetti Bowl, the engine lost power and a clanking noise erupted from the engine. With only miles to go, the piston rod broke. Limping into my parents' driveway, I thought about what a different story I would be telling if God had allowed the rod to come off anywhere else along the way. Instead, He had delivered me once again.

Father, I love You because I never need to worry about Your protection over my life. Amen.

Michael Stough II is the pastor of the Delaware, New Carlisle and Springfield First churches in Ohio.

Jesus, Take the Wheel!

"Be anxious for nothing, but in everything by prayer and supplication, with thanksgiving, let your requests be made known to God; and the peace of God, which surpasses all understanding, will guard your hearts and minds through Christ Jesus" (Phil. 4:6-7, NKJV).

At a young age, we are taught to have a goal-oriented mindset and to stay on top of things. We are given deadlines for homework and projects and tested on our ability to learn information we are taught, among other things. As we grow into adults, not only do we face our self-imposed deadlines, we also juggle expectations from our family, friends, co-workers and society. No wonder many of us are stressed out!

I cannot count the number of times this passage has helped me through turning points in my life. From preparing for a presentation or an exam to more complex events—buying a house; facing the loss of a loved one; dealing with a family member's illness; raising a child; and living through a pandemic—these verses have taught me to trust in God no matter the circumstance.

Paul is telling us not to worry about anything, but to, instead, and with a grateful heart, turn all our anxieties, fears and worries over to God. Sometimes we are so focused on the problem or crisis that we forget how God has turned our past problems into opportunities and/or blessings. God is always faithful, and if we submit our problems to Him, being grateful for what He has done for us in the past, He promises to give us such peace that has no comparison.

Father, please take the wheel of my life today. Amen.

Carolina Ramos is the administrative assistant of Ministries Development for the Columbia Union Conference.

No Place Like Heaven

"Now when He had spoken these things, while they watched, He was taken up, and a cloud received Him out of their sight. And while they looked steadfastly toward heaven as He went up, behold, two men stood by them in white apparel, who also said, 'Men of Galilee, why do you stand gazing up into heaven? This same Jesus, who was taken up from you into heaven, will so come in like manner as you saw Him go into heaven'" (Acts 1:9–11, NKJV).

Have you ever wondered what heaven will be like and if Jesus is coming back? Have you ever imagined yourself walking the streets of gold? Have you ever thought about sitting face-to-face with Jesus?

Heaven is a place where God and His angels live. It is a place of peace and joy, prepared for you and me. God is just waiting for us to be ready.

We have to pray, read the Bible and believe that He will return one day soon. I can't wait to see Jesus and meet the people I have read about in the Bible. I want Jesus to tell me how He felt when He reunited with His Father. I want to see His nail-pierced hands, a reminder of the price He paid for sin.

I can't imagine a better place than heaven! It will be amazing to see Jesus and the home He has made for His children. I can't wait to stand on the Sea of Glass and reunite with friends and family.

Dear Jesus, please help us to tell the world about You so all of us can go to heaven. Help us to love You and to be ready to go home to heaven with You. Amen.

Zionne I. Wydeman is a sixth-grader at the Mayfair Christian School in Ohio.

God's Message to Worriers Like Me

"The Lord your God in your midst, the Mighty One, will save; He will rejoice over you with gladness, He will quiet you with His love, He will rejoice over you with singing" (Zeph. 3:17, NKJV).

With my Type A personality, I tend to be a bit of a worrier. Too often I realize my mind has wandered to the "what ifs" in life. Being very experienced with this skill, it does not need to be a huge life or death type of concern. Oh no, my mind is also capable of making a simple fear seem very significant.

One day, a friend shared Zephaniah 3:17 with me, and it has since put a smile on my face on numerous occasions. I find this verse to be one of those "nutshell" texts that is packed with encouragement and speaks directly to my heart. It tells me that my God never leaves my side, even when I am needlessly stressing over small matters. He is happy to comfort and love me through it all, and He raises His voice in song for me! I am so thankful that fear and worry are not part of God's plan.

So on days when I allow Satan to magnify my worries and overpower my confidence that God is in control, I turn back to the Scriptures to renew my faith. I need these daily reminders that I do not need to worry, that He wants what's best for me and already has plans in motion to achieve them on His behalf.

God, what a blessing it is that You are always by my side. Amen.

Cyndee Grady is a member of the Waynesboro church in Virginia.

The Greatest Architect

"'Let not your heart be troubled; you believe in God, believe also in Me. In My Father's house are many mansions; if it were not so, I would have told you. I go to prepare a place for you. And if I go and prepare a place for you, I will come again and receive you to Myself; that where I am, there you may be also. And where I go you know, and the way you know.' Thomas said to Him, 'Lord, we do not know where You are going, and how can we know the way?' Jesus said to him, 'I am the way, the truth, and the life. No one comes to the Father except through Me'" (John 14:1–6, NKJV).

Jesus' words speak so lovingly and reassuringly, and say so much. In these verses, He gives us comfort, love, hope and guidance. He goes to prepare a place for us—our forever home.

To think that Jesus is designing my home, with everything else "on His plate," makes me feel so incredibly special. It's hard to fathom that He takes time out of His day to prepare a place for me!

In His promise, He reminds us that He will return, and we will be together. He wants to spend forever with us, and tells us exactly what we need to do to make that a reality. So when I feel overwhelmed and stressed, these verses comfort me and remind me that He is in control, down to the very last detail. All I must do is to follow Him.

The greatest Architect of all time is preparing a place for you and me. I can't wait!

Dear loving and gracious Father, thank You for the hope of spending forever with You. Amen.

Maria France is the executive assistant to the president at the Columbia Union Conference.

The Stone That Tells Lies

"A faithful witness will not lie: but a false witness will utter lies"
(Prov. 14:5, KJV).

My great-great-grandmother, Lassaphene Gant Segerson, died in 1884 at age 35 from complications giving birth to her 10th child. Sadly, this was a family tragedy that was all too commonly repeated in 19th century rural Tennessee. Usually the deceased were laid to rest with an engraved tombstone to mark their grave, but some were memorialized with only a crude, letter-less, hand-hewn stone. Surprisingly, there are two engraved tombstones for Lassaphene Segerson, lying some five miles apart! Oral family tradition says that during transport, the first tombstone was off-loaded prematurely by the roadside just after the wagon broke down or just before a large storm struck. The first stone was never moved again, and a second stone was placed on her grave at the Marl Bluff church, where her husband was eventually buried beside her.

In Proverbs, Solomon warns us of the difference between a faithful witness and a false witness. Do we faithfully present truth, the whole truth and nothing but the truth? Just like that first tombstone, we can passively tell lies without speaking a single word—by our silence or by our appearance. For almost 140 years, naïve passersby have believed that the first tombstone marks the final resting place of a young mother. The false witness testifies that the mother was buried alone in secluded woods, but the faithful witness declares that she sleeps alongside family on the church grounds of an active congregation.

O God of truth, may we never deceive by our words or deeds, or even by our silence or appearance. Amen.

David Taylor is a lay pastor of the West Chester church in Pennsylvania.

God Can Help You Do Anything!

**"I can do all things through Christ who strengthens me"
(Phil. 4:13, NKJV).**

This verse speaks to a specific challenge in my life that makes me feel weak at times. My story is an ongoing struggle. In fact, I am struggling right now to remain focused long enough to complete this assignment.

I have attention deficit disorder, which makes it hard for me to concentrate. Sometimes I ask myself, "Why can't I just be normal?" I remember one time in seventh grade I had to study for a science test that was coming up the next day. I tried to study on my own, but I wasn't able to stay focused.

My mom stayed up with me and quizzed me; we got through it, but I went to bed, still not confident in the material. When I woke up the next morning, I got dressed and headed to school. When I arrived at school, I sat in the back row. Not knowing what else to do, I closed my eyes, bowed my head and prayed for strength to focus on my exam. Immediately, a heavy weight lifted.

I took the test that day, and not only passed, but got an A.

There are times when I struggle. There are times when I get down and wonder why I can't stay as focused and organized as everyone else. But there is one thing I now realize: When I have done my best, even when I don't think it's enough, God will carry me the rest of the way. God can help you do anything.

Dear God, thank You for providing the strength that we need and for never being too busy for me. Amen.

Alex Jones is an eighth-grader at the Olney Adventist Preparatory School in Maryland.

Strength for the Day

"Even youths grow tired and weary, and young men stumble and fall; but those who hope in the Lord will renew their strength. They will soar on wings like eagles; they will run and not grow weary, they will walk and not be faint" (Isa. 40:30–31, NIV).

I have always loved watching the bald eagle, as it majestically and powerfully flies through the sky. In my travels, it makes my day when I see an eagle. Family members know my love for eagles, hence, I have many pictures of eagles in my office.

Over the years, I have also enjoyed running. Not the marathon-type running, but a simple, daily run, just enough to get my heart rate going and clear my thoughts. There is nothing better than a good 5K run to get the day going.

Lately, I have been feeling more body aches and have had to curb the running. And I've been reminded of this verse over and over: "Even youths grow tired and weary." The real key is to "put my hope in the Lord." I can sit in my office and look at the pictures of eagles flying and know that God promises me His strength for the day ahead. I can run the daily race through His power.

Father, please help me to depend totally on you. Give me Your strength so that I can soar, run and do Your work throughout the day. Amen.

Harold Greene is the director of the Information Technology Services for the Columbia Union Conference.

The Best of Friends

**"But I tell you, love your enemies and pray for those
who persecute you" (Matt. 5:44, NIV).**

This verse has made an impact in my life and in my heart. Because of
this verse, I try not to have any enemies. I still get upset at times, but
in those moments, I hear a still, small voice telling me to love everyone
I encounter.

For example, I have a friend whom I didn't like and she didn't like me
prior to us becoming friends. What was confusing was she didn't like me
because I didn't like her, and I didn't like her because she didn't like me.
We had never actually done anything to each other that caused us to
dislike one another.

Shortly after Vacation Bible School (VBS) one summer, I went with my
mom and brother on a hike where I encountered this girl. At VBS, the
leaders had taught us Matthew 5:44, and I was inspired by this verse. So
I took the initiative to talk to her. And after clearing everything up, we
eventually became the best of friends.

*Dear Lord, thank You. Because of You and Your Scriptures I have made the
best memories and my forgiveness and love for enemies grows stronger with
each chapter I read. Please show the people out there in the world who don't
know what forgiveness is what a tremendous impact it can make in their lives.
Amen.*

*Allyssa Jetter is an eighth-grader at the Manassas Adventist Preparatory School
in Virginia.*

God's Amazing Work

"And we know that all things work together for good to them that love God, to them who are the called according to His purpose" (Rom. 8:28, KJV).

The person that I am today is the result of God working in my life from the moment I was born. All of my experiences, the good, the bad, the ugly and the dark, went into the making of the individual that is present today. God used it all to fashion someone who I believe is caring, thoughtful, kind and considerate.

If there had been no pain, would I have learned how to be caring and considerate? If there had been no sadness, would I have learned how to be kind and thoughtful? If there had been no ugly and dark time, would I have sought wisdom from above? If there had been no good times, would I have been able to smile?

My smile has been constant, over the years, even in the midst of all the difficult times. My smile was like the sunshine on a cloudy day. It would occasionally disappear and hide behind the cloud like the sun, but then it would shine through again.

What about you? Can you see Gods' working in your life? Can you praise Him for who you are at this moment—that He fashioned someone unique and extraordinary using all the experiences you have had?

You and I are who we are today because God used what we thought was not good in our lives to transform us into who He wanted us to be.

Lord, I thank You that "Your thoughts are not our thoughts and that Your ways are not our ways" (Isa. 55:8, KJV). Amen.

Shirley B. Pritchett is the administrative assistant for the Sharon Temple Adventist School in Delaware.

Breathe

"Be still, and know that I am God" (Ps. 46:10, NIV).

One of my favorite songs is "Breathe" by Jonny Diaz:

Alarm clock screaming, bare feet hit the floor.
It's off to the races, everybody out the door.
I'm feeling like I'm falling behind, it's a crazy life!

Later, the music slows down and the chorus begins:

Breathe, just breathe. Come and rest at my feet.
And be, just be. Chaos calls, but all you really need, is to just breathe.

In 2016, my husband's job transferred him to a position out of state. The first few months were chaotic. With the added rent, the budget became tight. I missed my husband. My girls missed their father. I was exhausted doing everything alone. My devotions were nonexistent.

One morning, God stopped me with this verse: "Be still and know that I am God." He said: *Gabrielle. What's your hurry? Why are you worried? I have you and your family in the palm of My hand. Be still and breathe. I have you.*

That morning, I decided two things: First, I was going to spend more time resting at the feet of Jesus. Second, when chaos calls, I will be still, breathe and remember that God has me in His Hand.

Our family was split for 18 of the longest months of my life. Although our finances took a hit, our accounts were never overdrawn. Our house never needed a repair. Our cars never broke down. No one in our family fell ill. God carried my family and kept us in His care.

Father, help me to remember to be still. Amen.

Gabrielle J. Agwu is the computer teacher at Spencerville Adventist Academy in Maryland.

The Runaway Cardinal

"Who provides food for the raven when its young cry out to God and wander about for lack of food?" (Job 38:41, NIV).

Our family has a large lilac bush next to one of our windows. A few years ago, a Northern Cardinal couple decided to raise their young in this bush. After Mrs. Cardinal built her nest and incubated her eggs, the chicks hatched. We all enjoyed peeking into the nest and seeing the chicks, who most of the time were crying for food. Thankfully, both Mr. and Mrs. Cardinal were very faithful, taking turns feeding their babies. The chicks grew quickly before our eyes and cameras.

About one week later, my dad noticed the chicks were missing from their nest. We looked for them and were concerned when we only found one hopping on the ground, with no parents in sight. The chick wasn't strong enough to fly, but it was probably hungry, looking for worms, thinking its parents were taking too long to feed it. My dad scooped the chick up and placed it back in the nest, but, in a few hours, the chick was gone again.

This verse reminds me of the runaway Cardinal chick and humanity. When we have needs, we cry out to God, and He answers us in His own time and way. How many times do we roam aimlessly, trying to supply our own needs when we think He is taking too long? Perhaps God asks us to stay where we are for our safety.

Lord, thank You for providing my needs. Help me to trust in Your timing and not leave Your protection. Amen.

Caleb Palmer is a member of the Centerville church in Ohio.

The Three-Syllable Verse

"Jesus wept" (John 11:35, KJV).

From second through six grade, I attended a small Seventh-day Adventist church school. These were wonderful years, filled with joyful learning about God and what it meant to be a friend, among other lessons.

The older grades were assigned handwriting exercises to go along with Bible class. On one particular occasion, we were given the task of writing our favorite verse of the Bible. Without question, I knew mine, and proceeded to carefully write it out: "Jesus wept" John 11:35 (KJV).

The short verse was seen as my attempt to wiggle out of a writing assignment. I tried to explain that the text was indeed my favorite, and why: "Jesus, who knew the end from the beginning and knew He would raise Lazarus—not someday, but that day—was still affected by the impact Lazarus' loss had on his sisters and the whole town. Jesus really does know our sadness and hurts with us when we are hurting! Jesus is truly the best friend you can ever have!"

A passionate plea or not, I was asked to pick my next favorite verse.

"I don't have a second favorite," I honestly replied.

To replace the shortest verse in the Bible, I was assigned the shortest chapter of the Bible—Psalm 23.

With current events unfolding in increasingly tragic ways, this verse remains a deeply concise picture of God's love for us.

Thank You, Lord, for caring deeply about the big and little, public and private things we go through, and for always being right beside us! Amen.

Lisa A. Baich is the Pathfinder and Adventurer Steel City Club director at the Pittsburgh church in Pennsylvania.

God Strengthens Me

"I can do all things through Christ which strengtheneth me"
(Phil. 4:13, KJV).

This verse means that God gives me strength to do what I need to do. This verse speaks to my life because it gives me strength and keeps me motivated. My dad died two years ago, and I lost my mom around four years ago.

Although it has been a rough time for me, God gave me the strength to get through those times, and this verse has helped me a lot. God also gave me the strength to help others get through hard times too. My mamaw has had a really hard time with my dad's death. I have helped her when she was sad and grieving over my dad by telling her to go ahead and cry when she needed to and to let it out.

She has told several people that I have helped her through this time. I have learned that being sad is a waste of time. Life is better when you are happy. I pray that everyone learns how to be as happy as they can here on earth, with God's help, until we get to heaven where we can *really* be happy.

Dear God, thank You that You will come back soon and take us home. Thank You for the joy that only You can give. Amen.

Nathan Blanton is a sixth-grader at the Powell Valley Christian School in Virginia.

'Hath God Said?'

"Do not despise prophetic utterances. But examine everything carefully; hold fast to that which is good" (1 Thess. 5:20–21, NASB).

This inspired counsel has helped me safely navigate many storms and winds of doctrine that have buffeted the Remnant Church during my 45 years as a member and 20 as a pastor. The Bible often warns us against false teachers and false prophets (Matthew 7:15; 2 Peter 2:1), yet many are deceived and led astray from the truth. Many others have given up pillars such as the sanctuary, the Spirit of Prophecy and even the Sabbath.

How can we be secure from these deceptions and from the "strong, almost overmastering delusion" that is to break upon the world? How shall we stand firm when "the majority forsake us" and join the opposition?

We must rigorously, carefully test every idea by that which God has spoken through His chosen messengers—the prophets. We must "test the spirits to see whether they are from God" (1 John 4:1). False teachers twist the words of inspiration, disguising themselves as ministers of righteousness, and even the devil quotes Scripture (Matthew 4:6; 2 Corinthians 11:13–15; 2 Peter 3:16).

Remember this when presented with "new light," to keep you safe from deception. Satan prepares men to believe a lie by first leading them to question or to doubt that which God has plainly spoken. The enemy succeeded with Eve by first asking, "Hath God said?" We must do as Jesus did, standing firmly upon "It is written." To believe God's prophets is still good advice for us today! (2 Chronicles 20:20).

Father, help us to test all things by the Scriptures, and to "hold fast to that which is good." Amen.

Mark Cockerham is the pastor of the Blossburg, Canton, Hillcrest and Sayre churches in Pennsylvania.

A Clean Slate

"And we know that all things work together for good to those who love God, to those who are the called according to His purpose" (Rom. 8:28, NKJV).

In December 2019, I received an email notifying me that I was dismissed from my doctorate program. I had missed several assignments in a particular class that I was taking for the second time. My classes required daily posts and a major paper due every week. Devasted and discouraged, I felt like a failure and did not know what to do. I was overwhelmed with the workload and my daily schedule of being a wife, mom and educator.

I mustered the courage to speak to my advisor, who informed me that I would need to write a letter requesting to be reinstated. She reassured me of reinstatement upon the submission of the letter. Overwhelmed with fear, I hesitated to write the letter.

During this same time, my friends and I started 40 days of prayer and fasting that would conclude in a gathering in Nashville, Tenn. I didn't mention to them that my doctoral program had ended. In Nashville, I finally confessed the truth about my dilemma and entered into a pact to write my reinstatement letter.

We said our goodbyes and headed to the airport. While waiting to board the plane, I received a text informing me that my school was closing. My mind began to wonder. *How will I complete my program? Will I have to begin the doctorate program process all over? How will credits transfer from a school that was closing its doors?* While I was worrying, God was working. He allowed me to start a new school without losing any credits, and to pick up from where I left off without any penalty. He gave me a clean slate.

Lord, thank You for working things out according to Your purpose. Amen.

Shemika Campbell is the academic support specialist at Takoma Academy in Maryland.

The Lost Sheep

"What man of you, having a hundred sheep, if he loses one of them, does not leave the ninety-nine in the wilderness, and go after the one which is lost until he finds it? And when he has found it, he lays it on his shoulders, rejoicing. And when he comes home, he calls together his friends and neighbors, saying to them, 'Rejoice with me, for I have found my sheep which was lost!' I say to you that likewise there will be more joy in heaven over one sinner who repents than over ninety-nine just persons who need no repentance"
(Luke 15:4–7, NKJV).

Have you ever lost something very valuable to you? When you searched for it and eventually found it, you probably rejoiced because you were so happy to have it back! There is a parable in the Bible where a man lost one of his valued sheep. He searched diligently for his lost sheep because everyone of his sheep mattered to him. The shepherd left his 99 other sheep in the wilderness to find that one lost sheep.

When Jesus was giving this parable, He was referring to Himself as the Good Shepherd and the sheep as us. Sometimes we stray away from God, but He searches for us when we are lost because He loves us and cares about us.

If you are straying from Christ today, pray and ask Him to bring you back to Him. When you are brought back to Christ, all of heaven rejoices because another person has chosen to return to Him.

Dear Jesus, thank You for bringing me home to You. If we are straying from You, please help us to come back to You. Amen.

Petar Samardžić is an eighth-grader at the Mayfair Christian School in Ohio.

Just Like Ruth

"But Ruth said: 'Entreat me not to leave you, or to turn back from following after you; for wherever you go, I will go; and wherever you lodge, I will lodge; your people shall be my people, and your God, my God. Where you die, I will die, and there will I be buried. The Lord do so to me, and more also, if anything but death parts you and me'" (Ruth 1:16–17, NKJV).

I'll never forget receiving my first Bible from my mother. Maybe because my aunt's name was Ruth, I started with this book and fell in love with God and this story.

What kind of relationship spun out of a mother-in-law for her daughters-in-law to know her God? These women saw God through Naomi. As a mother-in-law, she must have been compassionate and gentle, lovingly treating them as God expected.

As Naomi bore the loss of her husband and sons, her faith in God was visible. Where did she find hope and encouragement? Where did she find peace in her storms? Who was her provider? No one but the great Jehovah-Jireh! Naomi's love for God was apparent in her daily living, acceptance of her situation and the hope she placed in Him.

No wonder Ruth couldn't and wouldn't leave. She told Naomi, "Entreat me not to leave you," and boldly stated, "Your God will be my God!" sealing it with an oath. That's exactly how I felt as a child when I read the book of Ruth. Like Ruth, I say to God each day, "Entreat me not to leave You!" My hope is in the redeeming, loving, hand-outstretched Savior.

Lord, whenever I step in a direction that is off course, may I always turn back to You. Amen.

Vanessa Waite is the senior accountant of the Treasury Department for the Columbia Union Conference.

Abide in Him

"I am the vine; you are the branches. If you remain in Me and I in you, you will bear fruit; apart from Me you can do nothing" (John 15:5, NIV).

I have many Bible verses that I love. But in light of recent times, John 15:5 has become my favorite. This verse became particular meaningful to me during the COVID-19 pandemic, because this crisis, and the other crises plaguing our world today, are sure signs of Jesus' soon return. I hear people saying, "Get ready, world! Get ready, church! Jesus is coming soon!" And while that may be true, the real question is, "How do I get ready?" By abiding in Him. Only those who abide in Jesus will thrive during difficult times.

So how does one abide in God? By surrendering all to Him. As the old gospel hymn goes, "All to Jesus, I surrender, all to Him I freely give."

In Matthew 11:28-30, Jesus bids us, "Come to Me, all you who are weary and burdened, and I will give you rest. ... For I am gentle and humble in heart, and you will find rest for your souls. For My yoke is easy and My burden is light" (NIV).

Lord, thank You for waiting for us. May we come to You, for Your arms are open wide. Amen.

Richard Klinedinst is a member of the York church in Pennsylvania.

The Lord Is the Best Defense

"Fear thou not; for I am with thee: be not dismayed; for I am thy God" (Isa. 41:10, KJV).

I became a Christian about 250 feet below the surface of the Mediterranean Sea onboard the nuclear-powered submarine USS Lewis and Clark (SSBN 644) in the early 1970s. I was a 19-year-old 2nd class sonarman when I became a Christian and a conscientious objector.

My job at battle stations was to aim the ship—by sound—at the enemy so the officers could formulate a firing solution to sink the enemy by torpedo. As a conscientious objector, I refused. As discipline, I had to stand before the captain at Captain's Mast. I was very afraid. I was facing middle-aged, Annapolis-trained line officers, and all I had was a high school diploma.

A Seventh-day Adventist chaplain instructed me to not answer any questions since they would be hypothetical and all they were trying to do was trip me up and confuse me. When given a hypothetical question, I was to reply, "That's a hypothetical question. Unless I was in that situation, I can't really say what I would do."

The Lord was not finished. My superiors posed a question to me at mast: "You're on a deserted island starving and there's nothing to eat but crabs and swine. What would you eat?"

The Lord gave me these words: "Sir, I would find what they were eating to stay alive and eat it." This flustered my accusers and immediately they closed my Captain's Mast. I was found guilty, fined and demoted, but letting the Lord defend me was more than I could have asked.

Lord, thank You for taking all the fear from me, then delivering me! Amen.

Ricci Sholock is a member of the Buckannon church in West Virginia.

A Bird's Eye View

"But ask the animals, and they will teach you, or the birds in the sky, and they will tell you" (Job 12:7, NIV).

Early one morning, before our 5-year-old triplets woke up, I found myself admiring a beautiful cardinal flying from tree to tree. It triggered a fond memory of how God sent me a woodpecker during my morning devotional. I smiled and whispered a prayer of thanksgiving for His watch and care over me then and now.

As I turned around, our children, who had apparently been there long enough to hear my prayer, greeted me. They asked me about God and His power. I noticed one of them got very quiet, then asked, "Mommy, do you think God would send us a bird?"

My heart smiled as my body became covered with goosebumps. I instantly knew that God was about to become real to them and that this experience would stay with them forever, if only they would believe. I asked, "Do you believe?" Immediately, they all chimed, "Yes!"

Before I prayed, I reminded them that "it's not about God doing what we want; it's about us trusting and believing that He is the Creator of the universe and that He is in control." That day, I not only asked God to send a cardinal to the tree near our house, but to have it perch on a branch at my kids' eye level.

As we opened our eyes, there sat a cardinal looking at us. They all gasped, as my eyes filled with tears of joy. Through a bird, they had just come face-to-face with God.

Father, thank You for using nature to teach our children life lessons. Amen.

Sonia Vazquez is a member of the Fredericksburg church in Virginia.

Follow the Signs

**"In this world you will have trouble. But take heart!
I have overcome the world" (John 16:33, NIV).**

Every morning, I run two miles in my neighborhood. I take this opportunity to speak and listen to God. One morning, He spoke to me through the street signs I passed while jogging. Below are some of the points He shared with me that day:

Speed Limit 30 MPH—We live in a society that is driven by immediate urgency. We expect God to have that same sense of urgency. We need to slow down and be patient. He's already told us that His ways are not our ways and His thoughts are not our thoughts, so obviously His timing is not our timing. Instead of trying to rush God and get our problems solved as soon as possible, let's learn to be patient through the tough times.

One Way—Some of us are in charge at home, are bosses at work and leaders in our local church. Sometimes we think that we can have that superior role in our relationship with God. Well, that is not how it works. There is only "One Way" that our relationship can work effortlessly. That way is for us to acknowledge and be aware that God is in complete control. We have to move out of the driver's seat and allow Jesus to take the wheel.

Caution: Speed Bump Ahead—There will be times where our journey will seem bumpy, and we may want to give up. When we are faced with challenges, we must remember what Jesus says in John 16:33: "In this world you will have trouble. But take heart! I have overcome the world."

Thank You, Father, that You are in control. Amen.

Tyson Bell is a member of the Ephesus church in Ohio.

What Is Good?

"He has shown you, O mortal, what is good. And what does the Lord require of you? To act justly and to love mercy and to walk humbly with your God" (Micah 6:8, NIV).

"Do you remember me? Do you remember when I came to visit you?" The woman wasn't yelling, but she was talking loudly as she moved purposefully toward the stage where I was presiding over graduation. Maybe it was because we were outside. Maybe it was because she was trying to get my attention. Or maybe it was because she might say something I didn't want to hear. In the moment, in that context, I couldn't place her face.

"I came to your office with my daughter because she was struggling at the college, and we asked you for another chance," she said.

I held my breath. Act justly. Love mercy. Walk humbly with God. What had justice required? What had mercy directed? My mind raced. In that instant, I desperately hoped that in that earlier encounter I had asked myself the question I often do: What would a good leader do in this situation? And I hoped that God had shown me in that situation what was good, and what justice, mercy and humility required.

"You gave her another chance," she continued. "And here she is on the stage with you today!"

Together, we three drank in the joy of that moment, basking in the thrill of a second chance, a hard-won victory, a completion, a *commencement*.

I cried then. I'm crying now. Tears of joy and praise to a God who still shows us what is good.

Lord, show us what is good, just, merciful and humble. Amen.

Nate Brandstater is the president of Kettering College in Ohio.

Miracle on a Sunny Afternoon

"Therefore I say to you, whatever things you ask when you pray, believe that you receive them, and you will have them" (Mark 11:24, NKJV).

In my life, there have been times when I have witnessed God answer my prayers. One such answered prayer happened on a beautiful, sunny day.

I had just returned home from school with our children. Our youngest son jumped on his bike and went for a ride. My husband and I were sitting in the kitchen when we heard an ambulance, and then another. Outside we called out to our son and ran to the end of the street. There, our worst nightmare stared us straight in the face—our son had been hit by a truck. He was in the middle of the road on a stretcher. Soon a helicopter transported him to a local hospital.

I called three people, asking them to tell everyone they knew to pray. In the helicopter, our son's head swelled around the straps that were holding it in place. The medic said that we had a very small window to get him into surgery to relieve the swelling.

At the hospital, we were met with a team of doctors and a chaplain. The next person I saw was our pastor, who happened to be visiting someone else in the hospital at the time. He prayed over our son.

After thoroughly examining our son, the doctors couldn't believe what they found: not one broken bone. No internal injuries. No need for surgery. He is our miracle.

The aftermath from the accident may have stumped the doctors, but I know what truly happened—God answered the hundreds of prayers.

Father, thank You for answering all of our prayers—big or small. Amen.

Jacqueline Messenger is the associate director of secondary education for the Columbia Union Conference.

He Has a Plan

**"'For I know the plans I have for you,' says the Lord. 'They are plans for good and not for disaster, to give you a future and a hope'"
(Jer. 29:11, NLT).**

To me, this verse means that I do not have to worry and that I can trust God. He knows what He is doing and has a plan for me. It tells me that I was made for a purpose. I can have hope in Jesus because He holds the future in His hands and always has my best interest in mind. He loves us so much and knows everything about us. Even though we may go through trials and temptations and stumble off His path, He is always ready to help us get back on track.

When my mom was about six or seven months pregnant with me, my family was in a car accident. A woman drove through a stop sign and hit our car. Everyone was fine besides minor scrapes and bruises. My mom's wrist hurt and the car was damaged, but she was scared that something had happened to me. She prayed and prayed that I would be OK, and was so relieved when the doctor found my heartbeat. I can confidently say that God saved my life that day because He has a special plan for my life.

Dear God, thank You for the special plans You have for each of us and for Your great love. Help us to stay on the right path. We love You. Amen.

Asha Caruthers is an eighth-grader at the Olney Adventist Preparatory School in Maryland.

"For we are God's handiwork, created in Christ Jesus to do good works, which God prepared in advance for us to do." EPH. 2:10, NIV

MAY

Plugged Into Christ's Power

"Knowing this, that our old man was crucified with Him, that the body of sin might be done away with, that we should no longer be slaves of sin" (Rom. 6:6, NKJV).

When I was young in the faith, I had a lot of trouble with my "old man." The King James Version said he'd been destroyed, but mine sometimes seemed to be alive and well! I wondered if I was not a true Christian, although I loved Jesus and had given my life to Him.

When I eventually learned some other meanings for "destroyed," it finally all made sense. "Made useless" or "disabled" are also possible translations. Think of the difference!

If I destroy my cell phone, it will never work again. Contrary to this, if it has no charge, if it is "dead," then it's useless and disabled—it doesn't work at the moment. But I can still charge it if I want to, and then it works fine!

Romans 6 tells me I have a choice of which master to serve: sin or righteousness. I have the choice of recharging my old man or being crucified with Christ every single day.

So now, when I wake up in the morning, the first thing I do is put myself in the arms of Jesus, recommit myself to Him and thank Him that His death and resurrection to newness of life are mine too. Then I ask Him to live His life in me through the Holy Spirit.

When temptations come and my old man wiggles a bit, I can keep him powerless by choosing Jesus and asking for His power to resist. Jesus is faithful, and it works!

Dear Jesus, thank You that, though I can't control my old man, You can. Please help me depend on Your power always! Amen.

Gillian Bethel is a member of the Amicus church in Virginia.

I Could Not Believe It!

"But Jesus beheld them, and said unto them, with men this is impossible; but with God all things are possible" (Matt. 19:26, KJV).

When I was just beginning ministry, Mary, a very missionary-minded sister, asked me to go with her to a Bible study that took 30 minutes by bike down an unpaved road. When we arrived, we found a family in extreme poverty. As we began studying the Bible, a mean-looking man suddenly stepped out from behind a curtain with a machete in his hand. I looked at Mary, my eyes urging us to leave. She remained calm and without fear. Fortunately, the man left the room.

When we said goodbye, Mary said, "Tomorrow, we will return." I whispered to Mary, "I am not coming back tomorrow." She immediately told me, "You study the Bible, but you do not apply it to your life. [As Matthew 28:20 states], the Lord said He would be with us."

We visited this family five more times, and every time the man appeared with his machete. I finally made the call for baptism and the lady accepted. She said to me, "I have a surprise for you. My husband also wants to be baptized." Seeing my surprised face, she explained, "My husband does not know how to read. He always pretended to be angry so you would not ask him anything. But he stayed behind the door and listened to the studies."

I could not believe it! The Word of God is powerful and can transform hearts. With God, all things are truly possible.

Father, thank You for the privilege of experiencing the power of Your Word. Amen.

Carlos J. Torres is the director of Family Ministries and Personal Ministries for the New Jersey Conference.

Are You Available?

"Be still, and know that I am God: I will be exalted among the heathen, I will be exalted in the earth" (Ps. 46:10, KJV).

How many of us enjoy being interrupted? I would argue that most of us do not. We have developed tools to prevent disturbance. Noise-canceling headphones, automatic replies to phone calls and emails are just a few. There are more subtle ways we do this, such as scheduling our lives so tightly there is no space for an unscheduled event. There is nothing wrong with preserving space in our lives where we can focus on our priorities. That is how we get work done. But it becomes a problem when our entire life is built around preventing interruptions.

Dietrich Bonhoeffer writes about this danger in *Life Together*: "We must be ready to allow ourselves to be interrupted by God. God will be constantly crossing our paths and canceling our plans by sending us people with claims and petitions. We may pass them by, preoccupied with our more important tasks ... it is a strange fact that Christians and even ministers frequently consider their work so important and urgent that they will allow nothing to disturb them. They think they are doing God a service in this, but they are disdaining God's 'crooked yet straight path'" (p. 99).

Now I don't think Bonhoeffer was recommending that we allow just anything to alter our schedules. The stipulation was to allow God to interrupt.

The Scriptures call us to "be still and know that He is God." He will reveal opportunities for us to share with others at any time, in any place. But if we are too busy, we will not be prepared for these types of interruptions.

Father, may we be open and receptive to divine occasions to share love—no matter how full our schedule may be. Amen.

Elliot Smith is a chaplain for the Kettering Adventist HealthCare in Ohio.

Nothing to Fear

"Even though I walk through the darkest valley, I will fear no evil, for You are with me; Your rod and your staff, they comfort me" (Ps. 23:4, NIV).

What does this verse mean? The first part says, "Even though I walk through the darkest valley, I will fear no evil." I think this means that even though we go through scary things, we have nothing to fear. I wonder why that is? The second part, "for you are with me," gives it all away.

We do not need to be afraid in those scary places or when we think about scary things, because God is with us. So the last part, "Your rod and Your staff, they comfort me," lets us know that God's presence comforts us. Simply put, we do not need to be afraid of anything, no matter what, because God is with us and comforts us with His gentle words of encouragement and love.

Sometimes we are scared, like when our parents have not come home yet, and we call them on their phones and they don't answer. We may think, "What happened to them? When are they coming back?" This can worry us a lot. God can help with that worry and fear. All we need to do is pray and ask. Let's practice this right now.

Dear Heavenly Father, right now I don't want to be afraid. I want to have the strength not to fear what's happening in my life. Lord, please let me put all fear aside so I can clear my mind and feel comforted by Your presence and love. Amen.

Nolan Johnson is a fourth-grader at the Mayfair Christian School in Ohio.

Looking Through Spiritual Lenses

"For our light affliction, which is but for a moment, is working for us a far more exceeding and eternal weight of glory, while we do not look at the things which are seen, but at the things which are not seen. For the things which are seen are temporary, but the things which are not seen are eternal" (2 Cor. 4:17–18, NKJV).

When I think of affliction, "light" does not come to mind in describing it. "Weighty" is much more accurate, in my opinion. But what I love about these verses is that God is once again showing me how a shift in perspective will tremendously benefit me.

Conflict is hard for me. Whether internal or external, I avoid it at all costs. Affliction shows up both ways in my life, and I constantly grapple with the uncomfortable intersection of walking through it—knowing that the eternal glory on the other side completely outweighs the journey.

What makes the difference? My focus. When I focus on affliction with my limited, human sight, my vision is clouded with the cares of the world and how I can fix my problems. But when I focus on the unseen with spiritual vision, which requires me to exercise faith and trust, I can lay hold on the better part of my story. It's not a simple task. In fact, I'm nearing 40 and I am still working through seeing with God's eyes instead of my own.

What we can grasp with our senses are temporary and will fade away. What we store up spiritually is eternal. But spiritual storehouses are not filled through a life of ease. Affliction, while not pleasant, is purposeful. I am learning with every trial to view it as such. I hope the same for you.

Lord, help us to view our affliction through spiritual lenses. May we be able to look back and say it was all worth it. Amen.

Quantrilla Ard is a member of the Restoration Praise Center in Maryland.

Love Yourself Like God Loves You

"Love the Lord your God with all your passion and prayer and muscle and intelligence—and that you love your neighbor as well as you do yourself" (Luke 10:27, MSG).

Joyce wasn't having a good day. The math assignment was so hard, and the new concept so confusing. She was discouraged.

"I'm stupid!" she exclaimed.

"You're not stupid. Don't tell yourself that. I'll answer your questions. You can do this," I responded.

"I can't do this!" continued Joyce.

"God made you smart, and He'll help you. Let's ask Him right now to be with you. He loves you, and will help you. I'm here to help you too," I promised.

A couple days later, I was struggling with a project that didn't work out well for me, and I said, "I'm stupid. I can't do it." I suddenly realized I was repeating the same words I had heard from my student.

At that moment, God's Holy Spirit spoke to my heart: You're not stupid. You can do this. Be kind to yourself, My child. I made you and love you. Love yourself just as I love you.

"Thank you," I prayed. "Help me to always remember to be kind and loving to myself, just as you are loving and kind."

God gave me the privilege to love and care for Joyce and many other children of His, and to help them learn of His love and care for them.

God loves you and me. He calls us to love Him, others and ourselves with all the power He has given us. What a wonderful invitation to be like God!

My kind God, may I be kind to myself and others just like You are. Amen.

Vicki Bernard is a member of the Hillcrest church in Pennsylvania.

Thankful for the People in My Life

"A friend loves at all times, and a brother is born for a time of adversity" (Prov. 17:17, NIV).

I like this verse for many reasons. First, a friend loves, but a brother is there for the hard things. It's not that a friend won't be there in times of need, but your brother is going to always be there, and he will understand what you're going through. There are things that brothers might not understand, but at least they are with you during the toughest times. Their love is stronger than a friend's love because your brother has been with you from the very beginning.

A brother doesn't have to be your physical brother; they can be any close family member. I was feeling down one day, and none of my friends could make me happy. A few days passed, and no one could help me, until the day I talked with my mom. She was able to fix my problem. She understood what I was going through.

Dear God, thank You for all You have done, and thank You for the people in our lives You have given to us. Please take care of everyone. Amen.

Nicanor Montiel dela Cruz is a seventh-grader at the C. F. Richards Christian School in Virginia.

He Supplies Our Every Need

"'Bring the whole tithe into the storehouse, that there may be food in My house. Test Me in this,' says the Lord Almighty, 'and see if I will not throw open the floodgates of heaven and pour out so much blessing that there will not be room enough to store it'"
(Mal. 3:10, NIV).

I became a Seventh-day Adventist and started tithing around the time I moved out on my own. Eventually, an elder explained that everything is God's in the first place, and we are just returning a small portion to Him. Tithing symbolizes trust in God that He will provide for all our needs.

My first winter on my own, a co-worker of mine lost her home to fire. Another employee thought of collecting groceries to help her. I went home and prayed, "Please, God, make sure I always have enough and some to share." I filled a grocery bag and still had enough for me. The next winter, I wrecked my car and had to come up with a deductible. A church member loaned me a pickup truck, and another gave me homemade canned green beans. And each workday, my employer provided me with lunch. As a result, I didn't have to buy groceries for an entire month, as I continued to faithfully tithe.

Now, 40 years later, I can attest that God did and still does supply my needs, for He is good.

Lord, may I stay faithful to You always. Amen.

Linda Brawner is a member of the Mansfield church in Ohio.

Calm in the Storm

"He will cover you with His feathers, and under His wings you will find refuge; His faithfulness will be your shield and rampart" (Ps. 91:4, NIV).

When I was a small girl, my mother hurried us down a tree-lined road. Before long, we heard the now familiar drone of a low flying bomber. My mother quickly pushed the stroller with my brother in it against the trunk of a large tree. She pulled my sister and me into the ditch. But I had already seen the plane's incendiary bomb released over the lone farmhouse in the nearby field. The fireball is clearly etched in my mind.

With her three little ones, my mother knew she could not remain where she lived, and so began her trek of fleeing from point A to point B to point C, always needing to stay ahead and out of the enemy's path. Her greatest fear was that in the crowds that pushed and shoved whenever transportation was available, she would lose us. "Hold tight to the stroller," she admonished us.

I owe all to my praying mother. We made it. And so did my father, who had chosen to drive an ambulance. God kept His word. His strong feathers as a protective shield saved us from a myriad of other mishaps.

Thank You, Father, for all the mothers who do whatever is necessary, often at the cost of their own privation, to bring their children safely through the thick and thin of this planet's times of turmoil. Amen.

Elfie G. Edwards is a member of the Elkins church in West Virginia.

The Gift That Gave Back

"The Lord your God is with you wherever you go" (Josh. 1:9, NKJV).

In 2017, I was living and working in Milan, Italy. I had a part-time job in a Chinese multinational company, lived downtown with my sister and did Bible work in my spare time. Life was comfortable and predictable. I was active in church and held a few offices. I enjoyed teaching Sabbath School and giving Bible studies, but I felt the need for a change.

Being a language lover, I enjoyed working with Chinese people and started studying Mandarin. I was so fascinated by my colleagues' work ethic and their exotic country that I began to look for opportunities to go to China as a missionary. I wanted to help them know God. I wrote my friend (and future husband) and asked if he knew anyone in China. He suggested I try a health center in Malaysia first and arranged for me to go.

During this time, I discovered that our CEO was Christian, and I decided to gift him the book *Steps to Christ*. One day, I left it in his office. He later came to me and asked who the book was from. I admitted it was from me. He walked into his office and came out with a beautiful painting for me, with Joshua 1:9 engraved on it.

As I prepared to tell my family, friends and boss that I was leaving for Asia, I felt scared, vulnerable and afraid to leave everything behind. But, as I walked past my living room, I looked up and read the promise on my gift and was again assured that God was with me, and He will be with me wherever I go.

Thank You, God, that wherever I go, You are with me. Amen.

Eugenia Baek is a member of the West Chester church in Pennsylvania.

He Heard My Prayer

**"God is our refuge and strength, a very present help in trouble"
(Ps. 46:1, KJV).**

I boarded the train for home after attending my sister's funeral in Georgia. A friend agreed to pick me up at the station, but after arriving, I waited and waited with no sign of him at all. Frustrated, I called the neighbor who had taken me to the train station several days before. I really didn't want to trouble him because he had just lost his job. Nevertheless, he kindly consented. I gave him clear instructions to wait on the street outside the station, reminding him not to wait at the entrance of the station where he first dropped me because it was a private Amtrak entrance for dignitaries.

I waited, but once again, no one came. I walked toward the entrance of the station, and, to my amazement, his car was by the same private entrance. Fear gripped me as I saw three security officers surrounding him. I walked quickly toward them. The officers told us that he was blocking a private entrance and had to pay a fine of $200. I cried to the Lord, "Oh, Lord, why is this happening? You know he can't afford to pay."

I was asked to get into the car, and an officer came around to my window. Holding up the ticket, he said, "I am tearing up my copy and you tear up yours too. I don't have the heart to fine you."

"Thank you very much. May God bless you and your family," I said.

Yes, "in my distress I called upon the Lord, and … He heard my voice" (Ps. 18:6, KJV).

Father, thank You for hearing and answering our prayers. Amen.

Adveria Thompson is a member of the Capital Chinese church in Maryland.

Where You Set Your Foot

**"I will give you every place where you set your foot,
as I promised Moses" (Josh. 1:3, NIV).**

In August 2007, I joined the Chesapeake Conference as the pastor of the
Baltimore Hispanic church.

My greatest challenge was getting used to a single congregation. Prior to
the invitation, I was directing a conference in Venezuela with more than
200 churches. It was difficult for me to adapt to a smaller size, but I was
convinced of God's divine direction and witnessed His every step.

When I arrived in Baltimore and saw a single congregation in a territory
with so many inhabitants, I asked God to give me the blessing of planting
new congregations. This text came to my mind: "I will give you every
place where you set your foot."

God told Joshua that He had given him land even before he stepped on it!
We have a God who keeps promises without limits! Sadly, we are the ones
who set the limits. His promise always remains the same, even today.

Inspired by this text, I encouraged the church members to move forward.
We started small groups, Bible studies and evangelistic campaigns to plant
the second congregation in Baltimore in June 2008. God blessed us, and
today, there are three Hispanic congregations in the center of Baltimore
city, five in Baltimore County*, one in Aberdeen and two in Columbia.

Although grateful, I endorse the words that God said to Joshua years later:
"There remains very much land yet to be possessed" (Josh. 13:1, NKJV).

*Thank You, God, for giving us the privilege of working for You and seeing Your
wonders. Amen.*

Orlando Rosales is the Hispanic Ministries director for the Chesapeake Conference.

*Two of them were established by two colporteurs.

The Best Cheerleader

"I have come that they may have life, and have it to the full"
(John 10:10, NIV).

I was blessed to have parents who always believed in me. I can't remember a decision I made in which my parents were not there to lend their support. They may not have agreed with every decision I made, but they were alongside me as I moved on from the outcome of my decisions. Their willingness to be there for me meant the world. It gave me strength and confidence to move forward when, at times, I didn't think I could. Maybe you had parents like that or maybe you had someone else in your life who cheered for you. Whether you did or didn't, know that in Christ we all have a passionate cheerleader.

When Jesus said, "I have come that they may have life, and have it to the full," He was referring to each of us—you and me. Let's stop and think about that. As His driving force, the Creator of the universe has an abundant life for us. I don't know about you, but that lifts me up.

God, thank You for being the best cheerleader of all time! Amen.

Wendy Pega is the interim associate superintendent for the Potomac Conference Education Department.

Don't Worry!

**"Therefore do not worry about tomorrow, for tomorrow will worry about its own things. Sufficient for the day is its own trouble"
(Matt. 6:34, NKJV).**

I am not supposed to worry about tomorrow, but still, I tend to worry.

My father is a pastor, and when he was relocated to a new district, we had to sell our beautiful home and move into an apartment. I miss my old house because it was bigger with more room and space to play. The apartment is smaller so our stuff is crammed together. Now that my older brother and I are growing up and need more space for schoolwork and play, the apartment is even smaller than before.

I began to wish for a new house with more space for my brother and me to play with our toys. I also dream of having a white Pomeranian puppy.

This year, I turned my wish into a prayer. I prayed for God to provide the best house with the best price for my family and our needs. My family joined me in prayer. After we prayed for several days, we started looking for homes. God provided several homes with all the necessary accommodations and within our budget.

I praise God for answering prayers and providing the best options at the right time. I learned that with a little faith God will provide. I don't have to worry; just trust in Him and be patient.

Thank you, Heavenly Father, for hearing and answering my prayer. Please strengthen my faith in You as I grow so that I will rely on You without worry for the rest of my life. Amen.

Austin D. Marton is a fourth-grader at Northern Ohio Adventist Academy.

Grace Freely Given

"Freely you have received; freely give" (Matt. 10:8, NIV).

When I stop and ponder that, in and of ourselves, we deserve nothing but eternal death, and that God has given us eternal life in Christ, I marvel at His grace. It is absolutely counter-intuitive. God's thinking and ways are not ours (Isaiah 55:8). He is infinite. We are finite. He is far beyond our vaunted logic, reason and sense of fairness.

His grace proves it and goes even further beyond by strengthening us in such a way that we are strong when we are weak (2 Corinthians 12:9–10)! As the song goes, it truly is "Amazing Grace." God freely offers us salvation (John 3:16), and when we receive Jesus as Savior and Lord, He freely gives us strength to live a life that is pleasing to Him and is best for us (Philippians 2:13).

In Matthew 10:8, Jesus instructed, "Freely you have received; freely give." We are God's modem to freely give grace just as we have received it. No security keys are required. We are only to give of ourselves freely as He gave of Himself freely.

Lord, make me weak so that You can be strong in and through me so others may know and experience Your amazing grace. Amen.

William Peterson is the executive secretary of the Pennsylvania Conference.

'Take No Thought'

"Therefore take no thought, saying, What shall we eat? or, What shall we drink? or, Wherewithal shall we be clothed? ... for your heavenly Father knoweth that ye have need of all these things" (Matt. 6:31–32, KJV).

I am a thinker, planner and need-to-knower. Accordingly, "taking no thought" was an enigma that both intrigued and challenged me. How does one "take no thought?" Our very training from childhood seems to negate that mandate: do well in school, get an advanced education, seek a lucrative career, work hard for advancement, save for retirement. In other words, take a lot of thoughts.

These verses challenged me to try to understand the heart-faith change God was seeking, and this became my daily reading. The power of "taking no thought" pulled me from the self-reliance of a steady paycheck to self-employment. A chance conversation with a contractor who stated that he never advertised but trusted God to send him business, strengthened my resolve to eventually trust God enough to allow Him to think for me. This powerful business model became mine, albeit with varying success.

Then, while I was in business-building mode, my husband decided to retire early to also build a business. These verses became my mental, emotional and spiritual survival tool. Finally, I had no thoughts! It was then that I accepted that my heavenly Father really did know what we needed as we saw Him provide repeatedly for us.

Though challenged, we were never hungry, homeless or helpless. I learned that, though His thoughts are not mine, His solutions are sure.

Father, I thank You for thinking of me continually. Help me to trust Your thoughts for my life. Amen.

Gloria Dorsey is a member of the Pisgah church in Maryland.

When Hope Begins to Grow

"Cast your cares on the Lord and He will sustain you; He will never let the righteous be shaken" (Ps. 55:22, NIV).

Each day, we are faced with millions of decisions. Some hold more weight than others, but, ultimately, all of them have consequences. Throughout our lives, we will be faced with choices that determine our outlook. We can choose to be pessimistic, negative and discouraged about our current situation—whether the pandemic or the array of other things happening in our lives—or we can look to God, trust that He has our best interest in mind and be optimistic about our situation.

I have dealt with anxiety and worry for a few years, and, while it has not been severe, any amount of it is overwhelming. It is very easy to be pessimistic. When I came across this text, I instantly connected with it. God asks me to give Him my worries and anxieties and then promises that He will never let me be shaken. When I read this, it helped to quiet my anxious thoughts. I am able to allow myself to trust God as He holds me safely in His arms.

Throughout the day, we fight a battle for our minds, hearts and actions. Satan's choice would be for us to live in fear and discouragement. When he can make us afraid and worried, he has won. But God is stronger, and He wants us to live without fear. As we start to let go of fear, hope begins to grow, and clinging to it will save us.

Dear Lord, please help us to choose You every day. Sustain us in Your arms through the storms of life. Amen.

Larissa Krueger is a 2020 graduate of Spencerville Adventist Academy in Maryland.

God Is With Us

**"Have I not commanded you? Be strong and courageous.
Do not be afraid; do not be discouraged, for the Lord your God
will be with you wherever you go" (Josh. 1:9, NIV).**

Sometimes we find ourselves in situations and wonder if God is paying attention. We might feel so alone that we can't feel God's presence; we need His guidance and help. Sometimes friends, spouses and parents don't completely understand what we are going through, but God does, and He cares. How comforting it is to know that wherever we go, God is there with us.

God told Joshua to be strong and have courage: "The Lord your God will be with you wherever you go." We don't have to feel alone, for God is with us. He is working out our problems, oftentimes without us even realizing it. We need to have faith to trust Him and receive what He has for us. If we need strength, peace, love, joy or hope, He has it all. He longs to pour out His favor and blessings on us.

As we read in Psalms 139:1-6, "You know when I sit and when I rise; You perceive my thoughts from afar. You discern my going out and my lying down; You are familiar with all my ways. ... You hem me in behind and before, and You lay Your hand upon me. Such knowledge is too wonderful for me to attain" (NIV).

There is nothing that God doesn't know and can't do for us. He walks with us every moment of every day.

Father, thank You for always being there. Amen.

Gloria Holland is the senior account clerk and administrative assistant for the Columbia Union Revolving Fund in Maryland.

God Knows Best

**"And we know that all things work together for good
to those who love God" (Rom. 8:28, NKJV).**

When I knocked on his door 30 years ago, I never imagined the conversation we had would impact me to this day.

He had been a leader of the church; a highly respected man of God of 96 years. His wife had passed away awhile back. My husband and I needed information on the cause of her death, as she had participated in the research my husband was conducting to obtain his Masters in Public Health.

After completing the interview, I dared to ask him a question that was haunting me. He had lived a life of hardship, but his spirit was young, filled with peace and joy.

I asked, "Pastor, if you had to give one piece of advice on how to live a life like yours, what would it be?"

Smiling, he answered, "Romans 8:28. Just love God, and, no matter what life brings your way, everything will work together for good."

I pray that by the time you read this message, humanity will have found a way to fight the coronavirus. As I'm writing, we're in the crossfires of a horrible battle. Our churches are closed. Many have lost their jobs. The list of the sick and dying grow with each passing day.

My husband recently conducted a virtual funeral for a dear Christian brother. As I heard family members of the deceased person share words of gratitude, I knew in my heart that even this, COVID-19, will work together for the good of those who love God.

Lord, how can this work for good? I do not know. But I know You do. Amen.

Carmen A. Esposito is the Hispanic Women's Ministries director for the Potomac Conference.

She Loved Me

"See how very much our Father loves us, for He calls us His children, and that is what we are! But the people who belong to this world don't recognize that we are God's children because they don't know Him" (1 John 3:1, NLT).

Every summer, for the first 8 years of my life, our family drove from our home in the metro-Detroit area down to our family farm in Boone, N.C. My brother and I would wake up at dawn to spend the day traipsing through the woods, fishing, riding in Grandpa Jim's old pickup and eating fudge-ripple ice cream with chocolate sauce. Those early years were the best.

Not long after I turned 9, we made that trip during a winter storm. Grandpa Jim, 65, had suffered a massive heart attack and stroke and died.

While our summer trips to Boone continued, I dreaded them. Grandma Annie had chores for me, criticized everything I did and publicly questioned the wisdom of eating my fudge-ripple treat. It seemed as if she detested me, and my heart began to grow cold.

Just before I turned 16, we again traveled to Boone. Grandma Annie had lost her battle with lung cancer. I went through the motions and attended the funeral. Imagine my surprise when the minister, neighbors and relatives shared stories of how my grandmother boasted about her smart, beautiful and gifted granddaughter.

It wasn't until that moment, that I recognized my grandmother had been hurting following the death of her husband. As I thought about the Father's love, I knew then that my grandmother loved me after all.

Father, thank You that You call us Your children. Amen.

Heidi A. Shoemaker is the executive assistant to the president and chief medical officer at Fort Hamilton Hospital, part of Kettering Adventist HealthCare in Ohio.

Shine for God!

"Arise, shine; for thy light is come, and the glory of the Lord is risen upon thee. For, behold, the darkness shall cover the earth, and gross darkness the people: but the Lord shall arise upon thee, and His glory shall be seen upon thee. And the Gentiles shall come to thy light, and kings to the brightness of thy rising" (Isa. 60:1–3, KJV).

Arise, shine! How beautiful are those words. These verses make me think of myself standing on a large stage with the whole world watching me. Everything I say has an impact and a meaning to every person, young and old. Because of this, I must choose my words wisely and point others to Christ. God is with me, and His light is shining on me. This is my opportunity to tell others about Him!

The world is covered in a dark haze of sin. But with God in my heart, I can be the one to shine and hasten His return. With God's help, I can bring others into the light of His glory, and they, too, can be witnesses. More and more, this family of light will grow, until everyone has had a chance to come into the light. When God returns, it will be easy for Him to find His children that love Him and who have witnessed for Him.

You also can be a witness and a light for Christ to others. Let our prayer today be an earnest request for God to live in us and shine through us.

Dear Father in heaven, please live in my heart. Let me be a light to those living in darkness. Please help me to remember each day to shine for You! I love You. Please come quickly. Amen.

Zora Edmondson is a member of the Frostburg church in Maryland.

He Overcame the World

"These things I have spoken unto you, that in Me ye might have peace. In the world ye shall have tribulation: but be of good cheer; I have overcome the world" (John 16:33, KJV).

My grandparents from India had planned to visit us the summer of 2016. Things came up and their coming was delayed. My grandpa thought about postponing the trip, but my parents disagreed, so my grandparents came.

That summer was one of the best. I really got to know my grandparents. Of course, I had been with them before, but I was younger at the time and understood less. They ended up staying into January of 2017. Afterward, we called my grandparents about twice a week to talk and see how they were doing.

Then it happened. I called my grandpa one Friday night, and told him we would video call them later that weekend. On Sunday evening, my family went fishing and got home late. When I woke up for school the next morning, my parents shared the tragic news with me. My grandpa had passed away from a heart attack. I was in shock. He was just in the house, laughing at my childhood antics. The first thing I did was hug my dad. In tears, he said to me, "We'll see him when Jesus comes again, Son."

John 16:33 is the verse that I have held on to. My grandpa's passing was just one of the many trials I'll face in life. Many people lose loved ones, but we have the peace that only Jesus gives—the peace that passes all understanding—and the assurance that He has overcome the world by conquering death.

God, help me to remember that You have already overcome the world, and You're by my side in whatever befalls me. Amen.

Sidharth Chavan is a junior at Takoma Academy in Maryland.

Categories and Mysteries

"'Are you for us or for our enemies?' 'Neither,' he replied"
(Josh. 5:13–14, NIV).

Categories, juxtapositions, contradictions, polarizations. The more we live, the more we understand that things are not black and white—that life is complex and messy most of the time. When it comes to faith, categorizing to avoid confusion and ambiguity seems paramount. It's like an ancient push we feel.

We see this in the Old Testament. Joshua was the leader and general of the Israelites. When he "was near Jericho, he looked up and saw a man standing in front of him with a drawn sword in his hand. Joshua went up to him and asked, 'Are you for us or for our enemies?' 'Neither,' he replied, 'but as commander of the army of the Lord I have now come'" (Josh. 5:13–14, NIV).

Reverently, Joshua fell to the ground and asked what message God had for him. "The commander of the Lord's army replied, 'Take off your sandals, for the place where you are standing is holy'" (verse 15).

This story is phenomenal. Joshua, as a commander, is used to thinking in categories and ranks. When he asks for them, God doesn't give them to him. When we ask for categories, God sometimes responds "neither" or, in the original Hebrew, "no," because sometimes reality does not fit into categories. In the presence of God, what matters is that everything that surrounds us is holy.

Maybe, as Eugene Peterson puts it, "mystery is not the absence of meaning but the presence of more meaning than we can comprehend." Worship is accepting this mystery.

Lord, help me to trust You when there are things I don't understand. Amen.

Nestor Bruno is the director of the Ministry Care Line for Kettering Adventist HealthCare in Ohio.

To Spend and Be Spent

"And I will very gladly spend and be spent for you; though the more abundantly I love you, the less I be loved" (2 Cor. 12:15, KJV).

Every choice we make, every course taken, has a cost. The apostle Paul was well aware of the cost of apostleship. In his second letter to the church in Corinth, he tenderly expresses how he felt about the believers. He announced that he was going to make a third visit to them and that in no way would he be a burden to them.

On the contrary, he told them: "I will very gladly spend and be spent for you." This is the mark of a servant of God who had come to know the heart of God as manifested through His Son. Jesus speaks these words of assurance today. When I understood that these words apply to a leader in God's work for the people, I was impressed. When I understood them to come from Jesus Christ to me, I was humbled in amazement.

The thought that Christ spares no blessing or good thing for His people is why we praise Him today. But to realize that He divested Himself of everything and became obedient unto death, even death on the cross— for you and me—is why we bow in surrender to Him.

"Though the more abundantly I love you, the less I be loved." Paul recognizes the tendency of the fallen human heart. It is easy to take for granted the one who loves you most. He experienced loneliness, ungratefulness and doubters along his journey. Scripture records the history that the greater manifestations of God's favor and blessings were often repaid with ensuing unfaithfulness and unbelief from His own. May we recommit our love to Him.

Dear Lord, help me love You more. Amen.

John Rengifo is the associate pastor of Evangelism and Discipleship for the Atholton church in Maryland.

Praying for My Enemy

"But I say to you, love your enemies, bless those who curse you, do good to those who hate you, and pray for those who spitefully use you and persecute you" (Matt. 5:44, NKJV).

Jason was my nemesis. When we were young, he beat up nearly every kid on our block, including me. Things worsened as we got older. He sexually assaulted a dear friend of mine, and, to my face, threatened to kill her.

For years, I harbored anger toward Jason. As a young Christian, I came across verse after verse in the Bible about forgiveness and praying for your enemies, but I ignored theses verses and would just turn the page. I was so deeply hurt; I didn't want to forgive or pray for him.

One day, I came to a passage and started to turn the page, when a vision came to my mind. I was in heaven and two beautiful girls were telling me how they came to Christ. They were sad that their dad wasn't there with them. "There was no one to pray for him," they said. Then they told me his name. Jason. I regretfully explained why I hadn't prayed. It was my fault he wasn't there.

This imagery shook me. I didn't want to pray for him, but what if my prayers could change him?

I began to pray for Jason—very reluctantly and minimally at first—but, over time, God's Spirit began to direct those prayers. He was a prayed-for man.

Years later, Jason reached out to me on Facebook. He apologized for everything. He had become a born-again Christian. He showed me pictures of his two little girls—two little girls who will have their daddy in heaven with them.

Father God, give me strength to forgive and to pray for those who hurt me, trusting that You hear and heal. Amen.

Jeremy Garlock is the superintendent of schools for the Pennsylvania Conference.

No More Night

"He will wipe every tear from their eyes, and there will be no more death or sorrow or crying or pain. All these things are gone forever" (Rev. 21:4, NLT).

This verse has always been a favorite of mine, so I recently read it in various translations. Surprised to find 28 translations online, I realized there are many different ways God shows us that because one day He will make death disappear, we can look forward to being happy forever.

My mom was very ill for four, long years and passed away three years ago. It still doesn't feel real that she is gone. God never intended for us to experience that kind of sadness, separation and death. He created us to live forever with each other and with Him.

Can you just imagine how wonderful it will be to have no crying, sadness or disappointment in heaven? It's almost beyond the realm of imagination. Almost. God has promised this, and He always keeps His Word, no matter the cost. He proved that at Calvary, and proves it every day, if we are willing to put our trust in Him.

The lyrics from the song "No More Night" tells of a wonderful time when there will be no more pain and no more night; instead, we will live in the light of His presence. Give God a chance to prove Himself. He wants you to test Him and see that He is faithful!

God, we look forward to the day when we will be with you in heaven forever! Amen.

Joannie Galbraith is a member of the Waynesboro church in Virginia.

A Mama's Prayer

"Refrain your voice from weeping, and your eyes from tears; for your work shall be rewarded ... and they shall come back from the land of the enemy. There is hope in your future ... that your children shall come back to their own border" (Jer. 31:16–17, NKJV).

I have a lot of favorite scriptures. Verses that give me hope, courage, inspire me, convict me, challenge me to action. Favorite promises from God's Word for different areas of my life. In Jeremiah, God spoke a new favorite verse directly to my mama-heart as I lifted my sons to Him.

"God, please ..." I managed to say.

Tears streamed down my face as I prayed for my sons, begging God to speak into their lives, reveal Himself and His love to them, and call them deeper into a relationship with Him. Teen and young adult years are hard, and trials were causing them to question faith and God.

Repeatedly, I sensed God saying, "I have loved you with an everlasting love; therefore with lovingkindness I have drawn you" (Jer. 31:3, NKJV).

I knew God loved my sons. What else did He want me to know?

Turning to Jeremiah, I began praying God's words over my sons. God saw my tears and knew my hurting heart. He challenged me to trust Him, and promised to work in their lives.

Now, as I pray for my sons, I take time to thank God for loving them, for wanting more for them than I even imagine, for having hopes and plans for their lives. I trust Him to persistently and consistently move mountains to remind them of who He is and call them deeper into friendship with Him.

God, please! Amen.

Tamyra Horst is the director of Communication, Family, Prayer and Women's Ministries for the Pennsylvania Conference.

Peace in Difficulty

"But now thus saith the Lord that created thee, O Jacob, and He that formed thee, O Israel, Fear not: for I have redeemed thee, I have called thee by thy name; thou art mine. When thou passest through the waters, I will be with thee; and through the rivers, they shall not overflow thee: when thou walkest through the fire, thou shalt not be burned; neither shall the flame kindle upon thee. For I am the Lord thy God, the Holy One of Israel, thy Saviour" (Isa. 43:1–3, KJV).

It was 1991, and I had just given birth to my daughter. The doctor came in to give me sad news: "You have cancer." I felt like my whole life was coming to an end. I was about to ask the doctor how much time I had, when I heard the voice of the Holy Spirit whisper, "Cursed is the man who trusts in man and makes flesh his strength" (Jer. 17:5, ESV). Then He said, "Even the hairs on your head are all numbered" (Luke 12:7, ESV), and I thought, *This is the word of God*. The doctor asked, "Is something wrong?" I replied, "No, nothing. Let's proceed with surgery."

The surgery was in a week; I was nervous and could not process the news. But when I woke up on the day of the surgery, I talked to God, and He answered me.

I opened my devotional, and the verse for that day was Isaiah 43:1–3. This promise gave me security and strength, and made me see that my case was not a matter of life or death, but a trial from which I would emerge victorious.

Thank You, Lord, for being with me in difficult times. I praise You! Amen.

Saylis V. Fuentes is the pastor of the Lorton Spanish church in Virginia.

He Healed Me Instead

**"And lo, I am with you always, even unto the end of the world"
(Matt. 28:20, KJV).**

The year was 2014. My mother had just been diagnosed with cancer. I had all the confidence and faith in the world that God would heal her; He didn't. Instead, He healed me.

During all the days of radiation, I continued to keep the faith. During the days of chemo, I claimed every scriptural promise that I could think of: on asking, receiving, believing and healing. Deep down inside, I just knew that God was going to heal my mom; He didn't. Instead, He healed me.

During one of her sickest days, I finally hit my breaking point. In anger, frustration and deep brokenness, I went to God expressing my sincere disappointment. And that's when He gave me Matthew 28:20 to not only strengthen me in that moment, but to carry me for years to come. It has anchored me in storms, comforted me when hurt, blanketed me when lonely, surrounded me when threatened and healed and restored me when shattered.

In the death of my mother, God, in His sovereign goodness, was delivering to me a "Beyond the Moment" faith. He was preparing me by giving me a word, a verse, that would transcend any situation that I would ever face: death, divorce, loss of job, family, home or health. He wanted me to comprehend that He would *always* be with me.

In 2014, I believed that God would heal my mother; He didn't. Instead, He healed me. My prayer is that He heals you too.

Dear God, please heal those who are hurting. Amen.

K. L. Watkins is the principal of the Sharon Temple Adventist School in Delaware.

Mirror, Mirror, on the Wall

"The wise woman builds her house, but the foolish pulls it down with her hands" (Prov. 14:1, NKJV).

The most dangerous household object is the mirror, with its ability to cut physically and emotionally. By amplifying our perceived flaws, wrinkles, cellulite and scars, it deceives us into believing that the imperfect reflection is who we really are. When that outer physical image doesn't measure up to our expectations, it shatters our identity and confidence.

My "house" for many years was a plus-sized body. When I lost nearly 150 pounds through healthier eating and walking, the outward change was so profound that old friends didn't recognize me. On the inside, I struggled with the same insecurities that caused me to turn to food. I was slimmer, but I still wasn't perfect, which made me feel unworthy and unlovable.

Instead of being wise as the Proverbs 14:1 woman and turning to the One who loves me with an everlasting love, I based my identity on the woman in the mirror and foolishly tore myself down with self-criticism. When we don't trust God's love but believe the voices that say we aren't good enough, we destroy our houses and self-sabotage with food, alcohol, drugs, sex and other temporary sources of pleasure, comfort and rebellion.

So cast off perfectionism, doubt and criticism by spending time with the God who desires to build up our bodily houses. We are worthy for the simple reason that our Creator says we are. After all, He is the one who knit us together in our mothers' wombs, whose thoughts of us outnumber the grains of sand and who has counted the hairs on our heads.

Lord, direct our hands to wisely build our houses and self-confidence. Help us to seek our reflection in Your eyes and not in the mirror. Amen.

Connie Kuykendall is a member of the Far West End church in Virginia.

Don't Lose Heart

"Consider Him who endured such opposition from sinners, so that you will not grow weary and lose heart. In your struggle against sin, you have not yet resisted to the point of shedding your blood" (Heb. 12:3–4, NIV).

One day in my youth, I felt really lonely and depressed. I wanted to cry! My friend had betrayed me. It was an awful situation, so I fell to my knees to pray to God. I told Him how I felt and asked Him to answer me as my Friend: "God, how can I overcome this situation?" Immediately, a thought came to mind: Go read Hebrews 12:3–4.

Initially, when I read the verse, I felt bad because I had a beautiful family, a house, food, friends and many other things, and I was being ungrateful to God. And second, I had never been in a situation like the one Jesus went through and suffered for me.

Since then, this verse has helped me in difficult moments, reminding me that I have many things for which I can be happy and grateful to God, and that, in my fight against sin, I have not yet resisted to the point of pouring out my blood.

Thank you, Lord, for the assurance that, because You faced incredible hardship, You are able to strengthen us in our time of need. Amen.

Deisy Bustamante is a senior accountant for the Columbia Union Revolving Fund in Maryland.

"Let us hold unswervingly to the hope we profess, for He who promised is faithful." HEB. 10:23, NIV

JUNE

Less Is More

**"I know what it is to be in need, and I know what
it is to have plenty. I have learned the secret of being content
in any and every situation, whether well fed or hungry,
whether living in plenty or in want. I can do all this through
Him who gives me strength" (Phil. 4:12–13, NIV).**

This is one of my favorite verses because it talks about being content. Sometimes it is easy to look at someone else's life and wish to have what they have. It is easy to see their big house, cool clothes or expensive car and want to have it. But, even though they have nice things, their life may not be all it seems to be.

The person could be struggling with problems unknown to anyone else. The life that God gave each of us was made just for us. God made each of us special with different talents and abilities. He placed each of us where we need to be. God has a plan, even if we do not see it.

This verse tells me that I can be content with the life that God gave me. I don't have to envy anybody else's life. This verse goes on to say that I can do all things through Christ who gives me strength. This means that if I ask Jesus to help me be content, He will help me do it. I am glad that Jesus loves us and that He talks to us through prayer. I am also thankful that He gives me strength.

Jesus, please give me strength to be content. Thank You for making us special and unique! Amen.

Darby Holder is a seventh-grader at the Harrisburg Adventist School in Pennsylvania.

Love Freely Gives

"But the fruit of the Spirit is love, joy, peace, longsuffering, gentleness, goodness, faith" (Gal. 5:22, KJV).

Love—one of the fruits of the Spirit—is represented in the parable of the prodigal son found in Luke 15:11–32.

We always talk about love, but what is it? Wikipedia describes love as "always seeking the highest good for others, no matter their behavior. It is a love that gives freely without asking anything in return."

How did the prodigal son behave? He was lazy, disrespectful and ungrateful. He asked for all his inheritance and wasted everything, living in ways his father had not taught him. He brought dishonor to his family and himself. When he found himself alone, sad, broke and without a single friend, he was reminded of how his father's servants lived and decided to return home.

The entire time he was away, his father thought of him and prayed for his return. The day he saw his son coming down the road, instead of asking lots of questions or shaming him, he ran out and immediately hugged him because of the pure love he felt for him. I encourage us all to practice this kind of love toward each other.

Dear Lord, please give us the unselfish love that You have toward people. Help us to see people with Your eyes. Amen.

Elyssia Sanchez is a fourth-grader at Vienna Adventist Academy in Virginia.

Legacy of a Christian Education

"Start children off on the way they should go, and even when they are old they will not turn from it" (Prov. 22:6, NIV).

I am the first of six children of Gilbert and Sylvia Spence. Much of the education we obtained was taught at home from parents who did not have an opportunity to obtain a college degree but were committed disciples of Jesus, the Master Teacher. Dad accepted the Seventh-day Adventist message in his teen years. Mom was already in the faith. I considered myself blessed to have parents similar to Jesus' parents—a homemaker teacher and an entrepreneur.

My dad served for many years as an elder of his local church in central Jamaica, and, in partnership with other dedicated leaders, grew a church school into a full educational center, offering elementary to academy education. Today it's known as May Pen Academy and is still operating in my homeland.

My parents saw to it that all of my siblings and I attended this school. When it was time to leave for college, my dad had a memorable conversation with me: "Son, I will not be able to leave a large monetary legacy for you," he said, "but I will invest in your education with the limited resources I have."

Before he passed in June 2015, I was able to invite him to a Washington Adventist University Alumni Sabbath gathering, and said to him publicly: "Dad, thank you for your support of Christian education and your wisdom of investing in me. Today, they call me the president of Washington Adventist University."

Thank You, God, for Seventh-day Adventist Christian education that made a positive difference in so many lives, and in my own. Amen.

Weymouth Spence is the president of Washington Adventist University in Maryland.

God Hears

"I call on the Lord in my distress, and He answers me"
(Ps. 120:1, NIV).

This verse is important to me because there have been times in life when I've felt down, like nobody could hear me. But God was always there. People have used me, and it would depress me, but praying to God made me feel like somebody cared and was listening.

When I was in sixth grade, something happened to me in which I blamed myself. One of my classmates took advantage of me constantly, and it tore me down. It affected my self-confidence greatly, and I felt useless. Unfortunately, I didn't tell any adult what was happening, because I thought nobody would care. But I was wrong. God showed me that I could talk to Him about anything and also to those I loved. I opened up to my older cousin, and that made me feel so much better. She ended up encouraging me to tell my parents, which was the best decision I made.

God hears and answers you when you call. Sometimes bad things happen. Sometimes it's even your fault. But He still loves you. No matter what you've done in the past, He will answer you in times of distress. If you are tired and helpless, He will help and comfort you. It's true because I've experienced it. God is real.

To this day, I still struggle with what happened to me, but knowing that God is there will always keep me going. God is my hero. And He can be yours too, if you ask Him to be.

Dear God, help us to remember that You're always here for us. Amen.

Sarai Myers is a seventh-grader at the Tree of Life Christian Preparatory School in Virginia.

Every Blessing

"Blessed be the God and Father of our Lord Jesus Christ, who has blessed us with every spiritual blessing in the heavenly places in Christ" (Eph. 1:3, NKJV).

I play the piano, and, as a result, have been able to experience so much in my life that I never dreamed of, like visiting Europe with my band and so many other things that I've only read about in books. Yet none of these adventures quite rival how music has brought my family closer.

My most cherished memories of piano and music aren't of playing it or where it has taken me; they are of driving to church, listening to hymn covers that my dad found for me to learn, and my mom and sister singing along to them. My number one hymn is "Come Thou Fount of Every Blessing." I love it so much that my dad had it arranged to a piano cover that is my all-time favorite; not for the notes, but for the memories and the meaning behind the notes on the page.

"Come thou fount of every blessing, Tune my heart to sing Thy grace."

The words that inspired these iconic lines come straight from the Bible: "Blessed be the God and Father of our Lord Jesus Christ, who has blessed us with every spiritual blessing in the heavenly places in Christ."

This verse talks about the glory of God, and how He has given us everything and every blessing. His streams of mercy are never ceasing. He calls for our songs of loudest praise. He calls us to sing to Him and to worship Him.

Lord, may we accept the invitation to come to Your fount of every blessing. Amen.

Ellie Sauser is a freshman at Spring Valley Academy in Ohio.

No Separation

"For I am convinced that neither death nor life, neither angels nor demons, neither the present nor the future, nor any powers, neither height nor depth, nor anything else in all creation, will be able to separate us from the love of God that is in Christ Jesus our Lord" (Rom. 8:38–39, NIV).

This is my favorite text in the Bible. So much of life is filled with heartache and pain: loved ones whom I have lost, political division and strife, famine, and pestilence with the COVID-19 virus.

Through it all, I find peace knowing that nothing can take God's love away from me. Though many question the existence of God, based on all the negativity in the world, this warfare confirms and reaffirms my commitment to God. His promises are a constant reminder of how good He is.

When we focus on negativity, we take our focus off of Christ. That makes Satan very happy. We often focus on the negativity within our church. As a result, many leave the church and sometimes God altogether. I have never understood that mindset, because for me, my salvation is not in the church but in Jesus Christ and Him alone. I love my church, but I also realize it is made up of human beings. Whenever human beings are in charge, there will always be mistakes and deficiencies because not everyone's focus is on Christ. That is where the problem lies. And this is a constant reminder of the great controversy.

Father, may we focus on Christ and let the Holy Spirit guide us so we will be ready for His soon return. "Even so, come, Lord Jesus" (Rev. 22:20, KJV). Amen.

Dunbar Henri is a religion teacher at Takoma Academy in Maryland.

God Saw Me Through

"Yea, though I walk through the valley of the shadow of death, I will fear no evil; for You are with me; Your rod and Your staff, they comfort me" (Ps. 23:4, NKJV).

One fateful Friday in 2015, my wife, Hellen, and I were celebrating our fifth anniversary in Cancun, Mexico. We spent the morning on the beach. Shortly after lunch, my head started aching severely. Back at the hotel, I felt sick and began to vomit. I thought perhaps it was due to food poisoning.

When I woke up several hours later, I had no strength to move. My wife helped me to the bathroom, where I began to vomit again. Then I experienced something that changed my life forever: "Sweetheart, I am seeing double," I told my wife.

After a few days in this condition, and feeling weak, we returned home. It turned out I didn't have food poisoning; I had a brain bleed. More precisely, a cavernous malformation. The best neurosurgeons at Johns Hopkins told me there was nothing that could be done. We would have to wait and see if the double vision subsided.

Today, I still see double when I look down, but I did not lose my sight. I experience dizziness every day, even now as I write this, but I can still walk. I thank God for sparing my life! In these past five years, Hellen and I have had the joy of raising two beautiful children—Gabriel and Hannah Belle.

The summer of 2015 was the darkest moment in my life, but Psalm 23 assured me that I was not alone. Jesus was right there walking beside me.

Lord, You are so good. Thank You for being with us in times of darkness. Amen.

Diego Boquer is the pastor of the Baltimore-White Marsh church in Maryland.

God of Love

**"The Lord hath appeared of old unto me,
saying, Yea, I have loved thee with an everlasting love:
therefore with lovingkindness have I drawn thee"
(Jer. 31:3, KJV).**

My first introduction to the Seventh-day Adventist Church was: "My mother doesn't eat pork, and she goes to church on Saturday."

After that startling introduction, I never thought I'd become a member. But when I walked into the Parkersburg church for the first time, I was met with love, the sermon spoke on love and I desired to come back to hear more about this love. Soon, I was encouraged to read the Bible more and join a Scripture memorization class.

It is my prayer that I can also draw those in my sphere of influence with lovingkindness so that they, too, can meet this God of love!

Lord, grant us a kind, loving and generous spirit that will bring others closer to You. Amen.

Amy Fullmer is a member of the Parkersburg church in West Virginia.

From Weakness to Strength

"And He said to me, 'My grace is sufficient for you, for My strength is made perfect in weakness.' Therefore most gladly I will rather boast in my infirmities, that the power of Christ may rest upon me. Therefore I take pleasure in infirmities, in reproaches, in needs, in persecutions, in distresses, for Christ's sake. For when I am weak, then I am strong" (2 Cor. 12:9–10, NKJV).

Anxiety filled my every waking moment. Being only 14, I never imagined enduring major back surgery to correct my agonizing scoliosis. Yet, here I was—tubes hanging out of me, pain wracking my body and feeling like I had been run over by a car. Little did I realize that the surgery I thought was going to end my physical suffering would introduce a whole new world of pain. Complications plagued me after the operation and took me on a multi-year journey of medical tests, dead-end diagnoses and challenging questions about my faith.

I cried out, "Lord, why aren't you healing me?" God was hearing my desperate prayers, but answering in His unique way. Over time, He miraculously healed a different part of me—my heart. The Holy Spirit drew me into the Word and daily devotions. There, He impressed me to share my story with others. As I did, God amazingly used my testimony to minister to other suffering hearts.

God used this text to show me that when I am at my weakest point, God's strength will shine brighter than ever before. Just as He is using my trial for His glory, He will do the same for you. Surrender yourself to God, and see His strength shine through your weakness.

Lord, please help me to be a light for You. Amen.

Christina Gibbs is a senior at Blue Mountain Academy in Pennsylvania.

Press On

**"But they who wait for the Lord shall renew their strength;
they shall mount up with wings like eagles; they shall run and
not be weary; they shall walk and not faint" (Isa. 40:31, ESV).**

I lived in Guatemala when I was 12-years-old. The church we attended was in need of toilets and children's classrooms. After the church board voted to build them, the members volunteered to help. Many assisted at first, but soon only two people stayed committed to the project—my dad and I.

Around this time, my family of five was planning to immigrate to the United States. We patiently prayed for our visas to arrive, but desperately wanted to finish the church upgrade prior to us leaving. Because my parents didn't have enough money to enroll me into school, I was able to work every day on the project with my dad.

When the community members only saw my dad and me working, they said, "Where are the others? Nobody is going to pay you anything!"

As a young man with dreams and goals, these words hurt. I looked to God: "They are right. Nobody is paying us. And why is nobody else helping?"

One day, an elderly woman approached me: "Son, you know what? As Isaiah 40:31 says, you just have to wait on the Lord." These words have forever been engraved in my mind.

After my dad and I finished the project, my family went to the immigration office, and I couldn't believe the news: "In a week, you will receive your five visas." We had finished the project just in time!

If you wait on the Lord, He will give you wings to fly.

Lord, when everything and everyone is against us, may You give us the strength to go on. Amen.

Darwin Jacinto is the youth director for the Langley Park Spanish church in Maryland.

Not Forever!

"I can do all things through Him who strengthens me"
(Phil. 4:13, NASB).

Full-time evangelism requires a lot of traveling and preaching, which can be very challenging for a family: uprooting every six weeks, moving your "house" to a new location, leaving friends you just made. But evangelism also "gives" a lot: meeting new friends, seeing new places and sharing Christ with people. Since we were on the go so often, my husband, Dave, decided our most ideal living quarters would be a mobile home retrofitted as a travel trailer.

While working for a conference in the Midwest, we experienced hard winters and hot summers. We moved a 12-foot by 60-foot mobile home numerous times. I would put plastic sheets down on the floor of the living room, then we would stack all the trailer jacks and boards on the floor. Almost every time we moved, we had a flat tire on the big trailer.

Dave drove a big toter truck—the type used to pull semis—and I escorted our wide-load home with our two young children in a 1937 Chevy Street Rod with a "wide load" sign and red flags.

Philippians 4:13 became one of my favorite Bible texts, as it pulled me through many difficult situations in the past, and still does. I've added my own spin to this verse to help me cope with life's demands: "I can do anything, as long as it's not forever!" This has become my motto. God will never give us more than He gives us the strength to handle.

Dear Lord, remind me throughout today that I can do all things through Your strength, and that nothing is forever except You and eternal life. Amen.

Becky Weigley serves as the director of the Ministerial Spouses Association for the Columbia Union Conference.

The Science of the Struggle

"And not only that, but we also glory in tribulations, knowing that tribulation produces perseverance; and perseverance, character; and character, hope. Now hope does not disappoint, because the love of God has been poured out in our hearts by the Holy Spirit who was given to us" (Rom. 5:3–5, NKJV).

Everyone has experienced something challenging in life. Though each struggle is unique, most have one key ingredient in common: Mohs. Designed by the geologist Friedrich Mohs, a mineral's hardness is evaluated on a scale from one to 10.

To grade its hardness, a mineral is scratched by other surfaces to see if it leaves a mark. The more a mineral can withstand a scratch, the higher it rates on the Mohs scale—a diamond having a rating of 10. Diamonds, however, do not start at 10. They begin as coal—a rating of three.

Paul tells us in the book of Romans that, with the help of the Holy Spirit, we are transformed, and our hardness or ability to withstand the struggles of life increases. We are changed by the love of God, and the struggles we endure shape our character and give us strength and hope.

The Bible tells us stories of how Job, Paul and even Jesus journeyed through struggles while keeping the faith and proving their "hardness." That first pressure-filled struggle you encounter may feel like the worst moment ever, but God's love and faith can keep you moving forward. In fact, others may marvel at the persevering character you show, or you can use that perseverance in your own future struggles. Hope is the evidence that you can endure life's pressures and transform into the diamond God desires you to be.

Father, thank You for hope! Amen.

Lamont Vaughan is a member of the New Life church in Maryland.

Lacking Nothing

"My brethren, count it all joy when you fall into various trials, knowing that the testing of your faith produces patience. But let patience have its perfect work, that you may be perfect and complete, lacking nothing" (James 1:2-4, NKJV).

I used to complain to my husband that nothing in life had come easy to me. Occasions that should have been joyous instead produced hardship, and I felt like the joy I could have obtained had been taken away from me. It was my wonderful husband, however, who reminded me to look at these experiences through a different lens—the Lord's. Where I saw obstacles, unfairness and resentment, the Lord saw love, endurance and character development. In each challenge, I felt heavily burdened, but I now realize the Lord gave me strength to overcome.

Life is full of trials, and God uses those difficulties to prepare us for bigger trials to come. We live in a harsh world, and, like a father who looks upon his child from a close distance and lets them occasionally fall to see if they can get back up, our Lord does the same. He watches us closely to make sure we are safe, but still lets us occasionally fall to prepare us for bigger trials of this world. In doing this, He teaches us patience. And through patience, we become perfect in character. As His children and reflectors of His grace, we will be prepared to be reunited with Him when He returns.

Lord, thank You for using trials and difficulties to refine and mold our characters. May we grow closer to You through these educational experiences. Amen.

Julia Kim is a member of the Ellicott City church in Maryland.

Learning God's Way

"In returning and rest you shall be saved; in quietness and confidence shall be your strength" (Isa. 30:15, NKJV).

I am typically a task-oriented person. It's like I have tunnel vision. When I see something that needs doing, I may ask for a volunteer to take it on. But if no one speaks up, I just go ahead and do it my way.

I have acquired a lot of jobs this way, and I didn't realize that, as I took on more and more responsibilities, I was hindering others from expanding their talents or discovering their God-given gifts. I just assumed everyone was OK with me doing things my way.

At one point, I was told, "It's either your way or the highway." I was shocked. I had no idea that people felt that way. You see, in my effort to getting things done, I unknowingly offended others. I wasn't considerate of their ideas or feelings. I was used to charging ahead and going to the next problem to tackle. But we serve a loving Father who disciplines those He loves (Proverbs 3:12).

I was in need of a pride check. I took the time out, stopped what I was doing and asked God to teach me. Isaiah 28:26 states, "For He instructs him in right judgment, His God teaches him" (NKJV).

I still struggle with my task-oriented tunnel vision. But God made me aware of it, and, in "returning and resting," I have learned that quiet time with my Savior is truly my strength for each day.

God, bless us as we continue our journey toward the Promised Land. Amen.

Kathy Decker is the church clerk of the Hillsboro church in Ohio.

100 Percent Chance

"For God so loved the world, that He gave His only begotten Son, that whosoever believes in Him should not perish, but have everlasting life" (John 3:16, KJV).

John 3:16 reminds me of how much God loves us. He loves us so much that He gave His only Son to take the punishment for our sins and die on a cross in our place. If God hadn't given Jesus to take our place, we would all be dead, as sin would have consumed us from the inside out.

Only adults are accepted or included in certain situations in life. But when it comes to Jesus, all of us—adults and children—are accepted and included and have a 100 percent chance of spending eternity with Jesus. All we have to do is believe in Him and accept His gift of life. On the other hand, if we reject God's gift, we will perish.

God gives each of us a choice to choose life or death. Which will you choose? "As for me and my house, [I] will serve the Lord" (Josh. 24:15, KJV).

Thank You, Lord, for giving Your Son to die for me so that I can have the opportunity of spending eternal life with You. Amen.

Jayden Gooden is a sixth-grader at the Roanoke Adventist Christian School in Virginia.

God's Building Project

"What? Know ye not that your body is the temple of the Holy Ghost which is in you, which ye have of God, and ye are not your own? For ye are bought with a price: therefore glorify God in your body, and in your spirit, which are God's" (1 Cor. 6:19–20, KJV).

I was involved in a church building project. Every thought and action that went into that project was about how beautiful we could design and make the building function as a place where God would be pleased. Once the building was finished, I would never ever think of filling it up with junk.

Notice that God is calling our bodies His temple—His building project. It belongs to Him. A temple is a place where God's Spirit dwells. The Holy Spirit wants to live within me.

The psalmist says that we are "fearfully and wonderfully made" (Ps. 139:14, KJV). That should give a person reason to rejoice, knowing that we were created by God.

Don't forget, we were bought with a price! That tells me that God came from heaven in the form of a man, and suffered the penalty of death that should have been paid by all of us sinners. His sacrifice gave us the privilege to believe and accept Him so that we can receive forgiveness for our sins.

Can I defile the bodily temple of God? Do I fill it with junk? How do I abuse it? Am I feeding it properly, both physically and spiritually? We need to take care of this body that God has created.

Lord, please allow the Holy Spirit to fill us up, and let us overflow. Amen.

Jim Buchanan is the pastor of the Cumberland and Frostburg churches in Maryland.

Learning to Rely on God

"Be anxious for nothing, but in everything by prayer and supplication, with thanksgiving, let your requests be made known to God; and the peace of God, which surpasses all understanding, will guard your hearts and minds through Christ Jesus" (Phil. 4:6–7, NKJV).

I clung to this Bible verse during one of the most difficult times in my life. It says that we shouldn't worry about things, but to pray to God, and He will guide and protect us.

When I was 13, my dad noticed an unusual and suspicious swelling on my skin. After I was tested, the doctors said I had nephrotic syndrome and that this disorder did not have an obvious cause or solution. They provided a treatment plan and hoped I would just get better.

I realize that humans have limits, and the only person I should rely on is God. As the verse says, I stopped worrying and being terrified about what I was going through, and started praying about it every day. Surprisingly, I started to believe that I could make it through this, and that I had the strength to fight it because God was taking care of me and had my back. My mind was at complete peace.

After several months of praying, I realized how arrogant I had lived my life up to that point, thinking that I could handle everything on my own. I thanked God for allowing me to "get away from everything" and talk to Him. And I praise Him for loving me.

Dear God, You are the miracle worker. Thank You for giving me peace in spite of pain. Amen.

Hailey Na is a junior at Blue Mountain Academy in Pennsylvania.

I Know He Cares!

**"Casting all your care upon Him, for He cares for you"
(1 Pet. 5:7, NKJV).**

This has been my comfort text since I was baptized at age 17. Just out of high school, and not knowing how I should steer my life, I cast all my burdens upon the Lord. I asked God for guidance in my career choice, overseas studies and job opportunities. At times, I wondered, *Does God really care for me? A teenager?*

Yes, Jesus cares! When several jobs fell through because of Sabbath keeping concerns, God opened a door for me to study at a Seventh-day Adventist junior college. The teachers were kind and loving; their Christlikeness transformed me. After graduating, I looked for a teaching job, with no success. All the government schools held classes on Sabbath.

There were times when I almost gave in to the voice that slyly said, "It's OK to work a few hours on Sabbath morning. You can still go to church afterward; surely God will understand!" Then I heard a much louder voice! "Get thee behind me, Satan."

In my darkest, most discouraging moments, God opened another door for me. A Seventh-day Adventist school principal invited me to teach their fifth- and sixth-grade class. My heart rejoiced with thanksgiving!

Psalm 55:22 says, "Give your worries to the Lord, and He will take care of you. He will never let good people down" (NCV). Let us cast our burdens of life on Jesus today, for He will take us through every storm.

Lord, as someone once said, "If we fall, our Good Shepherd is there to pick us up and help us mount the bike of life again." May Your guiding hands steer us through open doors. Amen.

Linda Mei Lin Koh is a member of the Capital Chinese church in Maryland.

God Loves Jesus

"Therefore My Father loves Me, because I lay down My life that I may take it again. No one takes it from Me, but I lay it down of Myself. I have power to lay it down, and I have power to take it again. This command I have received from My Father" (John 10:17–18, NKJV).

John 10:17–18 is one of my favorite scriptures because it takes God's love for us to a whole new level. In this verse, Jesus says that His Father loves Him because He laid down His life for us. Think about that for a minute. God loves Jesus even more for sacrificing His life to save us! This shows how massive God's love is for us!

Jesus didn't grumble His way down to earth to save us; He laid down His life of His own free will. Not only that, logic tells us if the Father loves us enough to sacrifice His own Son, He will take special care of us, for He wants us in heaven with Him.

When Jesus was on the cross, He felt that God had rejected Him. But I believe this verse says the exact opposite: The Father's love for Jesus was the greatest while dying on the cross for us.

This goes to show that, no matter how far away God may feel, He is always near. Look for Him in your everyday life—whether in big things, like narrowly missing a car crash, or small things, like a pretty sunrise or a good friend.

Dear Heavenly Father, as a result of your amazing love for us, may we live for You. Amen.

Olivia Hrovat is a freshman at Spring Valley Academy in Ohio.

In Our Darkest Moments

"Do not weep. Behold, the Lion of the tribe of Judah, the Root of David, has prevailed to open the scroll and to loose its seven seals" (Rev. 5:5, NKJV).

Some years ago, I was sitting down in an ultrasound room watching a sonographer perform an ultrasound on my wife. We were expecting our second child and were looking forward to the day we could hold him/her. This appointment was taking longer than usual, and I was getting impatient and nervous. I held my wife's hand and quietly prayed for her and my child's well-being.

After what seemed to be an eternity, the doctor came and proceeded to tell us they could not find a heartbeat. Our hearts sunk. Everything seemed to be lost. My wife and I began to cry as we embraced each other. This tragic moment was one we thought we couldn't overcome. When tragedy hits home, there are many questions we ask ourselves.

In Revelation, John finds himself without hope: If no one is able to open the scroll, then his life, suffering and the death of his friends will be in vain. When everything seems lost, we must remember that the "Lion of the tribe of Judah" has conquered death, and He is in control of our lives. He is able to help us in our darkest moments; to pick us up and lead us to higher ground. Regardless of what the situation may be, the answer to life's questions is always the same—Jesus!

As John wept, thinking all was lost, he learns that Jesus' sacrifice had been accepted, for He was able to open the scroll! This has given hope to my family, and it can do the same for you.

Lord, when faced with trials, may we seek Your face. Amen.

Walter Cárdenas is the associate ministerial director, youth director and Hispanic Ministries coordinator for the Mountain View Conference.

Anything and Everything

"Pray about everything" (Phil. 4:6, TLB).

I grew up in a missionary family, so we moved several times. The hardest part for me was getting attached to a country, and then having to leave it. My most challenging move was my Dad's call to serve at the General Conference in Maryland. That meant I had to leave South Africa. But all of my favorite things were there! My home, friends, delicious food.

When we arrived to the United States, I was even more sad because we didn't have a house, and I encountered people who were not particularly friendly to me. I did not understand why God would allow me to leave South Africa—where my true home and true friends were. Discouraged, I started to wonder if He had my best interest in mind after all.

Fortunately, during one of my gloomy days, I came across these Bible verses in my daily devotional: "Don't worry about anything; instead, pray about everything; tell God your needs, and don't forget to thank Him for His answers. If you do this, you will experience God's peace, which is far more wonderful than the human mind can understand. His peace will keep your thoughts and your hearts quiet and at rest as you trust in Christ Jesus" (Phil. 4:6–7, TLB).

I found comfort in these verses, and, even though the challenges did not immediately disappear, my first instinct now was to pray. When we pray, we are reminded of God's mighty hand at work in our lives, and we experience an incomprehensible peace. We don't always understand the steps in our journey, but God, who sees the bigger picture, knows that they lead to His glory and our well-being.

Heavenly Father, thank You that I can pray to You about anything and everything. Amen.

Tania Moorooven is a 2020 graduate of Shenandoah Valley Academy in Virginia.

Unconditional Love

"For I am persuaded, that neither death, nor life, nor angels, nor principalities, nor powers, nor things present, nor things to come, nor height, nor depth, nor any other creature, shall be able to separate us from the love of God, which is in Christ Jesus our Lord" (Rom. 8:38–39, KJV).

I joined a book club in the summer of 2020. The book, *Redeeming Love*, by Francine Rivers, is a Christian novel based on the biblical account of Hosea. As I read how many times the husband took back his wife, who willingly left him time and again to take up prostitution, I continuously questioned why he stayed married to her. This particular verse kept reminding me about God's love for us—an unconditional and redeeming love that nobody can comprehend, not even the heavenly angels.

If a husband is willing to accept and embrace his wife to that extent, it is no surprise that God does the same and much more for us. It is reassuring to know that we can always count on His love, as undeserving as we are. Our good Father is always ready to forgive and take us back, no matter what we have done.

God loves us so much that He gave His Son to die on the cross for us. All we must do is accept Him and lay everything at His feet. He invites us to openly talk to Him, not holding anything back, and He will do the rest. What a wonderful Savior!

Abba, You are a good Father. Thank You that nothing can ever separate us from Your love. Amen.

Sabine Thomas-Belizaire is a member of the Beltsville church in Maryland.

Blossom Like a Flower

"Watch out for false prophets. They come to you in sheep's clothing, but inwardly they are ferocious wolves" (Matt. 7:15, NIV).

My daughter is as cute as a flower, and, when she was little, she would dress like one too. One day she dressed and adorned herself from head to toe as a floral arrangement. She had a big yellow daisy on her white T-shirt, small, white and yellow forget-me-nots on her blue shorts and a flower design on her headband. I told her she was the cutest blossom I'd ever seen. Smiling, she floated outside to play with all the other flowers.

All at once, she turned around with terror in her eyes and darted back into the house. Hyperventilating and crying uncontrollably, she told me she had seen a bee.

"Oh sweetheart, bees don't want anything to do with you," I said.

"No, Daddy. They will come for me," she responded. "They will think that I'm a flower, and when they see I am not, they will get mad and sting me."

I told my floral daughter that although she was dressed as a flower and was the bouquet of her daddy's heart, she wasn't really a flower. Bees can smell the difference.

Like bees, who can smell what's real or not, so can people. They can tell if you're genuine and kind or only pretending under that Christian T-shirt.

So today, open your heart wide and truly care about those around you. I guarantee that you will blossom and that people will respond to your true, authentic, caring heart as never before.

God, may we open like a flower to You and others. Amen.

William J. Largo is the network director for Mission and Ministry at Kettering Adventist HealthCare in Ohio.

He Delivers Us

"Many are the afflictions of the righteous, but the Lord delivers him out of them all" (Ps. 34:19, NKJV).

Recently, multiple mishaps bombarded our household. First, our carpet and furniture were damaged by a leak we discovered in the basement. Frantic calls to plumbers were of no help. Meanwhile, water continued to come into the house from an unknown source. As if this wasn't enough, the dehumidifier, blow dryer and washer broke. All this took place in just three days! How was I going to deal with these issues all at once?

Feeling overwhelmed, stressed and discouraged, I wasn't sure what to do next. Finally, a retired plumber came to the rescue, cutting the wall in several places to discover the problem. The solution wasn't simple. The replacement part was nowhere to be found, but, thankfully, the plumber eventually found a creative fix.

After all the stress and extra work caused by this chaos, blessings came to mind that helped soften the unexpected headache: A friend rushed over to help. The plumber did a good job and was reasonably priced. A dehumidifier was on sale. A washer was also on sale and could be delivered right away. We had just paid off a bill, so there was enough money to put toward these unforeseen expenses.

Many times it feels like everything is turned upside down and life isn't fair, but Jesus has promised to be there. Psalm 34:19 has often provided me with comfort and strength, knowing that, no matter what happens, God is there.

The devil may try to discourage us, but praise the Lord for blessings in the midst of trials!

Father, when life brings us challenges, may we search for the blessings. Thank You that You will deliver us from all our afflictions! Amen.

Shelly Lowe is a member of the Williamsport church in Maryland.

A Wonderful Gift

"For the grace of God that bringeth salvation hath appeared to all men, teaching us that, denying ungodliness and worldly lusts, we should live soberly, righteously, and godly, in this present world; looking for that blessed hope, and the glorious appearing of the great God and our Saviour Jesus Christ; who gave Himself for us, that He might redeem us from all iniquity, and purify unto Himself a peculiar people, zealous of good works" (Titus 2:11-14, KJV).

God's grace, in the person of Jesus Christ, brought us salvation. Jesus also came to teach us how we should live. His grace does not free us to live in sin, giving in to the temptations of this world and go against His will.

Instead, we should live just and godly lives in such a way that shows the rest of the world that we serve God and belong to Him. We should live this way now, today, as we wait for our Savior's return to take us home. And this is possible, because Christ died to pay the price for our sins, and, when we accept Him as our Savior, He works in us to purify us to make us His own.

This should get us excited to do good works, not in order to save ourselves, but to express our sincere love for Jesus and appreciation for the gift He has given to us.

Lord, when You died on the cross, You gave us hope. May we accept Your love and grace and live according to Your Word. Amen.

Rich Fullmer is an elder at the Parkersburg church and the school board chair at Parkersburg Academy in West Virginia.

A Beautiful Promise

"For I know the thoughts that I think toward you, says the Lord, thoughts of peace and not of evil, to give you a future and a hope" (Jer. 29:11, NKJV).

This is my favorite verse because of the promise God gives us. He promises that He is in control of our future and tells us that He has a good purpose for us, no matter what happens. God takes on a proactive role in this relationship. We may think we know what is good for us, but He knows what is best.

A good father won't spoil or harm his child. He may allow his child's character to grow through difficulties, but that is to develop a good and righteous person. That is how God is.

Whenever we are confused about why something has happened in our lives, let us remember the promise in this verse: God knows us, He is with us, He has a good purpose for us.

God, when I don't know what tomorrow will hold, hold me close. My future is bright, as long as my life is in You. Amen.

Minming Liu is a member of the Capital Chinese church in Maryland.

The Ultimate Gardener

"Being confident of this, that He who began a good work in you will carry it on to completion until the day of Christ Jesus" (Phil. 1:6, NIV).

Every spring and summer, I spend hours each week in my garden beds—planning, planting and weeding—trying to enrich the soil and finding the best plants for my semi-shaded plot.

In 2019, I followed the same guidelines, planted everything in the same time period as past years, but took an extra action that made all the difference.

I patiently waited and relaxed.

Instead of worrying, I decided to pause and see how they would do. I also prayed over my garden and decided to just enjoy it. I resolved to not be disappointed if my perennials didn't fill in just the way I had imagined.

The spring brought just the right amount of sun and rain, and the garden blossomed much better than the last three summers.

What was my secret? It wasn't mine at all. I just let go of the growth process and watched God work. He sent the rain, set the temperature and beamed the right amount of sunshine on my backyard.

I still had to weed and fertilize, but I know my flower beds weren't thriving because of me. If that were the case, they would have flourished better than the last several years. As my garden grew, so did my faith—reminding me that God will help my life blossom too.

Seek God today. Learn about His good ways, and then trust Him to grow your life in the way He knows best.

Dear Lord, may Your results in our lives bloom brighter than we could ever plan ourselves. Amen.

V. Michelle Bernard is an assistant director for the Office of Strategic Communication and Public Relations at the Columbia Union Conference.

The Honest and False Witness

**"An honest witness does not deceive,
but a false witness pours out lies" (Prov. 14:5, NIV).**

This verse has been close to my heart for a long time. I remember how my sister used to lie to me, and I could easily tell she was lying. I can also tell that my mom is always honest.

Obviously, God knows when someone is lying. There are many stories in the Bible about truth and lies. For example, the story of the two sons and their father. One son says he will not work in the field for his dad, but does. And the other son promises he will work in the field, but doesn't (Matthew 21:28-32). Did they both lie?

Even though we don't always tell the truth to our parents, God knows. He sees everything. He knows us better than we know Him or ourselves. It is because of sin that we lie to people. Many times we do this to avoid getting caught in a bad act.

I encourage you to avoid telling lies. If you're a kid, it's better for your parents to know what you did than for them to find out later. You can even pray to God to help you change your lying ways. You can tell Him anything, and He can help, because He always listens.

Dear Lord, I pray that I will avoid lying, and that You will help others to do the same. Amen.

Taran McWilliams is a sixth-grader at the Rocky Knoll Adventist School in West Virginia.

Peace in the Middle of Life's Storms

"Do not be anxious about anything, but in every situation, by prayer and petition, with thanksgiving, present your requests to God. And the peace of God, which transcends all understanding, will guard your hearts and your minds in Christ Jesus" (Phil. 4:6–7, NIV).

What does "do not be anxious about anything" mean? Sitting around, relaxing and letting everything come our way? Ignoring daily challenges and issues, whether big or small? In order to answer these questions, we must first define "anxiety."

Webster's dictionary defines anxiety as "a feeling of worry, nervousness, or unease, typically about an imminent event or something with an uncertain outcome." Anxiety and fear are often part of our daily lives, but does this mean we sin when we feel uneasy or nervous?

It may depend on the circumstance, but one thing is clear: With Christ, there is never a need to be anxious. He has promised that, when we present our requests to Him, with thanksgiving, He will give us the peace "which passes *all* understanding" (Phil. 4:7, RSV, emphasis supplied).

The fact is, we like to be in control of our lives and circumstances—but this produces anxiety. Instead, we need to intentionally and purposefully lay our worries down on a daily basis and be willing to surrender and wait for God's peace to cover us!

Father, in the middle of life's storms, help us to hold onto You. Today, we choose to give You our anxieties and fears. Amen.

Luci Sloan is an elder at the Beltsville church in Maryland.

Little Things Matter Too

"Diligent work gets a commendation; shiftless work earns an angry rebuke" (Prov. 14:35, MSG).

During my junior year of college, I applied for a job as a laborer for a man who owned several businesses and needed help around his house. He lived just outside of the college campus and was within walking distance. I enjoyed working for him, and he liked and appreciated my work ethic.

In late spring, he asked if I wanted to work for him at his hotel in Ocean City, Md. I was stunned and overjoyed! What a dream job! I worked hard that summer. But one thing I didn't do well was my personal housework. I was tired from the long days and hours and procrastinated on my chores.

One day, my employer did a surprise inspection of the apartment where he had allowed me to stay. He found the floor unvacuumed and a week's worth of dishes piled in the sink. He saw the mess and called me to the apartment. He was disappointed that I thought so little of his property that I would treat it like this. He sternly told me: "Clean up this place on your own time now, and don't let it get like this again!"

His words cut like a knife; I had never felt so ashamed. I had taken so much pride in doing my other work but neglected the little things that mattered as well. From that time on, I vowed to remember that little things matter too.

God expects us to be good stewards in all that we do—the large tasks as well as the little ones!

Dear Father, may I work in such a way that I bring honor to You in all I do. Amen.

George Dutton is a member of the Kettering church in Ohio.

"And the peace of God, which transcends all understanding, will guard your hearts and your minds in Christ Jesus." PHIL. 4:7, NIV

JULY

Called for His Purpose

"And we know that all things work together for good to those who love God, to those who are the called according to His purpose" (Rom. 8:28, NKJV).

This verse has taken on many meanings throughout the course of my life. I remember first hearing it while listening to the radio program *Your Story Hour*. Throughout the story, the main character kept saying that "all things work together for good." To my young self, this meant that, no matter what, everything would be OK, and nothing too terrible would happen to me because God wouldn't let it. Of course, now I think a little differently.

This verse stuck with me as I went through high school and into college. If I was going through a particularly tough time, I gleaned encouragement from knowing that God works everything for good. And, in hindsight, I still believe He did. Just not in the way I thought He would.

Often, we believe that whenever we call on God for help, He will do it our way. But that isn't what the verse says. It says "all things work together for good." Not our plan. Not anyone else's plan. God's plan.

I now see this Bible verse very differently from the first time I heard it on *Your Story Hour*. We can find comfort in our pain, knowing God will bring good from any situation. It may not be immediate, or in an expected way, but it will come "to those who love God, to those who are the called according to His purpose." And everyone on earth is called to do God's purpose. That means you and me!

Thank You, Lord, for the comfort that You have our back, even when we feel You are far away. Amen.

Jacklyn Ruth is the communication specialist for the Communication Department at the Chesapeake Conference.

Love Is the Greatest

**"And now these three remain: faith, hope and love.
But the greatest of these is love" (1 Cor. 13:13, NIV).**

As I look at 1 Corinthians 13, it is clear that prophecy, the gift of tongues and other gifts of the Spirit will come to an end because they will no longer be of value. But verse 13 has the wonderful word, "remain," which expresses the idea of permanence for the three basic elements of our Christian experience: faith, hope and love.

This verse signifies that love is the element used to describe the very nature of God. That's the reason Paul clearly says that, above all gifts of the Spirit, this one is the greatest.

Yes, God's love in our lives is the element that makes the biggest difference: "Dear friends, let us love one another, for love comes from God. Everyone who loves has been born of God and knows God. Whoever does not love does not know God, because God is love"(1 John 4:7–8, NIV). In Scripture, we have the greatest news: He loved us when we did not love Him, even while we were His enemies. Yes, that is true love!

God has given us His love without measure. "And hope does not put us to shame, because God's love has been *poured* out into our hearts through the Holy Spirit, who has been given to us" (Rom. 5:5, NIV, emphasis supplied). When God's love is *poured* in us without measure, it's because He wants His love to overflow from our lives so we have enough to share with those in desperate need of His love—no matter who they are or how they act. Let's remember: His love is not selective, for He died for the entire world.

Father, may our faith and hope be intertwined with Your eternal and unlimited love. Amen.

Oswaldo Magana is the executive secretary for the Ohio Conference.

Experience His Goodness

"For I resolved to know nothing while I was with you except Jesus Christ and Him crucified" (1 Cor. 2:2, NIV).

Paul took great joy in knowing, walking with and loving Christ. His personal mission was to spread the good news of Jesus' life, death and resurrection. But that hadn't always been the case. Earlier in his life, Paul was against Christ and His divine message, and destroyed anyone who believed in it.

However, this all changed one day as he was traveling to Damascus. On his journey, Paul came into direct contact with the same Christ he despised. That interaction transformed his life and the way he thought. The same man who sought to destroy Jesus' message now proclaimed it to all who would hear. This dramatic change happened because Paul decided to journey to the heart of God, and the "beginning of a lifetime" was within reach.

What does this mean for us? That pursuing an intimate relationship with God can take place anytime and anywhere. For Paul, it took a Damascus experience to get his attention. How about for you? How far will you go to seek God's heart? You saw what a dramatic change choosing God made in Paul's life. Imagine what He can do in your life. It only takes a decision to experience His goodness.

Lord, may we be willing to seek Your heart and enter into an eternal journey with You today. Amen.

Gustavo Parada is the pastor of the Spencer, Ripley and Charleston Spanish churches in West Virginia.

'God Found It!'

"He replied, 'Because you have so little faith. I tell you the truth, if you have faith as small as a mustard seed, you can say to this mountain, "Move from here to there," and it will move. Nothing will be impossible for you'" (Matt. 17:20–21, NIV).

My family vacations in North Myrtle Beach, S.C., at our family beach home every year.

One particular Fourth of July, we were relaxing by the pool overlooking the beach. A strong breeze blew a lot of sand in my direction, irritating my contact lenses. I reached up to brush the sand out, when the wind caught one of my contacts, blowing the tiny lens off to beach neverland. Immediately, I started looking for it, crawling on the pool cement on my hands and knees. Everyone around me said, "It's gone," and "You'll never find it." It was upsetting! I was now stuck on vacation with my thick glasses.

I left the pool and went upstairs to our condominium. After shedding a few frustrated tears, I knelt down in the quiet room alone and prayed an earnest prayer to God. I remembered His promise that faith as small as a mustard seed could move a mountain, and I knew that this kind of faith applied to a teeny, tiny lens too. Determined to find it, I went back down to the pool deck.

Right near the beach sand lay my perfect lens! "I found it!" I screamed. At first everyone doubted me, but soon they were amazed.

"Wait," I said, "God found it for me!" I then testified about my answered prayer.

Thank You, God, for caring about the little things that are big to me. Amen.

Lisha Weber is the software support specialist for the Information Technology Services at the Columbia Union Conference.

He Completes Us

"Behold, I stand at the door, and knock: if any man hears My voice, and opens the door, I will come in to him, and will sup with him, and he with Me" (Rev. 3:20, KJV).

This verse gives me comfort because it reassures me that God will always be there for me, ready to come to my aid at any moment. I grew up in a Seventh-day Adventist home, but I didn't have a personal relationship with God. When I got older, I felt like something was missing.

I grew up thinking about love and how I wanted someone to make me feel complete. I began dating, and every relationship started out great, but some of the guys wanted more than just love. This made me feel like I wasn't good enough for anyone. I was tired of chasing guys and looking for someone to love me.

One day, I talked to my pastor, and he made me realize that all I needed to do was to truly turn to God. I felt so guilty because I thought God wouldn't forgive me for all my past sins. My pastor told me about Mary Magdalene and how, despite all of her mistakes, God was still there for her.

That day, I realized how close God was and how willing He was to help me. He was the only One who could truly bring fulfillment in my life. As my favorite verse says, He's at the door, waiting for us to open it and let Him in!

Dear Heavenly Father, please help us to open our eyes and see that You are ready to come into our lives and make us complete. Amen.

Andrea Huaytalla is a 2020 graduate of Shenandoah Valley Academy in Virginia.

Never Forsaken

"Hear me when I call, O God of my righteousness! You have relieved me in my distress; have mercy on me, and hear my prayer" (Ps. 4:1, NKJV).

When I was 3 years old, my mother left me with family in Guatemala to immigrate to the United States. She wanted to give me a better future. My aunt guided me in the ways of God, but I asked Him why my mother left me. I suffered every Mother's Day because all my friends hugged their mothers and gave them gifts, and I did not have my mother. I could not tell her about my sufferings. When I felt alone or needed a hug, she was not there.

I began asking God to hug me to give me strength, but I didn't feel any answers to my prayers. One day, a friend offered me drugs, and I accepted. My friend told me that with drugs I would forget all my problems. I kept doing drugs for a few years, until I had a dream that showed me that God did not want that for me; He wanted something better. I felt like I had spoiled everything and had disappointed my family and God. But I was still loved.

Sometimes, God doesn't give us answers to our questions right away, but He will answer them in His time. God does not work within human logic; He works within His logic. Maybe you think He has forgotten you, but He will never forget you. God tells you to cry to Him, and He will answer you. He always listens when you humbly kneel and tell Him everything you feel in your heart. He will never leave you alone.

Father, thank You for promising to never leave us or forsake us. Amen.

Erick Hernandez is a freshman at Richmond Academy in Virginia.

God's Adoption Plan

"For ye have not received the spirit of bondage again to fear; but ye have received the Spirit of adoption, whereby we cry, Abba, Father" (Rom. 8:15, KJV).

My daughter recently adopted a little girl whom she was fostering since she was two days old. It amazes me to see a person have so much love for a child that isn't biologically theirs.

It took two years and fostering a total of five children until my daughter was able to adopt this girl. During this time, my daughter experienced heartache, sleepless nights, court dates, social workers, parental visitation and more. She battled tremendous emotional upheaval every time she bonded with a child, then had to send him or her back home.

God legally adopted us into His heavenly family, but it came at a price. The emotional and physical pain this caused Him is beyond comprehension. Yet He says we are worth the cost. "Who for the joy that was set before Him endured the cross, despising the shame, and has sat down at the right hand of the throne of God" (Heb. 12:2, NKJV).

When we contemplate on God's unlimited love for us—that He would go through so much to legally bring us into His heavenly family—it moves us to cry out "Daddy" and receive His loving embrace.

When we accept that we are adopted by the Creator of the universe, we adopt His Son's character. We become like Jesus when we associate with our heavenly family through reading and meditation. As 2 Corinthians 3:18 says, we "are being transformed into the same image from glory to glory, just as by the Spirit of the Lord" (NKJV).

Thank You, Lord, for adopting us. Amen.

Daniel Morikone retired after 20 years of ministry in the Mountain View Conference.

Unchanging Love

**"And he arose, and came to his father. But when he was yet
a great way off, his father saw him, and had compassion, and ran,
and fell on his neck, and kissed him" (Luke 15:20, KJV).**

Except for the cross, the most convincing evidence that shows the Father's love is found in Luke 15:20.

The prodigal son left his father's house to travel on the pathway of sin. After wasting his entire inheritance, he had no money or friends. While feasting on slop with the hogs, he thought of his father's house and of the comforts of life. Pulling himself out of the slimy pit, he headed for home, hoping his father would let him be a servant. At least he would be able to survive.

Before he reached his destination, His father was waiting with open arms, running to meet him, giving him the best robe money could buy and welcoming him back into the family. What love! What marvelous love!

The path of sin has many pitfalls, some very deep, like murder, incest, child abuse. Others very shallow, like gossip, white lies, harsh words, backbiting and pride. But they are all on the path of sin. The longer one stays in a pit, the deeper it gets, until it is almost impossible to step out of it.

At times, I wander from my Father's house, stumbling into some of the more shallow pits. When I fall, I realize I can't stay there. I climb out of the pit and head for home. My Father is always waiting for me, running to meet me, clothing me with His robe of righteousness and welcoming me back into the family. Why such grace beyond all measure? Love. Unconditional, unselfish, unchanging love.

Heavenly Father, thank You for Your welcoming arms. Amen.

Beverley Phipps is a member of the Hamlet church in Ohio.

Look at the Heart

"For the Lord does not see as man sees; for man looks at the outward appearance, but the Lord looks at the heart" (1 Sam. 16:7, NKJV).

He landed on our doorstep, without an invitation, nor in swaddling clothes. He answered, on occasion, to "Buddy." He was a white, 40-pound fur ball. My wife, Jackie, lacked enthusiasm regarding this unexpected addition to an otherwise empty nest. She had never liked big dogs, especially at grooming time. She never liked boy dogs for the obvious reasons, and she did not like the fact that he was all white, too hard to keep clean. And to boot, he came without papers. By all outward appearances, this pooch was a loser.

That "blessed event" was 10 years ago. Today we love Buddy, whether he's barking at the deer in the yard or pretending he's a lap dog. He's no longer too big, too much of a boy dog or too white. He's now an official member of the family. We've taken the measure of his "heart" and he of ours.

Samuel was tasked by God to anoint the next king of Israel. His first instinct was to choose Jesse's eldest son, the good looking one. But God knew the heart of the youngest of Jesse's sons, David, and chose him.

Unfortunately, we live in times when people are judged by the color of their skin, their language, speech or religion. We tend to be impressed by a person's resume, how they dress and where they live, instead of the leaning of their hearts. And we forget that Christ died for all people, not just a privileged few.

Today, God, may we resolve to touch the lives of all people, and not permit prejudice or stereotypes to blind us to the fact that we are all children of our heavenly Father, Who looks at our hearts. Amen.

Walter Carson is vice president and general counsel for the Columbia Union Conference.

God of the Impossible

"With men this is impossible; but with God all things are possible" (Matt. 19:26, KJV).

At six months pregnant, I found myself facing the repercussions of severe marital distress. As a result, I was placed on hospital bed rest until I gave birth—a blessed event that seemed incredibly far away.

Upon admission to the hospital, I was so devastated by what was happening in my relationship that I was too crushed to pray. All I could do was cry out, "Jesus." Almost immediately, the Lord's peace began to flood my mind, heart and room. Rescuing me from the depths of despair, He reminded me that He was with me, that I could face everything with Him and that His grace was sufficient.

Due to my leaking amniotic sac, the doctors mandated that I keep my body as flat as possible, use a bedpan, receive injections and take rounds of giant vitamins. Though the medical world has made tremendous strides, no one has discovered how to reseal an amniotic sac. Specialists visited one by one to tell me all the ways my baby would be challenged.

As loved ones rallied around me in prayer, I begged the Lord for a miracle. I needed Him to restore my amniotic sac. I recommitted my baby to Him, claiming Matthew 19:26, and asked Him to continue to fill her with His Holy Spirit and make her whole. Each week, the perinatologist remarked, "Wow, I've never seen fluid levels so high for a confirmed leak!" The Lord had answered my prayer!

Safiyya was born a month early, but perfectly healthy! In the 19 years since, He has indeed used her for His glory.

God, thank You for being in the miracle-working business! May we keep trusting in You! Amen.

Naeemah Shakir Phillip is a member of the New Market church in Virginia.

Strength to Soar

**"But those who hope in the Lord will renew their strength.
They will soar on wings like eagles; they will run and not grow weary,
they will walk and not be faint" (Isa. 40:31, NIV).**

I had persevered through law school for four years while working to pay tuition, spent months taking classes after work and eliminated everything fun in favor of studying for two weeks. Now the event I had prepared for was looming, and I would soon take the two-day Maryland bar exam.

My butterflies had long since flown away, leaving me with a sick feeling in my stomach. My heart raced periodically when I thought of what was to come. I knew a calm spirit and a good night's sleep were imperative to success. So what could I do?

Prayer had been part of this process for four long years, and I did not abandon it now. After praying for God's presence, I was impressed to go to my Bible to seek encouragement, but not a single text came to mind. So I did what any panicking, sleep-deprived young adult would do. I closed my eyes, opened my Bible and pointed.

As I read, I was overcome with peace. On this journey, I had done what I could. Imperfect. Unpolished. But here, God was allowing me to shut down fear and trust in Him, promising that I could not only get through this trial but "soar on eagle's wings!" That visual brought such comfort, such peace and such a revelation of God's power.

God was with me that day, and, since then, I have returned to this text many times when overcome with trouble, doubt, fear, uncertainty, sadness. It always brings me comfort and assurance of God's almighty hand.

Lord, thank You for Your power that brings peace. Amen.

*Lisa Saveikis Burrow is the assistant to the general counsel at the
Columbia Union Conference.*

Amazing Love

"For God so loved the world that He gave His only begotten Son, that whoever believes in Him should not perish but have everlasting life" (John 3:16, NKJV).

Early in my childhood, my mom made decisions that were best for me. She chose warm clothes, healthy food and safe toys. When I was older, my mom chose Desmond T. Doss Academy for me because she wanted me to have a "solid foundation." I didn't grow up going to church. My mom taught me prayers and read me stories from a children's Bible, but she wanted me to know *more*. I knew who God and Jesus were, but it wasn't until later that I learned how I could be saved.

I know how much my mom loves me. I also know that my mom would do anything for me. I cannot imagine how she would feel to give me up. God made the ultimate sacrifice to give up His Son to save sinners like me.

This Bible verse was the first verse I memorized. I often think about what God must have felt, what struggles He went through as He made this decision. How do you choose to sacrifice Your child? It amazes me that God chose me; that He thought I would be worthy of His kingdom. How can anyone love me *that* much?

If God could sacrifice His Son, the least I can do is believe, listen and follow His commandments and pray. I know that I have a purpose in this life, and I need to share the gift of salvation with others.

Thank You, Father, for Your sacrifice! Help me to pass on to others the message of how to receive Christ in their hearts. Amen.

Logan Johnson is a freshman at the Desmond T. Doss Christian Academy in Virginia.

Take a Stand!

"Then choose for yourselves this day whom you will serve. ... But as for me and my household, we will serve the Lord" (Josh. 24:15, NIV).

Israel had witnessed the Lord's powerful hand at work during their campaign to conquer the idolatrous inhabitants of the land of Canaan. Despite this—and without excuses—they weren't fully devoted to God.

From the crossing of the Red Sea to the water that gushed from the rock at Horeb to manna that fell daily, they should have viewed each miracle as an opportunity to firm up their allegiance to God. They had witnessed so much of His love, and each instance should have brought them closer to their Lord, solidifying their total devotion to Him.

But they simply didn't allow themselves to submit fully to His leading. Even after His divine hand protected them during their battles against the Canaanites, they tended to drift away. I believe Joshua proclaimed the words of this text because he saw that, in the coming centuries, they would continue to slowly and deeply drift back into idolatry. This happened years before they worshipped the golden calf, and later caused the men of Israel to lust after Midianite women and become lured into Baal worship. Sadly, this same sin would continue to haunt them for hundreds, if not thousands of years. Do our choices cause us to become susceptible to idolatry?

When we devote ourselves to anything other than God, we fall into the same trap as Israel. Naturally, we don't fall identically as they did, but the result is the same. As Christians, we must take a stand! I can't speak for you, "but as for me and my household, we will serve the Lord."

Lord, may our choices bring glory to You. And when faced with hard decisions, may we stand up and stand firm! Amen.

Jared Briggman is a church planter for the Mountain View Conference.

24/7

"How precious it is, Lord, to realize that you are thinking about me constantly! I can't even count how many times a day your thoughts turn toward me. And when I waken in the morning, you are still thinking of me!" (Ps. 139:17–18, TLB).

I love this verse because it paints a beautiful picture of God's unfailing love for me. He truly values me by reminding me that He is always thinking of me, even on the days when I think I am forgotten.

This verse reminds me that I am important, worthwhile and special enough for the God who created all things and made the universe to think of me continually.

This verse reminds me that I am loved, and nothing I have done or any mistake I have made will keep Him from loving me and thinking about me. His thoughts about me are not just random thoughts, but beautiful, wonderful and lovely thoughts. How awesome is that?

At times, I try to understand how Someone can think of me so often? So I reflect on the many times I have thought of my family and those who are special to me. And yet I fall short. No matter how many times I try or how intentional I am about thinking of my loved ones constantly, I can never come close to the number of times God thinks of me. This tells me I must be significant and worthy enough to be thought of.

Lord, remind me constantly that You are the eternal, all-powerful, all-knowing, mighty God who thinks about me nonstop because You love me and that, no matter what I go through in life, I am not alone, for You are with me. Amen.

Joanne Cortes is the pastor of Beltsville church's DC Campus in Washington, D.C.

Trust in the Lord

"Trust in the Lord with all your heart, and lean not on your own understanding; in all your ways acknowledge Him, and He shall direct your paths" (Prov. 3:5-6, NKJV).

I have had my share of trials over the years, as all Christians experience. Lessons learned have matured my faith and trust and have taught me to seek the Lord's will rather than my own.

In 1995, I was diagnosed with a life-threatening illness—Non-Hodgkin's T-cell lymphoma. Having embraced an alternative medicine mindset years earlier, I wanted to find a treatment that would support my body and strengthen my immune system. I turned to the Lord, knowing He already had a plan, and asked Him to make it so clear to me that there would be no question in my mind.

Several days later, after much prayer, three acquaintances of mine—with no knowledge of each other—contacted me with identical information for a cancer treatment—a "natural" treatment. I cannot express in words what my heart felt, as tears of overwhelming gratitude welled up in my eyes. The message couldn't have been clearer.

About the same time, a friend shared with me the name of her oncologist whom she highly recommended. I recognized I'd need monitoring to know when I was in remission. After talking with the doctor about the natural treatment plan, he was willing to do it, but not without expressing his apprehension about my choice of treatment.

I strictly adhered to the treatment. After nine months, my oncologist, totally amazed, said the words I longed to hear: "You are in remission."

Heavenly Father, help us daily to have complete faith and trust in You. Amen.

Sandra Jones is the advertising and circulation manager for the Columbia Union Conference Visitor *magazine.*

A Solution for Every Problem

"And David was greatly distressed; for the people spake of stoning him, because the soul of all the people was grieved, every man for his sons and for his daughters: but David encouraged himself in the Lord his God" (1 Sam. 30:6, KJV).

This verse is my source of comfort and peace, because it shows both the problem and solution to everyday stress.

Problem: David was greatly distressed.

Solution: David encouraged himself in the Lord his God.

It doesn't matter what happens around us, if friends turn against us or we cannot see the light at the end of the tunnel. What matters is that we remember that God is still on His throne and that we seek comfort and encouragement from Him.

I remember a time when, like David, I made a series of unwise decisions that put me in a significant bind. I didn't know where to turn or who to trust. Worse yet, the weight of guilt from these decisions was almost unbearable. This verse gave me considerable hope that God would hear me, so I encouraged myself in the Lord my God. I asked Him to forgive me of my errors and to deliver me.

God not only brought me tremendous peace, but delivered me from my distress. That's when the purpose of this passage became real to me.

Lord, please help us to remember that we don't have to wallow in our guilt, mistakes and sins. Instead, we can encourage ourselves in You for restoration. Amen.

Andrew S. Baker is a member of the Braxton church in West Virginia.

Serving Is Leading

"But it shall not be so among you: but whosoever will be great among you, let him be your minister" (Matt. 20:26, KJV).

Leadership roles, whether large or seemingly small, are given to each of us by the Lord. God gave kings like Saul, David and Solomon the responsibility of shepherding His people and building His kingdom. Like parents, who are entrusted to nurture, protect and guide their children, or church elders, who are called to shepherd Christ's people, God has given each of us a unique role in His work of salvation.

One thing I have learned through my years as a husband, father and a pastor in various ministry leadership roles is that a leader does not mean you play a more important role than anyone else; a leader is one who serves alongside others in order to meet a united goal.

Servant leadership is not about standing above others but of humbling ourselves so that God may work in and through us so His will may be done.

Heavenly Father, remind us today that our leadership roles in all forms come from You. Impress on our hearts the responsibility to care for Your people. Please help us to see the opportunities and open doors in front of us. Help us to serve others selflessly and to serve You wholeheartedly, like Jesus. Amen.

Marvin C. Brown III is the president of the Allegheny West Conference.

Make God's Day!

"Casting all your care upon Him, for He cares for you"
(1 Pet. 5:7, NKJV).

God cares for us so very much. This care is not superficial like how we care about our favorite sports team or favorite food. He truly thinks positive thoughts toward us each and every day, and He wants the best for us.

God is a relationship-focused God who shows this throughout the Bible in countless ways. He pulls out all the stops to establish and deepen relationships with whomever—be they Jew or Gentile.

In a relationship, one of the ways a couple bonds is by sharing positive and negative feelings with each other: joys, desires, aspirations, wants, happy memories, stresses, hurt, struggles, areas of needed growth. This is what God wants from us in our relationship with Him. He wants to hear about everything in our lives—the good, the bad and the ugly.

Maybe today ...

- you are feeling happy or sad. God wants to know.
- you are excited about the future or regret the past. God wants to know.
- you wish the day would last forever or "this day will never end." God wants to know.
- you are proud of a life success or have not seen a success in years. God wants to know.

Whatever is currently happening in your life, God longs for you to share it with Him. Why don't you take a few moments to open up to Him. You would make His day!

Lord, thank You for taking our cares and concerns and giving us peace.
Help us to trust in You. Amen.

Andrew Moll is a member of the Ellicott City church in Maryland.

Watch Out for Seagulls!

"Do not let any unwholesome talk come out of your mouths, but only what is helpful for building others up according to their needs, that it may benefit those who listen" (Eph. 4:29, NIV).

My family loves the beach. One summer, we went to Hampton Beach in New Hampshire.

After setting up, we went down to the shore. The water was freezing! While my brave sister boogie-boarded, I relaxed in the sun. I thought about how nice it was to be on vacation, and before I knew it, I fell asleep.

Suddenly, something hot and soft hit me. I immediately felt around to see what it was. But that was a mistake. I opened my eyes and saw that it was seagull poop! I entered the freezing cold water to get it off my hand and favorite swimsuit.

This whole unpleasant experience was a good reminder though. Birds are pretty to look at and nice to hear, but not when they "go" on you. Christians can be pretty to look at and nice to hear, but none of that matters if we are mean and selfish. The worst part is we can't take back what we say. It is so important to be careful about what we watch, read and listen to. When we let something into our lives—good or bad, whether through our eyes or ears—it will eventually come out.

Lord, help us speak words that uplift others and bring glory to You. Amen.

Rebecca Savoy is a sophomore at Richmond Academy in Virginia.

'God Is Love'

Whoever does not love does not know God, because God is love. This is how God showed His love among us: He sent His one and only Son into the world that we might live through Him. This is love: not that we loved God, but that He loved us and sent His Son as an atoning sacrifice for our sins" (1 John 4:8–10, NIV).

This verse has been very powerful to me. I have gone through some very tough times, like when my mom passed away from cancer. When this happened, I felt like I wasn't loved, and I was very lonely. However, people—especially church members—noticed how sad I was, and they helped me every day.

One church member shared 1 John 4:8–10 with me. He explained that it meant that God loves us no matter what, and, when we feel very lonely, He is always right next to us. What spoke to me the most was: "God is love." After hearing that, I didn't feel lonely anymore. I now had Someone who was there for me, comforting me, and, most importantly, always loving me.

If someone you know is going through something difficult and is lonely or sad, share this verse with them because it can change a person's heart—like mine.

Dear God, thank You for always loving me. Thank You for Your comfort and the assurance that You will be with me always, even until the end of the world. Amen.

Kyle Williams is a junior at Blue Mountain Academy in Pennsylvania.

The Road Trip

"So do not fear, for I am with you; do not be dismayed, for I am your God. I will strengthen you and help you; I will uphold you with My righteous right hand" (Isa. 41:10, NIV).

One summer, my family decided to take a road trip to Tennessee. We started off very early, and, by the time we stopped for a bathroom break, it was already noon. My sister dashed to the restroom while the line was short. By the time I got there, the line had grown, so I had to wait.

When I finished and walked back to the parking lot, to my shock and dismay, our van was nowhere in sight. After five minutes of searching for my family, panic set in. *Had they left me?*

I had no phone to call my dad. Still trembling, the first thing on my mind was to pray for protection, that no one would try to kidnap me in this strange place. Second, I prayed that my family would come back for me.

In that moment, God reminded me of Isaiah 41:10. I held onto the hope that He would reunite me with my family. God provided a kind stranger who helped call my family, and they came back for me.

Because we cannot see Him, sometimes we forget that God is truly with us. But He is and will always be there! No matter how things may look now, when we reflect on our lives, we will see how God's hand worked through it all.

Lord, even when I am at my lowest point, help me to always remember to trust in You. Amen.

Drusilla Apola is a 2020 graduate of Shenandoah Valley Academy in Virginia.

David's Story

"But Jesus said, suffer little children, and forbid them not, to come unto me: for of such is the kingdom of heaven" (Matt. 19:14, KJV).

One hot July, I was working as a literature evangelist. That morning, I held just one lead card—the person I had been requested to visit that day. The name David was scribbled on the card, obviously a child's handwriting. The house was more than an hour away on narrow roads.

It was two days before payday, and my tires were bald. I had enough fuel to make the trip, and $1.76 in cash.

Dear Lord, tell me what to do.

I prayed and opened my Bible, wishing for a sign that I should canvass in a nearby town. My eyes fell on Philippians 4:19: "And my God will supply every need of yours according to His riches in glory in Christ Jesus" (ESV).

I immediately got into my car and drove to the town. The house was humble and inside was a weary mother and her 9-year-old son, David. He had leukemia and a short time to live. His eyes lit up when he saw *The Bible Story* book. As he caressed it, I wrote the contract with tear-filled eyes. I left my demo books and drove home with my down payment: two rabbits.

Three months later, David went to his final sleep. His mother told me that he first saw *The Bible Story* book in his doctor's office. He knew very little about Jesus, but he wanted the book. He spent his last days reading and talking about being with Jesus.

That morning, I had prayed for a divine appointment. God's loving answer was priceless. I pray that one day in heaven, I will meet a healthy, happy David.

Lord, may we never miss an opportunity to share Your love with others. Amen.

Naomi McKey-Tricomi is the assistant pastor of the Wheeling church in West Virginia.

God Heals, Leads, Restores

"I have seen his ways, and will heal him: I will lead him also, and restore comforts unto him and to his mourners" (Isa. 57:18, KJV).

Heal, lead and restore—these are the promises that abound in this short verse. This text resonates with me because it came at a time when I was fervently praying for someone dear to me. As I poured out my heart to God, He spoke to me clearly by providing this verse, and reassured me that He would heal and lead that person.

How many times have we followed our own heart and wisdom, decisions that only lead to pain? The good news is that, no matter how bad our poor choices may hurt ourselves or others, He is always there to heal, lead and restore. He promises to heal us and those we have hurt, and to heal those who have hurt us. People who may have violated us ultimately need healing, comfort and restoration too. We are all in need of freedom and victory in Jesus.

When we truly see God for who He is, we truly see ourselves. It is then that we are led to hunger and thirst for righteousness. God's mercy is unending. He will never turn His back on a heart that is broken and humble. No matter what you have done in this life, God promises He will heal you, lead you and restore you. Just keep your eyes on Him.

Lord, thank You that, although You know everything about us, You still love us. Amen.

Jessica Manantan is the youth leader and prayer coordinator of the Grafton church in West Virginia.

All I Need and Want

"Whom have I in heaven but You? And there is none upon earth that I desire besides You" (Ps. 73:25, NKJV).

It was 25 years ago, and I've never experienced anything like it before or since; not that anyone else hasn't had the same issue. In my mid-30s, I experienced depression for the first time in my life. Being a very positive person who is known for my laugh and optimistic demeanor, it was such a stark contrast from my usual state of mind.

It was close to nine months before I felt like myself again. About halfway into my depression, I experienced a dark night of the soul that overwhelmed me. I went to church one evening, walked down the aisle to the front and poured my soul out to God. At the time, God not only seemed distant but wholly non-existent. I craved Him more than air in my lungs and thought, *If only I could sense God again I would be able to face anything that might happen to me for the rest of my life.* It was then that a sweet relief came over me, and I knew once more that God was real and loved me.

No, the depression did not immediately go away, but I never forgot what I experienced that evening. I still truly believe that no matter what happens to me, if I have God, then I have what matters most. "Whom have I in heaven but You? And there is none upon earth that I desire besides You."

God, thank You that I have You. There is absolutely nothing else I need and want as much as You. Amen.

Rick Labate is the associate director of Pastoral Ministries for the Potomac Conference.

He Gives Us Grace to Trust

"Trust in the Lord with all your heart, and lean not on your own understanding; in all your ways acknowledge Him, and He shall direct your paths" (Prov. 3:5–6, NKJV).

This text became especially significant to our family when we planned to move from Nigeria to the United States, where I was to study in the seminary at Andrews University (Mich.). I applied for a visa for myself, my wife and our little boy. Well-meaning people shared horror stories with us of their visa application denials, and suggested that perhaps I should apply for the visa alone and try to apply for my wife and child later. Maybe we would have better luck that way.

We had been married less than two years at the time, and we didn't think being apart was good for our marriage. I resolved that we would all go together, and, if it was God's will for me to study in the U.S., He would make it happen, regardless of the circumstances. Bible promises strengthened my resolve and made it clear to me that my wife and child are blessings from the Lord (Psalm 127:3; Proverbs 18:22). God's blessing would not become a curse to me at the embassy. To make a long story short, we all arrived in the U.S. during the summer of 2016.

Trusting God means believing His promises and moving forward with them, assured that He will fulfill them. God has always directed our path as a family because He gives us the grace to trust Him in difficult situations.

Father, thank You for assuring us that You will direct us in the way we should go, as long as we trust You. Amen.

Femi Fabiyi is a member of the Miamisburg church in Ohio.

Calm in the Storm

"He calmed the storm to a whisper and stilled the waves. What a blessing was that stillness as he brought them safely into harbor!" (Ps. 107:29–30, NLT).

Since the time I was young, I have loved storms. Storms have so much power. Once when I was working at Camp Pugwash in Nova Scotia, Canada, a storm began brewing over the ocean. Camp Pugwash is situated by the sea, which makes it a great place to watch storms roll in.

It was nighttime when this particular storm came. In the distance, I could see orange bolts of lightning light up the sky. As the storm drew closer, everything grew quiet.

A friend and I went down to the beach to watch the storm come in. As we watched, we heard a distant roar. We didn't know what it was. Suddenly, the wind picked up and the waves came crashing in. A few seconds later, a lightning bolt struck the water 200 feet from where we were.

We ran back up the hill from the beach as the rain started pouring down. We knew the camp horses would be spooked by the strong wind, rain and lightning, so we ran to the horse barn to calm them down. When we got there, each of us took a horse by the reins and began to stroke their necks, whispering in their ears that everything would be OK.

How many of us are like those horses? When life gets too difficult and the "storms" of life get to us, we get scared. We need to remember that Jesus is beside us, whispering to us every step of the way.

God, may we remember that, when afraid, You whisper in our ear that everything will be OK. Amen.

Todd Casey is the youth director for the Pennsylvania Conference.

The Plaque in My Kitchen

"Love is patient, love is kind. It doesn't boast. It isn't proud. It doesn't dishonor others, it isn't self-seeking. It keeps no record of wrongs. Love doesn't delight in evil but rejoices with the truth. It always protects, always trusts, always hopes, always perseveres" (1 Cor. 13:4–7, paraphrased).

This paraphrased version of 1 Corinthians 13:4–7 is written on a plaque and hangs on a wall in our kitchen. It means something special to me. God's love is unconditional. Everyone should follow and live by these words throughout their lives, and certainly in marriage. My parents live by these words daily, and I want to follow their example. I want to keep learning to follow our Father's Word.

Dear God, thank You for parents who teach me about You and show Your love in their lives. Help me to continue to learn more about You. Amen.

Henry Brenner is a fourth-grader at the Roanoke Adventist Christian School in Virginia.

Perfect Love

"There is no fear in love; but perfect love casteth out fear: because fear hath torment" (1 John 4:18, KJV).

This verse has meant a lot to me through the years because I've always feared that people wouldn't like me or accept me because I was not good enough. This lack of confidence kept me from trying a lot of things for fear of rejection or failure.

Fast forward through many years of heartache and a broken first marriage, and I met someone who didn't want to change me. He accepted me just as I was. It took a long time to be convinced that someone could truly love me, as imperfect as I thought I was. But after five years, he won me over by his kindness, compassion and love, and we married. Shortly thereafter, we heard about the wonderful message of Jesus Christ and joined God's church body.

Looking back, I realize today that it was the perfect love of Jesus shining through him that won my love and confidence. Because of my husband, I learned that I was valuable to Jesus. When you learn about the unconditional love of Jesus—to the point of death—and the wonderful truths of the Gospel, you find your self-worth in Him and not in people, jobs or worldly treasure. When you have Jesus, you find He is all you need. There is no fear. You can live in peace and happiness.

Even though my husband has since passed, I still have Jesus with me every day. I share His love with others, so that they can trust in Him and be rid of all their fears, no matter what life brings their way.

Thank You, God, that I find my self-worth in You. Amen.

Phyllis Curry is the treasurer for the Elkins church in West Virginia.

God's Got It

"Cast all your anxiety on Him because He cares for you"
(1 Pet. 5:7, NIV).

To be honest, when I was first asked to write a devotional, I desperately wanted to decline. I felt my heart beat a little faster and my breath become shorter—symptoms associated with anxiety. The fear of not being good enough was so overwhelming, and I was just about to say no until I remembered 1 Peter 5:7. I've heard this verse multiple times, and right at that moment, it stuck with me.

About five years ago, I started to have panic attacks, and I developed symptoms of anxiety. These symptoms are often hard to handle, and sometimes I feel I don't have control of my own body. But when I read this verse, all my worries, stresses and anxieties are washed away. I feel like the words were written just for me. It reminds me that, even when I feel out of control, God's got it.

God knows we will go through hard times, but He will never leave our side. He cares too much for us!

Thank You, God, for having my back! Amen.

Faith Davis is an eighth-grader at Worthington Adventist Academy in Ohio.

From Pieces to Peace

"For we are His workmanship, created in Christ Jesus for good works, which God prepared beforehand that we should walk in them" (Eph. 2:10, NKJV).

It seems I was born to suffer. The physical and emotional abuse at the hands of my father began when I was 4-years-old. I was always sick, to the point that the doctors diagnosed that I could be either mute or deaf for the rest of my life. I was bullied during my school years and always struggled to "fit in." I got into a toxic relationship that destroyed my heart, my identity and self-esteem. I felt sick, lonely, rejected and purposeless.

Tired of fighting hard for belonging, love and health, it crossed my mind to take my own life. I was missing something; rather Someone.

It wasn't until I surrendered all my broken pieces to Jesus, that God told me: *"You are my workmanship, created in my image for good works, which I prepared for you beforehand that you should walk in them "*

Since then, Jesus has been restoring each broken piece. My father is now a wonderful man of God; my health and habits have been restored; my husband is my soul mate; I have a job that I love; and I found my purpose—to serve with my voice through different platforms.

We are all a work in progress. Jesus will help us break free from the feelings of failure and worthlessness. The divine Potter will be faithful to refine and shape us into His image, for we are His masterpieces.

The goal is knowing Jesus and persevering in Him. He will give us His peace and joy that surpasses all understanding. We are hopeful, secure, free and whole in Jesus!

Lord Jesus, thank You for faithfully shaping us into Your image. Amen.

Nancy E. Cabrera is a member of the Spencerville church in Maryland.

God's Riches At Christ's Expense

**"For this son of mine was dead and is alive again;
he was lost and is found" (Luke 15:24, NIV).**

Demanding and receiving his inheritance while his dad is still alive, Jack packs his convertible and leaves home for the West Coast. There, he quickly makes friends, rents a great apartment and parties hard until he runs out of money. Deserted by his friends, he is evicted from his apartment and is forced to sell his car to buy food and lodging. In desperation, he takes the only job he can—a pig slaughtering factory.

Reflecting on his situation, he realizes that even the housekeepers at home live better than he does, so he decides to return home, practicing his speech on the long walk back.

"Father, I have sinned against both heaven and you. I am no longer worthy of being called your son. Please take me on as a housekeeper."

Back home, Dad has been waiting and looking for his boy to return, every day hoping to see a familiar figure. Then it happens. He sees his boy, thin and bedraggled, trudging up the long driveway. His boy has come home!

The boy begins to make his speech, but his dad hears none of it. He clothes the boy in his own best suit, invites the neighbors and throws a welcome home party. His older brother, jealous and angry, refuses to attend or rejoice.

"Dad, you never threw a party for me, and I've been faithful." To him, the dad says, "You've always been here, and what's mine is yours."

I rejoice every day because this story explains that God never treats me how I deserve. In my Father's world, it's all about His amazing **GRACE**.

*Lord, thank You for **G**od's **R**iches **A**t **C**hrist's **E**xpense. Amen.*

Maurice T. Battle, Jr., is the pastor of the Lewisburg church in West Virginia.

"Now is your time of grief, but I will see you again and you will rejoice, and no one will take away your joy." JOHN 16:22, NIV

AUGUST

Be Like David

"Don't let anyone look down on you because you are young, but set an example for the believers in speech, in conduct, in love, in faith and in purity" (1 Tim. 4:12, NIV).

While studying graphic design my senior year at Andrews University (Mich.), the Seventh-day Adventist Church offered me a job. However, I had always envisioned myself at an agency, so I eagerly accepted a position at the design studio where I had interned the year before. But God had other plans. Less than two years later, the Adventist Church would call again.

I was 23 years old when I started working for the Church. Unfortunately, the opportunity wasn't what I hoped it would be. Time after time, I felt as though my contributions weren't valued because I was too young and inexperienced. Though I knew people's intentions were good, I was regularly "schooled" in the "ways of the church." Again and again, I received the response: "Because this is how we have always done it."

I watched my friends slowly leave church work, until I was the "last one standing." Thankfully, I had an administrator who encouraged me toward perseverance and grace. And now, 21 years later, I'm still standing.

The Bible describes David as a musician and poet. He ministered creatively. Designers may not be pastors, but we, too, effectively bring His message to members and beyond.

Young adults, whatever your vocation, you have an important role in the church. Your fresh opinions and ideas are valuable. Like so many young Bible characters, who began in a position of unimportance, you can make a difference. Be like David: humble, devoted and appointed by God to lead.

Heavenly Father, help us to be men and women after God's own heart. Amen.

Kelly Butler Coe is the associate director of communication and art director for the Columbia Union Conference.

His Plan and Purpose

"Trust in the Lord with all your heart and lean not on your own understanding; in all your ways submit to Him, and He will make your paths straight" (Prov. 3:5–6, NIV).

When my daughter was 3-years-old, she offered to help me "mow the lawn." In other words, it was a hint to ride on my shoulders. As I mowed, I was in deep turmoil about the seemingly insurmountable challenges and obstacles that life had sent my way. I was so buried in my angst that it took me nearly an hour to actually hear and truly listen to the words my daughter had been singing over and over in her little angelic voice.

"Trust and obey, for there's no other way. To be happy in Jesus, but to trust and obey."

When her voice finally caught my attention, I heard it in my heart and soul. I realized that I had been trying to understand and solve all of my problems on my own. And if I continued down that path, I would keep failing and feeling overwhelmed.

That song is based on Proverbs 3, and those verses instruct us to recognize our own limited ability to understand, because God is in control. We will not be disappointed if we trust Him and believe that His understanding is greater than ours. It may take time to understand His ways, and, in many cases, look back to see that His plan and purpose for us were there all along.

Lord, help me to trust You completely and to have faith that You always have a plan for me. Amen.

Scott Bennie is the dean of Health Professions, Graduate Studies and Institutional Effectiveness at Kettering College in Ohio.

Lost in Chicago

"So do not fear, for I am with you; do not be dismayed, for I am your God. I will strengthen you and help you; I will uphold you with My righteous right hand" (Isa. 41:10, NIV).

When I was 5-years-old, I took a trip with my family to Taste of Chicago—the world's largest food festival. There were innumerable amounts of food to try: Mexican, Indian, Italian, you name it. While there, something interesting caught my dad's attention, and he crossed the street to check it out. Seconds later, my 5-year-old brain decided it was a good idea to follow him. I ventured across the street to find my dad. I got in the line where I thought he was, tapped his back and said, "Dad?"

A random man turned around. Terrified, I walked away, sat down on the sidewalk and started to cry. A stranger came up to me and asked what was wrong. I looked up, crying as I described my situation. Sitting with me, she put a caring arm around me and told me it would be OK.

A few minutes later, I felt a hand grab me and pick me up. My mom had found me! Hysterical and happy, she turned to thank the lady, but she was gone. To this day, I believe that lady was my guardian angel protecting me.

Isaiah 41:10 really speaks to me because it says God is always with me and will always strengthen me. In that moment, when I was completely and utterly lost, He was protecting me and bringing me back to safety. If you keep God in your heart, there is no reason to fear, because He will guide you, keep you and strengthen you all the days of your life.

God, when we're scared, may we hold onto Your righteous right hand. Amen.

Alexis Dulan is a freshman at Spring Valley Academy in Ohio.

Speak Life

"In the beginning, God" (Gen. 1:1, ESV).

It was a rainy Monday morning. I stood in front of my seventh-grade class ready to teach Bible. My head cloudy, my heart in pieces from trials in my personal life, I struggled to hold back the tears.

"Good morning, class! Let's pray! There will be no singing today for Bible class," I said as quickly as I could. "We will go right into our lesson. It will be a review because you all know the creation story!" I allowed a student to pray because I knew the darkness I felt would cause me to cry.

I then opened the Bible and began reciting Genesis 1:1–3: "In the beginning, God created the heavens and the earth ..." As I continued about how the earth was first empty and void, and darkness covered the face of the deep, the Holy Spirit hovered over the void in my heart. Tears began to roll down my cheeks.

God spoke light and life into my heart that day, and my journey with Him has never been the same.

Sometimes, studying the Bible becomes a duty, not an encounter with our Best Friend. God wants to meet us through His Word and speak life into our lives. Maybe words of comfort, maybe words of reproof. Whatever we need, He has a timely word in His Word. Will you allow Him to meet you in His Word today and speak light and life to you?

Father, in any and every beginning, be God! Amen.

Gladys S. Guerrero is a member of the Sligo church in Maryland.

Blessings Upon Blessings

"The Lord is my shepherd; I shall not want. ... I will fear no evil; for You are with me; ... Surely goodness and mercy shall follow me all the days of my life" (Ps. 23:1, 4, 6, NKJV).

These verses mean a lot to me because I know God is always with me and looking out for me.

When one of our teachers resigned in August 2019, we all thought that the school was going to close. So we prayed and prayed, and then Mrs. Smith offered to come out of retirement to teach us. I feel God has really blessed me by having her as my teacher.

Also, the Lord has blessed me with two wonderful grandparents—Nana and Pop. They have been my parents since I was 2 years old. Since the time I started living with them, Nana has taught me the Bible. That is why I am in a Christian school.

From the time I was 4, I've wanted to be a pastor. The Bible is so interesting, and I feel that everybody should know about God and His protection over us. I love waking up and seeing His creation. I enjoy the air we breathe and the food we eat—blessings that all come from God.

Dear Heavenly Father, thank You for keeping us safe and healthy. Please help the scientists to find a cure and a vaccine for the coronavirus. Please help the people who have the virus and their relatives. Please watch over all of us and protect us. Amen.

Laken Carroll is a sixth-grader at the Roanoke Adventist Christian School in Virginia.

The Mountain That Moved

"He replied, 'Because you have so little faith. Truly I tell you, if you have faith as small as a mustard seed, you can say to this mountain, "Move from here to there," and it will move. Nothing will be impossible for you'" (Matt. 17:20, NIV).

Six years ago, when I was preparing to graduate with a master's degree in Children and Family Ministry at Bethel University (Minn.), I noticed that graduation would be held on a Saturday—my Sabbath. I spoke to one of my classmates about whether the administration would ever consider switching it to a different day. My classmate doubted they'd change the day for just one person.

I gave it a try, praying for God to intervene. Unfortunately, the registrar explained that it wouldn't be possible to change the day, but I could graduate on a Sunday as a guest from another university. I was heartbroken and wondered why God didn't intervene, but went ahead with the preparation for graduating elsewhere.

Two months later, I received an email from the registrar's office notifying me that graduation had been changed to Sunday. I couldn't believe it! Did God really answer my prayer to graduate in person with my classmates? I had never seen Him change a situation to fit my exact request, especially a seemingly insurmountable mountain—an event that had been the university's tradition for years. This experience humbled me, and I learned to be more dependent on God.

Lord, when life isn't easy, and we are met with many challenges, may we put our trust in You, believing that You will come through. Amen.

Tanya Muganda is a member of the Sligo church in Maryland.

A Heart Yearning

"Teach me Your way, O Lord; I will walk in Your truth; unite my heart to fear Your name" (Ps. 86:11, NKJV).

This verse has made a great impact on my life. Just below the chapter title, my Bible also includes these words: "A prayer of David." Other than his incredible victory over Goliath, David is also remembered as a man after God's own heart. Verse 11 gives us further proof of this. When you read through the Psalms, one thing is evident: David yearned for the Lord. He often praised God and declared His excellence. He meditated on the words of God throughout the day and night. He would ask God to examine his heart and prove him. These verses left a deep impression on me.

During my sophomore year of college, I decided to study the Bible for myself. Before then, I didn't know much about Christianity, nor did I grasp the depth and power of God's Word. As I began to study the Bible and pray more sincerely, the Holy Spirit began to change my heart. Psalm 86:11 resonated with me more and more. I added that verse to my prayers, and asked God to reveal His ways and His will to me. Like David, I began to desire a close and meaningful relationship with Jesus. Looking back, God has brought me a long way.

I'm still a work in progress, learning more each and every day, but I praise God that one thing hasn't changed: My heart still yearns for Jesus. God has been so faithful to me. He is merciful and gracious. His promises are my hope and strength, and I continue to hold onto them.

Jesus, help us to devote ourselves to You and seek Your heart daily. Amen.

Jonathan Kim is a member of the Ellicott City church in Maryland.

The Father Himself Loves Me

"In that day you will ask in My name. I am not saying that I will ask the Father on your behalf. No, the Father Himself loves you because you have loved Me and have believed that I came from God" (John 16:26–27, NIV).

I like verses that surprise me. This verse certainly did that, given that I grew up primarily with a courtroom-based image of the Father, standing in judgment over me, with Jesus interceding as my Advocate.

This verse reminds me that the members of the Godhead are united in their love for me and their desire to save me. Jesus has no need to advocate before the Father on my behalf, because the Father is not my accuser. Satan, the adversary, and sin itself, are my only enemies. In the Godhead, I have nothing but friends.

Understanding and believing this verse helped me to let go of many fears and to see that the Father is just as loving and gracious as His Son. It has been incredibly freeing to comprehend that Christ died to save us from sin, not from God.

Dear Heavenly Father, thank You for letting me see Christ—the clearest representation of who You are. Amen.

Robert Fuller is a member of the Spencerville church in Maryland.

The Power of Worry

"But my God shall supply all your needs according to His riches in glory by Christ Jesus" (Phil. 4:19, KJV).

I find myself worrying about the future, like, "Will I get accepted into the college I want?" In my worries, this verse reminds me that "God supplies all my needs." He knew our future even before we were born. He has a plan and purpose for everything.

In December 2019, I was diagnosed with scoliosis. I had been getting severe back pain since April of that year, but now things started to get real, and I was scared. The doctors ordered X-rays, and they looked dissatisfactory. Then they ordered an MRI to rule out brain tumors, since the X-rays and the curve numbers were unexplainable.

The MRI was clean. It was time to see a surgeon. I wanted the surgery right away, but the surgeon said the best treatment would be to wear a brace until I finished growing. I thought, *What! You are going to put me in a brace with two 50-degree curves? My spine looks like an S!* However, my parents agreed with the surgeon. I prayed about it, and, in February, I got a big, tight, scary brace!

As I write this in 2020, I'm graduating from the eighth grade, and I must wear the brace until my sophomore year. Honestly, I am not excited about wearing my brace in high school, but I know everything happens for a reason and that I don't have to worry because everything is in God's hands.

Are you troubled, anxious or worried? Your present, past or future may scare you, but ask God to free you today. Release your worries into His hands forever, and never look back.

Lord, may we feel Your Holy Spirit's peaceful presence today. Amen.

Princess Alcantara is an eighth-grader at the Shenandoah Valley Adventist Elementary School in Virginia.

A True Friend

"Two are better than one, because they have a good reward for their labor" (Eccl. 4:9, NKJV).

One day, two new girls enrolled at my school. They were surrounded by a crowd of girls who wanted to meet them during recess. As I made my way over, I recognized I had met one of them in church that past Sabbath! We immediately became best friends. We were the only Seventh-day Adventist girls in the entire public school.

I loved my friend. She was funny, happy, smart and kind. After we graduated from eighth grade, we attended different high schools, but still spent every Sabbath together, studying our Sabbath School lessons and enjoying potluck with the youth.

How wonderful that my Father granted me such a friend! We went through joys and heartbreaks together, and she always encouraged me to put my trust in God. I admired her love for Him and observed that, although she loved me as her best friend, Jesus was her "bestest" friend.

The two of us were better than one, because when I fell, she was there to lift me up, and vice versa. When I was spiritually cold, she provided comforting words from Scripture. In tough times, we prayed for each other.

Prior to meeting my friend, Jesus had always been there for both of us. He was the first to delight in our joys and wipe our tears. So now, the three of us formed a threefold cord together.

When Jesus is included in a relationship, that relationship will not easily break. Ask your Father for such a friendship. And, while you wait, be that friend to those around you.

Father, thank You for friends who strengthen us in our walk with You. Amen.

Yolanda Bocanegra is the director of the Adventurers club for the Paterson Temple church in New Jersey.

He Is All-Powerful

"Then [Jesus] said to the tree, 'May no one ever eat fruit from you again.' ... Peter remembered and said to Jesus, 'Rabbi, look! The fig tree you cursed has withered!'" (Mark 11:14, 21, NIV).

Here is an odd story about Jesus. Hungry, Jesus sees a fig tree with leaves because it was out of season. Finding it has no fruit, He curses the tree, and it dies. Why does Jesus do that? Doesn't it seem unreasonable? Why does Mark tell this story?

The gospel accounts are not collections of random stories of things Jesus *did*. Each gospel book is a revelation of who Jesus *is*. So either Mark wants us to think Jesus is an unreasonable tree killer, or something deeper is happening here.

I feel like in this passage Jesus is showing that He has the power to do all things. He can even tell a tree that it will have no more fruit, and just from those words alone, the tree will wither up and die.

It is just amazing to see what God can do. People either fear Him for it or are in fear of Him. Two completely different fears, but if you ask me, I love to fear Him—to be in awe of Him and respect Him.

So let us come closer to Him and build a stronger relationship every single day for the rest of our lives.

Dear God, please help us grow closer to You each day. Thank You for being all-powerful. Amen.

Tallen Forrey is an eighth-grader at the Harrisburg Adventist School in Pennsylvania.

Outside Forces Have Nothing on Us

"Peace I leave with you; my peace I give you. I do not give to you as the world gives. Do not let your hearts be troubled and do not be afraid" (John 14:27, NIV).

The law of inertia states that an object at rest or in motion will remain so unless acted upon by an outside force. Maybe not intentionally or consciously, but when things don't go our way, we reason it's the outside forces' fault, not ours!

So *that's* the reason I'm stressed and miserable. No one wants their progress halted or rest interrupted by "outside forces," but can these forces really halt and interrupt? Do they have that power and control over us? Jesus tells us not to worry.

God never gives us a directive or command that is not in our best interest and that is not possible to accomplish! He knows about the alarm clocks of life, the traffic, deadlines, migraine headaches, rude co-workers, disrespectful family members, car problems, bills, layoffs, distractions, delays, disruptions, disappointments, disasters, depression, disease. He faced it all Himself (Hebrews 4:15). So He can be trusted when He says He will give us peace.

Inertia is a real thing. It's a "law." We have a more powerful God though. Believe and exclaim this verse to the "outside forces" in your life. Make it your own because it is yours.

As you promise, Lord, give us peace, and may we receive it and represent You as You deserve. Amen.

Rick Downes is a deacon and lay teacher at the Shenango Valley church in Ohio.

The Power of Words

"Death and life are in the power of the tongue, and those who love it will eat its fruit" (Prov. 18:21, NKJV).

This verse reminds me of the power that words have, and that I have to watch what I say. Words can either encourage or destroy, and, because they can stick in one's mind forever, they can positively or negatively affect the lives of others. This is important to me because I have not always been careful with my words, and have hurt people as a result.

I once read a story about a group of frogs that were traveling through the woods, and two of them fell into a deep pit. When the other frogs saw how deep the pit was, they told the two frogs that they were as good as dead. The two frogs ignored the comments and tried to jump up out of the pit with all their might. The other frogs kept telling them to stop, that they were as good as dead. Finally, one of the frogs took heed to what the other frogs were saying and gave up. He fell down and died.

The other frog continued to jump as hard as he could. Once again, the crowd of frogs yelled at him to stop the pain and just die. He jumped even harder and finally made it out. When he got out, the other frogs said, "Did you not hear us?" The frog explained to them that he was deaf. He thought they were encouraging him the entire time.

Destructive words can tear others down, but encouraging words can lift them up and help them. Choose your words wisely, for words are forever.

Lord, teach me to be careful with my words. Help me to be encouraging to everyone. Amen.

Nicole Daneker is an eighth-grader at the Shenandoah Valley Adventist Elementary School in Virginia.

Jesus, Please Come Soon!

"He will wipe every tear from their eyes. There will be no more death, or mourning or crying or pain, for the old order of things has passed away" (Rev. 21:4, NIV).

In the time we are living, especially with this pandemic, Revelation 21:4 fills me with hope and happiness because Jesus is coming soon, and there will be no more pain or crying. Recently, in a class in my Pathfinder's club, we studied the first vision of Ellen White. That gave me even more hope, knowing that this will all happen, and that very soon we will live in a better place.

Pain or sadness can come in many ways, like the death of a loved one, a sickness, parents divorcing, hunger, poverty, injustice, etc. A few months ago, I lived an experience that for many would probably not be important, but for me it was. Jesus tells us to be obedient, which makes each of us different. Being different brought big changes in one of my most important friendships. The moments that we were together started to disappear, and there were times when I felt like I was alone, but Jesus never leaves me alone. I know that everything that I went through was one of the many difficulties that I will have during the time we are in this world.

We all go through difficult times, but we should always remember the promises of God and that soon He will come again.

Dear Jesus, I want You to come soon! Amen.

Marianna Guzmán is a sixth-grader at the Takoma Academy Preparatory School in Maryland.

All You!

"And I will turn my hand upon thee, and purely purge away thy dross, and take away all thy tin" (Isa. 1:25, KJV).

I grew up in a nominal Seventh-day Adventist home where guilt abounded. "I'm going to be good," my cousin and I would say. But we drifted away from God.

At 21, I was sincerely, miraculously converted. For 18 years, I struggled with guilt and could never quite "be good enough." So I drifted away again.

Fast forward to 25 years of being "in and out of the world." The tender pleading of the Father's Spirit—wooing, entreating and drawing this wanderer to the Father's heart of love—awakened my soul to return to God.

He began a good work in me, and was performing it, as Philippians 1:6 states. He called me, and sanctified me wholly. He preserved me blameless unto His coming. He called me, and He is the One Who will do it for me (1 Thessalonians 5:23–24). Jesus set me free from sin; from the desire for sin, the running to it, the search for it, the love of it, the restless reaching. Not that I have attained (Philippians 3:12), but that I no longer want to sin.

Lord, I want Your purity and holiness. You broke the chains that bound me in sin that encompassed my every thought. You took away my desire to "be good" and are teaching me to look to Your goodness and wear Your robe of righteousness. You brought me to a longing for You and Your kingdom. You are purely purging away my dross and taking away all my tin. It is all You! Amen.

Kathleen E. Brooks is a member of the Mount Vernon Hill church in Ohio.

Think on These Things

"Finally, brethren, whatsoever things are true, whatsoever things are honest, whatsoever things are just, whatsoever things are pure, whatsoever things are lovely, whatsoever things are of good report; if there be any virtue, and if there be any praise, think on these things" (Phil. 4:8, KJV).

I became acquainted with this verse as a young adult, and it quickly became a favorite of mine. Being raised in the Seventh-day Adventist Church, I often felt completely out of sync and appalled by pop culture, which only continues to deteriorate and get worse. So this verse, which extols all that is good and pure, was very comforting and inspiring to me.

As the years have passed, sadly I have also seen how easily seemingly "little" things without any virtue or praise have crept into my own life. For example, I now more easily shrug off viewing certain things on TV that would've made me uncomfortable in the past. As discouraging as that is, this verse reminds me of the importance of focusing on and filling my mind with that which is good. In fact, it tells me to focus on Christ—the One who perfectly embodies truth   with honesty and all that is just, pure, lovely and of good report. It is only by being in Christ and allowing Him to live in me that I can avoid evil in my own life.

As I write this, there are riots in multiple cities across our great nation. The looting, arson and violence exemplify the worst in humanity and stand in stark contrast to the beautiful virtues in this verse. More than ever, we all need Christ!

Dear Lord, may we give our lives fully to You so that we may reflect Your character to the world. Amen.

Jane Cermak-Faver is an associate treasurer for the Columbia Union Conference.

A Thousand Hills

"For every beast of the forest is Mine, and the cattle upon a thousand hills" (Ps. 50:10, NKJV).

Graduation had just ended. The tired mommy shifted an infant girl from one side to the other. "I would love to have my children at your school," she said. "I can see from this graduation program how much your church members love their school."

I searched her face. Our church had just finished a six-week evangelism campaign, but she hadn't attended. *Does she have enough money to pay the required tuition?* I thought, then stopped myself. *This is God's school, and He sends the seekers.* Just then, one of her sons came running by.

"Mom, if I have to go here, I'm not going to be marching up the aisle for any graduation program." With that he went defiantly off to join the others.

"That's Jeremy, and he'll be in the eighth grade," his mother remarked.

"That would be nice," I responded. "We need more upper-grade students."

She continued, "I really want all four of my boys at your school, but I have no money, and my husband is out of work." Emotion crept onto her face.

"It's OK! Let's keep praying," I encouraged. "A small church school like ours is a huge faith-growing enterprise. We don't know how God will provide. Sometimes the money comes through the parents or family; other times the money comes from the church; and sometimes the money multiplies miraculously like the widow's mite."

That first day of school began with all four of her sons enrolled. And guess who marched down the aisle in that May's graduation service?

Father, thank You for Your miraculous providence. Amen.

Rose Gamblin is the principal/teacher at the Gettysburg Adventist Christian School in Pennsylvania.

Forward-Thinking

"I'm not saying that I have this all together, that I have it made. But I am well on my way, reaching out for Christ, who has so wondrously reached out for me. Friends, don't get me wrong: By no means do I consider myself an expert in all of this, but I've got my eye on the goal, where God is beckoning us onward—to Jesus. I am off and running, and I'm not turning back" (Phil. 3:13-14, MSG).

Life is a journey, and it's important to remember that my spiritual walk is just as important as my destination. Would I prefer life to be worry-free with no more cares, pain or fear of the unknown? Absolutely! However, this text reminds me that even though this life's journey is riddled with challenges, I can move forward with confidence in Christ. To dwell on yesterday's failures is not part of God's plan. Instead, I learn from the past and move forward toward the heavenly prize—home with the Lord. By pressing on, I thrive.

The dark night of the soul can be a nurturing time with the Father. Sometimes we are in conversation; other times we are silent. His quiet love encourages me: "Look in my eyes and see the deep love I have for you." His presence makes the desert a place of solitude. I am reminded that my pilgrimage is not a scorecard but rather a love relationship with Jesus that He continues to nurture. So when I walk through the darkest valley, I fear no evil, for He is with me (Psalm 23:4).

Has my voyage with Him reached its zenith with no more room to grow? Not at all. For you see, I'm not the guide. He is.

Lord, may I keep moving forward with You, my Friend. Amen.

Steve Laing is the vice president of Education for the Potomac Conference.

Good Like Medicine

"But the fruit of the Spirit is love, joy, peace, longsuffering, gentleness, goodness, faith, meekness, temperance: against such there is no law" (Gal. 5:22–23, KJV).

I believe that a Christian must have the fruit of the spirit. If all Christians would read and take to heart these verses daily, along with Philippians 4:8, which tells us to think on whatsoever is true, honest, just, pure, lovely and of good report, we would not have the problems in church we are faced with today. But the only way to attain, retain and maintain that fruit is by steadily focusing on Jesus; to "think on" Him continuously.

We are living in the last days, and this world is fast drawing to a close. Having that early morning devotional time gives me strength to make it through each day. The Bible says, as we see all these things happening, to "look up ... for your redemption draweth nigh" (Luke 21:28, KJV).

Many people mockingly tell me that I view life through rose-colored glasses. Maybe so, but I'd rather see Jesus through these glasses than look at the wickedness of the world and not see Jesus at all, ending up a broken, downhearted and depressed human being. And I am reminded that "a merry heart doeth good like a medicine: but a broken spirit drieth the bones" (Prov. 17:22, KJV).

Lord, I pray that You will continue to abide in me and encourage me to always look to You. Help me to point others to You so they will experience the same peace, love and tranquility that I enjoy each day—and, ultimately, eternal life with You. Amen.

Peggy J. Koch is an elder at the Charleston Boulevard church in West Virginia.

God's Love for a Sinner

"This man is My chosen instrument to proclaim My name to the Gentiles and their kings and to the people of Israel" (Acts 9:15, NIV).

God loves us very much. No matter what we do, He will still forgive us because His love for us is unconditional.

Before the apostle Paul became a follower of Jesus, his name was Saul. Saul thought he knew all about God and that Jesus was a false messiah. He even convinced people to kill Stephen. Saul was angry that the disciples were preaching about Jesus.

On his way to Damascus, Saul was confronted by a voice in heaven. It was Jesus—the One he was persecuting. As a result of this encounter, Saul became blind. There was a man named Ananias in Damascus, and, in a vision, Jesus appeared to him and told him to baptize Saul. When Ananias asked why, Jesus said: "This man is My chosen instrument to proclaim My name to the Gentiles and their kings and to the people of Israel."

Saul was filled with the Holy Spirit after his baptism, and he was no longer blind. How could God give a person like Saul, now Paul, a second chance? Because God's love was and is unconditional. He loved us so much that He sent His Son to die for our sins.

Paul used his second chance to become a vessel for God, writing 13 books in the New Testament. And, as a result of his ministry, many people have come to Christ.

Dear Lord, please help us to work for You, not against You. May others be drawn to Your love by how we live. Amen.

Josue Ayala is an eighth-grader at Vienna Adventist Academy in Virginia.

Before We Call

**"Before they call, I will answer; and while they are
yet speaking, I will hear" (Isa. 65:24, KJV).**

My husband and I live in rural Ohio with our two daughters, sons-in-law
and five delightful granddaughters. Our family farm is named "Winds of
Faith Farm." One day, God did something incredible.

I was busy in the house in southern Ohio, when all of a sudden my
youngest granddaughters, Lydia and Gabrielle, bolted through the front
door with terror on their young faces.

They screamed that our beloved mini-horse Dumplin had somehow gotten
out of his stall and was galloping toward the road. The thought of what my
granddaughters might witness was too much! But what to do?

For sure we could not catch up to him. I looked into the faces of my frantic
granddaughters and did the only thing I knew to do. I prayed that God
would send an angel to stop Dumplin before he got to the road.

My granddaughters and I looked up to see a truly unbelievable sight.
Only a few yards from the road, Dumplin suddenly stopped and turned
around, as if an unseen hand was leading him. He trotted back to the barn,
stopped at the barn door and gently walked into his stall. We quickly slid
the stall door closed and immediately knelt down to thank God for sending
his angel to bring Dumplin back to us unharmed. What a faith builder!

As unbelievable as this story may sound, I know that two little girls and
their grandmother will always remember the day an angel led their little
horse away from danger back to safety. Never underestimate the power of
prayer and the love of our wonderful God who hears us before we call.

Lord, thank You for always hearing and answering. Amen.

Madeline Whittle is a member of the Hillsboro church in Ohio.

Don't Stop Short

**"But you, be strong and do not let your hands be weak,
for your work shall be rewarded" (2 Chron. 15:7, NKJV).**

This scripture caused me to reflect on my spiritual condition, and ask, *Have I done enough? Have I gone far enough?* As Christians, we may do "enough" to satisfy ourselves, or even our pastor. But is it enough to please God?

When Asa became king, Judah was a total mess. The people had rejected the true God and boldly worshipped idols. Asa made some courageous moves to reform the nation: "He removed the altars of foreign gods and the high places, and broke down the sacred pillars and cut down the wooden images. He commanded Judah to seek the Lord God of their fathers, and to observe the law and the commandment" (2 Chron. 14:3–4, NKJV). Judah flourished under his reign. There was, however, still more work to be done. The reformation was incomplete. So God sent Azariah to encourage Asa to be strong and finish the work.

Like many Christians, I took aggressive measures to align my life with the Scriptures. Major changes took place and were eradicated: harmful behaviors, shameful practices and filthy language. But was that enough? Did I stop short of God's goal for me? Did I trade His standards for the standards of men?

Maybe we should re-examine our habits and thoughts. Is our reformation complete, or is there more work yet to be done? May we all be encouraged by the words of Azariah: "But you, be strong and do not let your hands be weak, for your work shall be rewarded!"

Dear Lord, let us not grow weary of doing good. Please strengthen our hands and finish Your great work in us. Amen.

Jeffery Thomas is the head elder of the Calvary church in Virginia.

Claim His Promise!

**"The angel of the Lord encampeth round about them
that fear Him, and delivereth them" (Ps. 34:7, KJV).**

I love Psalm 34:7 because you can claim it in so many situations. For
example, if you're afraid of the dark, you can declare this promise when
you're scared. I personally claim this promise every night before I go to bed.

God has protected me in so many ways. I almost died twice as a baby, and
I've been in several accidents. One incident took place at another school
that I attended. Jaydon jumped on Nehemiah and stole his lunch box. Then
a bunch of bullies—Evan, Jeremiah and Rafael—started pushing Nehemiah
around. I tried to keep them from hitting Nehemiah, but then they started
hitting me instead! At that point, Rafael walked away, but Jeremiah started
punching my ankle, and Evan was hitting me in the chest! The Lord
protected me that day. After my ankle healed, all I had left was a scar.

*Dear Father, help me to remember what I have learned: not to focus on the
fear in this world, but on the promise in Psalm 34:7. Amen.*

*Joshua Montes de Oca is a fifth-grader at the Roanoke Adventist Christian School
in Virginia.*

You Can Depend on Him

"Look at the birds of the air; they do not sow or reap or store away in barns, and yet your heavenly Father feeds them. Are you not much more valuable then they? Can any one of you by worrying add a single hour to your life?" (Matt. 6:26–27, NIV).

This is my favorite Bible verse, as it became my mantra in 2017. My husband moved from Iowa to Columbus, Ohio, to take a job at Amazon. One month after he started, he had a stroke while he was at work. The stroke changed every part of our lives. I became the breadwinner. He became dependent on me for basically everything. As my carnal nature is to worry all the time, this verse gave me great comfort, and I felt that God was helping me realize my need to depend on Him always.

God was ever-present during that time, and we were abundantly blessed. Money would literally show up when we least expected it. We never lacked food, clothing or housing. We were also able to afford our daughter's tuition at Worthington Adventist Academy.

Try God, trust God and see if He will show up when you need Him most.

God, thank You for providing for my every need. Amen.

Linda Davis is the first- and second-grade teacher at Worthington Adventist Academy in Ohio.

His Way or Yours?

"Trust in the Lord with all your heart, and lean not on your own understanding; in all your ways acknowledge Him, and He shall direct your paths. Do not be wise in your own eyes; fear the Lord and depart from evil" (Prov. 3:5-7, NKJV).

This was a verse I loved while I was growing up, however it took me a few years to actually understand it. Some people read it and say, "Oh, it's just such a complicated passage." But it really isn't. The verses hold one message: His way or yours? In other words, do you trust Him?

A boy was playing with a ball, and it bounced up and got stuck on the roof. He tried several times to get it, but to no avail. The father watched all this from the porch in amusement and wonder. The boy then gave up and went to his father for help. The dad, chuckling, hit the roof, and the ball bounced off. The dad then asked his son a question: "Why didn't you ask me to help you in the first place?"

In this passage, God is indirectly asking this question: "Why don't you just come and trust Me to help you?" Who is this someone, or what is this thing that is giving you a hard time? What is it that you are trying to do but just can't? What is that class you don't like because you can't understand it? Just trust Him. Always keep this in mind if you are tempted to leave Him out. Leaning on our own understanding = being wise in our eyes = hard times and problems.

Today, just let Him have His way in your life and see quick and easy results.

Dear Jesus, help us to trust You to direct us today. Amen.

Inioluwa Jobi is a sophomore at Takoma Academy in Maryland.

Be My Strength

"God is within her, she will not fall; God will help her at break of day" (Ps. 46:5, NIV).

Today, I feel stressed, alone and overwhelmed. I am missing my class, our memories together and all of our missed opportunities. I feel like I don't have enough time to get my schoolwork done, and I feel like quitting. However, this verse reminds me that I am not alone. God is with me, and He will help me today and tomorrow. With Him, I will not fail.

I once survived a major car accident. God was with me and I didn't even know it. My mom, dad, and their dog, Moby, were going to Lake Anna in Virginia for the Fourth of July. Suddenly a spinner hubcap flew off the car in front of us. My dad swerved, and our car's wheel fell off! We ran off the side of the road and into a tree at 70 mph! The tree traveled halfway up the hood of the car, and all of the side windows shattered on them. Moby ended up on my dad's lap, unharmed. My parents had to crawl out of the rear doors, and my mom was taken to the hospital.

The ER doctors told my mom, who was 12 weeks pregnant with me, that she could go home, but if she started bleeding, it would be due to a miscarriage. Fortunately, my grandpa was an attending doctor at the hospital and ordered an ultrasound of his grandchild. At first my parents didn't hear a sound and got really scared. Finally, they heard my heartbeat! God was with us.

Thank You, God, for always being with me, even when I don't know it. Please help me to turn to You every day. Be my strength. Amen.

Katie Pacylowski is an eighth-grader at the Shenandoah Valley Adventist Elementary School in Virginia.

God Is With Me

**"When you go through deep waters, I will be with you.
When you go through rivers of difficulty, you will not drown.
When you walk through the fire of oppression, you will not be
burned up; the flames will not consume you" (Isa. 43:2, NLT).**

I like this verse a lot because it reminds me that, no matter what happens, God is with me. There have been times when I have struggled with things such as math or science. But I have always gotten through these classes, thanks to my parents and God.

God will be with me at all times. When I'm going through deep troubles, God will not abandon me. I'm having troubles right now because I have been worrying about this pandemic. More and more people are getting infected and dying every day. It makes me wonder if my family is next. I believe God is with me though, and He will keep us safe.

God is also with me when I walk through the fires of oppression. We are told that during the final days before Jesus' second coming, people will use their authoritative power to stop Christians from worshipping God on the Sabbath. Even then, God will be with us. Like He says, "The flames will not consume you." When the time comes, we will be protected.

So when you go through deep troubles such as losing a loved one, God will stay with you. When you struggle with something, no matter what it is, God will help you. When someone abuses their power to stop you, God will help you out. No matter what happens, God will always keep you safe.

Dear God, help me to trust You no matter what happens. Amen.

Jacob Chapman is an eighth-grader at the Harrisburg Adventist School in Pennsylvania.

He's in Control

"For I know the plans I have for you, declares the Lord, plans for welfare and not for evil, to give you a future and a hope" (Jer. 29:11, NKJV).

This verse has impacted me greatly because it reminds me that I am not alone. Whatever it is that you are going through in life, God will always be by your side. If it's school, friends, future decisions or anything else, God will help you prosper. He wants us to succeed and to get far in life.

Now that I am a senior in high school and I will be going to college soon, I am not 100 percent sure what I want to do with my life. I have been praying constantly for God to show me what His will is and to reveal His plans for me.

Every time I think about college and making decisions, my anxiety increases greatly because this is a life decision. Studying for a career that you might not enjoy is a dangerous path to go down. But constantly reminding myself of this verse and that God has plans for me keeps me motivated and knowing that it will be OK. It is all in God's hands, and by letting Him take control of it, I will prosper.

We need to be patient with God, because, in time, He will give His response. He will not always respond right when you want Him to, but He will when you need it. By listening to God and following His will, He will bless us and use us to bless others.

Father in Heaven, thank You that You have good plans for us and for being in control of everything. Amen.

Antonia Hess is a senior at Blue Mountain Academy in Pennsylvania.

The Choice

"Jesus said to him, 'I am the way, the truth, and the life. No one comes to the Father except through Me'" (John 14:6, NKJV).

I have always believed that logical thinking, risk analysis and dealing with life in a sensible and realistic way would guarantee success. I used to consider myself pragmatic, focusing on the processes behind any task, initiative or goal.

When you are pragmatic, you are practical. You follow the rules and expect to be rewarded. You are usually successful, but are often still searching for "the answer." You may attend church, but a true understanding of the Bible eludes you; it stays hidden.

You often ask yourself, *Is this real? There must be truth somewhere, I just need to work harder. I need to do more to reach the next level.* You continue to take on more tasks, but you do not find the way, the truth or the life. You continue to use every practical, matter-of-fact, realistic, sensible and down to earth approach to resolve your quest.

One day, God spoke to me through this verse. He said, "I am the way. You need to get to know Me. You need to see My character. You need to trust Me. When I tell you I am always with you, I am. When I show you how to live with love, follow Me. When I show you how to be courageous, follow Me. When I show you mercy, learn from Me. When I share joy with you, experience it. Get to know Me. Spend time with Me."

I answered, "I believe in You! I choose You today!"

Will you choose Him to be your way, truth and life?

Lord, today we choose You above our own plans. We trust You. Amen.

David Forbes is the principal at Richmond Academy in Virginia.

Claim It Every Day

"I can do all things through Christ who strengthens me"
(Phil. 4:13, NKJV).

Philippians 4:13 helps me achieve so many things. When I take a test in school, I always think about this verse to remind me that God will help me do well. Or if I have a competition and I am scared, I think of this verse to remind me that God is on my team. God can help me through anything.

In my young 10-year-old life, I have been taught that God's grace is His free gift to all, and that I have a chance to receive His blessings. The grace of God is sufficient for all my needs and covers all my errors, sins and mistakes. God's grace is with everyone, so He will stand for us, no matter what.

I feel this verse is saying that God is praying for me and helping me through everything. I do not need to fear when things are hard or when I feel lonely. I only need to trust that God is with me.

God, thank You for Philippians 4:13. I want to claim it every day of my life. Amen.

Tije Adediran is a sixth-grader at Worthington Adventist Academy in Ohio.

'Jesus, Save Me!'

"I call on the Lord in my distress, and He answers me" (Ps. 120:1, NIV).

The wind and the waves crashed against the small fishing vessel, threatening to sink the boat and all its occupants. The boat pitched and yawned in the waves. The wind howled, and the ocean roared. The disciples were terrified. Out of the mist and gloom of the storm, the disciples were astonished to see Jesus walking toward them on the water. Peter, the most outspoken disciple, was the first to act.

Not truly believing that it was Jesus, Peter says, "Lord, if it's you, tell me to come out on the water." Jesus replies, "Come." So out Peter comes, hauling himself over the side of the boat, and tentatively placing his feet on the water. With shaking hands, he lets go of the sides of the boat and begins to walk toward his Savior. As he walks, he feels the tempest wind, tastes the angry sea spray and his eyes drift from Jesus to the chaos around him. He begins to sink. "Jesus, save me!" Immediately, Jesus reaches down and lifts Peter up.

In Peter's distress, he cried to God, and God heard him. In my distress, I cry out to God and He hears me. In your distress, cry out to God and He will hear you.

When going through storms in life, it's easy to focus on the chaos and tempest around you. It's easy to lose sight of God and focus on the problem. However, Psalm 120:1 testifies that when we call on the Lord, He will answer. "Jesus is the same yesterday and today and forever" (Heb. 13:8). The same God who answered Peter's desperate prayer, can and will answer yours.

Lord God, save me! Hear my prayer. Amen.

Gabriel Morency is a sophomore at Takoma Academy in Maryland.

NOTES

"Surely the Sovereign Lord does nothing without revealing His plan to His servants the prophets." AMOS 3:7, NIV

SEPTEMBER

Safe and Sound

"That the creation itself also will be set free from its slavery to corruption into the freedom of the glory of the children of God" (Rom. 8:21, NASB).

When I was a little boy living in the Dominican Republic, I used to save ants from the flood my mother created when she cleaned the concrete floor in our garage. I would take little leaves, straws, whatever was around, to save them. How terrible it was when even one didn't make it. It pained me.

Imagine how many people God has not been able to save since the beginning of creation—because they haven't chosen Him in return. Jeremiah 17:9 says, "The heart is deceitful above all things and beyond cure. Who can understand it?" (NIV). And Romans 3:23 says, "For all have sinned and fall short of the glory of God" (NIV).

However, there is hope in Jesus: "But the gift of God is eternal life in Christ Jesus our Lord" (Rom. 6:23, NIV). What wonderful news! When I hear these words from the Bible, that sensation I felt when I used to save those little ants rejuvenates me. How much more excited does God get when a little child He created turns to Him to be saved?

God, save us, for we cannot save ourselves. Amen.

Jaime N. Rodriguez Arjona is the pastor of the Summersville and Vida Nueva Spanish churches in West Virginia.

Angels Watch Out for Us!

**"For He shall give His angels charge over you,
to keep you in all your ways" (Ps. 91:11, NKJV).**

Angels are watching out for us today and every day. God is always there and will send His angels to protect us.

One day, I was going into work with my dad, but he stopped to get the mail first and told me to stay in the car. But I decided to get out and help him. When he got back in, he didn't realize that I had gotten out of the car, so when he drove off, he rolled over my foot.

I screamed, and my dad got out and carried me to his warehouse where I sat down on a chair. I cried and cried. My dad told me that I could either go to urgent care or home. I just wanted to be home. My foot hurt badly, but it wasn't seriously damaged. It could have been a lot worse. I think angels came and lifted the car a little so that it didn't crush my foot.

Angels protect us, and we should rejoice and thank God for His mercies. Remember God is always there for you. And today and every day, remember you can always reach out to Him, and He will answer your prayers.

Dear God, thank You for everything You do for us and that I am alive today. Thank You for sending Your angels to protect us. Amen.

Leia Stefan is a fourth-grader at Frederick Adventist Academy in Maryland.

His Plans Are Perfect

"'For I know the plans I have for you,' declares the Lord, 'plans to prosper you and not to harm you, plans to give you hope and a future'" (Jer. 29:11, NIV).

One Friday afternoon, I was given some devastating news that interfered with my cherished plans. I was emotionally distraught that evening, and still upset as I entered church Sabbath morning. As I listened to the pastor's sermon, I struggled to maintain my composure. My husband's comforting arm around my shoulder did little to stop the flow of my silent tears.

I was acquainted with Jeremiah 29:11 in the King James Version, but not in the New International Version—the translation the pastor was using in his sermon. It became clear that God was speaking to me through that sermon.

As I reflected on the text, I realized I was grieving over my plans, what I wanted to do, and not what God had planned for me. God's plans are always better than ours, no matter how good we think our plans are. That "devastating" news became a blessing to me several months later. It was a lesson I have never forgotten.

Jeremiah 29:11 has become one of my favorite texts. It helps me remember that God is in control of my life. He wants me to rely on Him and to implement His plans. When I think of Joseph and Daniel and how they trusted God through the most trying of circumstances, it inspires me to seek and follow His will for me.

Father, You have my best interest at heart. You will never leave me nor forsake me. Help me to always implement Your plans. Amen.

Carole Smith is the head teacher at the Roanoke Adventist Christian School in Virginia.

A Matter of Confidence

"Being confident of this, that He who began a good work in you will carry it on to completion until the day of Christ Jesus" (Phil. 1:6, NIV).

I used to pretend with my brother and sister that I was a teacher, but, after I graduated from high school, that dream flew out the window. I didn't have confidence that I would do well in college and be able to fulfill my dream.

A few years ago, my life took an unexpected turn, and I was in a quandary. So I prayed! Our local church school needed a teacher's assistant. I inquired about the position, but decided to shelve the plan because of lack of training. Again, I had no confidence.

Last year, the principal approached me to reconsider the position. I prayed long and hard about it. Like Moses, I was skeptical. The phrase, "God doesn't call the qualified; He qualifies whom He calls," came to my mind. "Is this You calling me to this, Lord?" I asked. I eventually accepted the position.

I met many challenges and made some mistakes, but I was supported by the teachers and God Himself. As the saying goes, "If God calls you to it, He will lead you through it." It isn't what I can do or what I know, but who God is and what He knows. Amazing things can be done through one who is willing and dependent on Him. This year has had its ups and downs, but God is good, and I have confidence in Him.

Dear Lord, thank You for building me up and making all things new. Amen.

Deb Zuch is the teacher's assistant at the York Adventist Christian School in Pennsylvania.

God Came Through

"But those who wait on the Lord shall renew their strength; they shall mount up with wings like eagles, they shall run and not be weary, they shall walk and not faint" (Isa. 40:31, NKJV).

It happened in the summer on a Sunday morning. I was awakened by my wife who said, "Wake up, the babies are here!" This was no dream; this was reality. This was the day. You see, we were expecting the surprise of our lives: three babies. Yes, triplets! We lived in Berrien Springs, Mich., and made our way to the only hospital in Kalamazoo that performed multiple births.

There were three beds—one for each baby—and a team of nurses and other medical personnel was assigned to each bed. All kinds of emotions went through my mind: excitement, concern, joy, worry.

A few minutes into the surgery, the first baby was delivered. Then the second. Everything was going as planned until the last baby arrived. As soon as he was placed on the bed, he stopped breathing. His color changed from a rosy pink to blue. The doctors did everything possible to make him breathe, but to no avail.

At that moment, I closed my eyes and lifted up a prayer to God. His answer came in the form of Isaiah 40:31. It was as if God was speaking this verse directly to me. A peace came over me that is hard to explain. As I opened my eyes, Daniel began to breathe again. God came through in my moment of need.

Dear Father, thank You for the assurance that You will come through in our moment of need. Amen.

Jose Vazquez is the vice president of administration for the Potomac Conference.

The Great Commandments

**"This is My commandment, that you love one another
as I have loved you" (John 15:12, NKJV).**

What obsessed the Pharisees of Christ's day? Keeping the law, as
they knew it to be. Biblical scholars, including George R. Knight, have
concluded that the Pharisees identified in the Scriptures and sought
to adhere to "613 commandments, 365 prohibitions and 248 positive
injunctions." Their adherence to these determined their faithfulness to
the law of Moses.

Today, there are many who believe that true fidelity to Christ is the
keeping of myriad commandments, prohibitions and injunctions—
viewed as righteousness, and, as such, the "ticket" to eternal life.
While the apostle Paul reminds us of the importance of keeping the
commandments of God (Romans 3:31), Christ reminds us what the heart
of the law is—to love the Lord with all heart, soul and mind; the second
being to love your neighbor as yourself (Matthew 22:36–40).

I have often wondered how anyone could not love the Lord. His
love, tenderness and goodness make anything short of loving Him
unfathomable to me. Now, loving one's neighbor—*that* is sometimes
truly challenging. As I look back over my 70 years, I cannot say that I
have always been a good neighbor. My obedience to the second of the
great commandments is constantly evolving because I want to love my
neighbors by the Master's standards, not my own. How about you?

*Father, today I openly profess to others my love for You. Through Your sweet
Spirit, help us all to be the kind of neighbors that Your Son spoke of in the
Scriptures. May we be living and loving testaments to true Christian love for
all others. Amen.*

*Hamlet Canosa is the former vice president of Education for the Columbia Union
Conference.*

Weeds and Spider Webs

"The sacrifices of God are a broken spirit, a broken and a contrite heart—these, O God, You will not despise" (Ps. 51:17, NKJV).

The morning after Tropical Storm Isaias brushed through my neighborhood, I went outside to check my garden beds. The soil along the slope of a small pine grove where the summer weeds were normally difficult to pull up was now unusually saturated, and the weeds came out easily.

I began pulling the weeds that had previously built strong roots within and around those beautiful evergreens. I thought about the "storms of life" that sometimes break us, revealing all of humanity's weakness, and our need of a Savior whose everlasting arms are willing and able to pull us out of the gutter.

When I was done weeding, I saw woven spider webs at the top of the pine trees and gently swept them away. Right then I realized that nature was showing me God's complete plan of salvation. He wants to cleanse us from our sins and renew our minds, where the "cobwebs" of life so frequently lodge.

Consider the spider web, so destructive and yet so frail. Those cobwebs are beautifully crafted, yet they trap flies and other insects.

Like spider webs, our habits can attract deception, selfishness and covetousness. But through a personal relationship with God, daily prayers, reading His Word and experiencing the presence of the Holy Spirit in our lives, our Heavenly Father can sweep away our mental cobwebs.

Lord, have mercy on us all. Clean the weeds and the webs of sin from our lives, and give us Your heart. Amen.

Lama Garvey is an elder at the Hackettstown church in New Jersey.

How I 'Log in' to God

"So do not fear, for I am with you; do not be dismayed, for I am your God. I will strengthen you and help you; I will uphold you with My righteous right hand" (Isa. 41:10, NIV).

College is a hard time for most young adults. Personally, that period of my life was lonely and discouraging, full of seemingly endless work on top of regular everyday life while figuring out how to be and act like an adult.

In 2017, the American College Health Association conducted a survey of nearly 48,000 college students that revealed 64 percent felt "very lonely" and 62 percent felt "overwhelming anxious" within the previous 12 months. For some students, college is just a bunch of lonely people together.

My university required passwords that needed to be constantly reset, so I picked Bible verses to log in; they included numbers and easily fit the requirements of nondictionary words. Throw in a few special characters, and voila! Plus, it was a nice way to incorporate pick-me-up scripture verses throughout my day. Thus, I came to know Isaiah 41:10:

"Do not fear"—a command and a common negative emotion.

"For I am with you"—a rationale encouraging us that we are not alone.

"Do not be dismayed, for I am your God"—a reminder we need to hear again and again.

"I will strengthen you and help you"—a promise.

"I will uphold you with My righteous right hand"—a hope and security.

Let this verse be the password you need to log in for a more confident life moving onward and upward with Christ.

God, thank You for being my password. Amen.

Jasmine Jiao Valenti is a member of the Capital Chinese church in Maryland.

The Prayer Under the Umbrella

"For with God all things are possible" (Mark 10:27, KJV).

My husband and I received a call to be Bible workers in Florida. We rented a moving trailer and car carrier for our trip. On our moving day, it started to rain, and because our car sat low to the ground, we had trouble getting it onto the carrier. The moving company upgraded the carrier so that the whole car could go on top instead of just the front wheels.

For a half hour, the church's head elder and I watched under an umbrella as my husband tried to drive the car onto the carrier. Seeing this, the gentleman from the moving company said, "It is impossible; you will never get the car on the carrier."

I asked, "What did you say?"

He repeated, "You will never get that car on that carrier!"

I immediately motioned to my husband to join the elder and me under the umbrella. I relayed to him what the employee had said. My husband looked at me and agreed, "Yes, I know that!"

I encouraged, "Well, we believe it is God's will for us to go to Florida to be Bible workers, and with God all things are possible, so let's pray."

Right after, my husband got in the car and drove it right onto the carrier.

Bewildered, the man questioned, "How in the world did you do that?"

Smiling, I said, "With God all things are possible, so we prayed, and He sent His angels to help."

Lord, when confronted with difficult situations, remind us that You always come through. Amen.

Elaine Buchanan is a Bible worker for the Cumberland church in Maryland.

Walk With God

"And Enoch walked with God; and he was not, for God took him"
(Gen. 5:24, NKJV).

As a child, I was desperate to know more about God. From what I can remember, I was introduced to God in grade school by neighbors. I proceeded to invite myself to many different church denominations with several of my neighbors and relatives. Looking back, I realize something was missing in my life, and I believe that, even as children, the Holy Spirit works to draw us closer to God.

Since the time I was baptized into the Seventh-day Adventist Church as a teenager, I must admit my faith has teetered. I finally embraced the fact that having a daily scheduled time with God is imperative to my survival. Satan knows that if he can distract us from time spent with God, our relationship with God will surely suffer. Reading the Bible and communing with God adds peace when diversions encircle me. Living out Genesis 5:24 has helped me to grow spiritually, and it secured my devotion and unwavering trust in God.

Enoch did not live in seclusion, but he purposely sought God's will in every aspect of his life. Decades later, my "daily" time has turned to a joyous moment by moment walk with God. As we believe we are living in the last days, let us remain focused and embrace a relationship with an all-powerful Father who cares about every aspect of our lives.

God, You desire to walk with each one of us and communicate just how much You love us, so may we share with You our joys, sorrows and fears. Amen.

Carla Benjamin is a member of the Seabrook church in Maryland.

Hope Is Found in the Next Chapter

"That where I am, there you may be also" (John 14:1, NKJV).

One of my favorite passages begins in John 13. Peter loves Jesus so much that he believes he would never fail Him.

In this story, Jesus says He will be with the disciples only a little while longer. The disciples are distraught by these words, which leads Peter to say, "Lord, where are You going?" Jesus replies, "Where I am going you cannot follow Me now, but you shall follow me afterward" (John 13:36, NKJV).

In verse 37, Peter passionately responds, "Lord, why can I not follow You now? I will lay down my life for Your sake." Jesus replies, "Will you lay down your life for My sake? Most assuredly, I say to you, the rooster shall not crow till you have denied Me three times" (verse 38).

Peter thought He was walking so closely with Jesus that he would never fail Him, but Jesus makes it clear that Peter, who is relying on his own commitment and strength, was going to deny Him three times.

Like Peter, I have felt strong in my faith and commitment, only to later fall and hang my head in shame. *Fortunately, this passage does not end here.* When the Bible was written, it did not include chapter and verse divisions. These were added later by translators. This means that chapter 14 is a continuous thought from chapter 13.

Jesus continues, "Let not your heart be troubled. ... I go to make a place for you [in heaven]. ... [and] will come again" (Luke 14:1–3, NKJV). Jesus was determined to save Peter, and I praise God He is determined to save you and me.

Lord, help us to stay close to You and never leave Your side. Amen.

Mike Hewitt is the president of the Mountain View Conference.

Pray With Confidence

**"Likewise the Spirit also helps in our weaknesses.
For we do not know what we should pray for as we ought,
but the Spirit Himself makes intercession for us with
groanings which cannot be uttered" (Rom. 8:26, NKJV).**

My prayer time often goes like this: I close my eyes and try to talk to the Father, but the words that come out feel forced and meaningless. I try to apologize for all of the sins I have committed, but it never feels genuine. I try to tell God about my problems and express all of my emotions, but there are some things that just cannot be said. I find myself distracted by other things of life, and I often give up. I just stop talking. If the words I say don't mean anything, why say them? I feel so confused, weak and separated from God.

When this happens, I find comfort in Romans 8:26. The Holy Spirit understands that some things are just too deep and meaningful to say out loud. When I don't know what to say, the Holy Spirit intercedes for me. The Spirit knows exactly what I am trying to say. By this, I am able to connect with the Lord. The Spirit helps me pray.

So now when I pray, I pray with confidence that God will know what I am trying to say, and He will listen to me. This verse helps me feel less alone in my walk with God. It provides comfort when I feel separated from Him, and for that, I am thankful.

God, when I don't know what to say in my prayers, say it for me. I trust in You. Amen.

Beka Shull is a freshman at Spring Valley Academy in Ohio.

Where Moth and Rust Can't Destroy

"Let not your heart be troubled: ye believe in God, believe also in Me. In My Father's house are many mansions: if it were not so, I would have told you. I go to prepare a place for you. And if I go and prepare a place for you, I will come again, and receive you unto Myself; that where I am, there ye may be also" (John 14:1–3, KJV).

These are very trying times that we live in, with the COVID-19 pandemic, as well as the racial pandemic that has always existed. This world is not my home, I am just passing through, but how am I to pass through without being affected by the things that are going on around me? I have heard many times that no man is an island. That is when I remember these verses which give me a promise, a hope and a future.

This promise assures me that Jesus said I should not worry about anything, including COVID-19, racial tensions, buying a home, family issues, health problems and so on. Why should I not be concerned? Because He is preparing a mansion for me. All I have to do is to trust Him and believe what He says, because He does not lie. He is the Author and Finisher of my faith.

Whenever I feel like I'm losing control, I need to remember His promise: "Let not your heart be troubled." Do I always remember? No. But He who has promised will indeed never leave me nor forsake me.

I have hope that "He that shall come will come, and will not tarry" (Heb. 10:37, KJV). I believe in the heavenly dream that moth and rust cannot destroy.

Thank You, God, that my future is hidden in the One who holds this world in the palm of His hand. Amen.

Winifred Hylton is the receptionist at the Columbia Union Conference.

Our Refuge and Strength

**"God is our refuge and strength, a very present help in trouble"
(Ps. 46:1, NKJV).**

I greatly appreciate the words of Psalm 46:1 that promise that our God is a very present help in times of trouble. We think in terms of being present or absent. Here we are reminded that God is very present in those times when we have no other hope. Somehow, God manifests Himself in a special way just when we need Him the most. We have those times when we need Him to sustain us. Often in health care and spiritual care, the people we minister to find themselves in very serious situations — even the loss of loved ones.

I am so thankful that even in those terrible times, we can point people to a God who is very present. My prayer today is that we always know that God is with us.

Father God, even in the most difficult times, may we will always remember that You are very present. Amen.

Ron Swiger is the chaplain of Greene Memorial Hospital for the Kettering Adventist HealthCare in Ohio.

The Trouble With Rearview Mirrors

"Remember Lot's wife" (Luke 17:32, KJV).

I was introduced to the mirrors on my father's car at the age of 16 while learning to drive. There were side mirrors and a mirror in front called the rearview mirror. When properly adjusted, the twin left and right mirrors allowed me to see advancing vehicles on either side. But it was the vehicle's rearview mirror that permitted me to see objects through the back windshield. I quickly learned the value of this mirror in spotting objects to my rear, especially when parking. But I also discovered I could not drive the vehicle forward if I lingered viewing what was in the rearview mirror. Driving forward required that my vision remained fixed on what lay ahead.

Perhaps three of the most powerful words in Scripture lie in the verse above. They have kept me grounded over the years: "Remember Lot's wife." Lot, his wife and two daughters were given the opportunity to flee Sodom before its destruction. Genesis 19:17 gives the directive: "Look not behind thee" (KJV). But the allure of life in Sodom was not something Mrs. Lot could leave behind. She did not fix her vision on a better life ahead. One look to her rear resulted in her death.

The question for us is, are we learning to look to the future? Or are we allowing the trappings of this world to linger in our rear view? Fixing our eyes on Jesus is the only answer. His plans are so much greater than our own. Lot's wife missed her opportunity. Let us not miss ours. Remember Lot's wife.

Father, thank You for Your Word and its instruction for daily living. May we apply these words to our hearts. Amen.

Yvonne Curry Smallwood is a member of the First church in Washington, D.C.

Open My Eyes

"And Elisha prayed, and said, 'Lord, I pray, open his eyes that he may see.' Then the Lord opened the eyes of the young man, and he saw. And behold, the mountain was full of horses and chariots of fire all around Elisha" (2 Kings 6:17, NKJV).

Early in his childhood, my friend Igor was often corrected for his inability to name colors. It wasn't until elementary school that he learned he was color blind, a condition that affects one in 12 men and one in 200 women in the world. Later in life, he found it difficult to accomplish basic responsibilities like shopping for clothes. Driving was also a challenge, as he could not distinguish red from green.

However, on June 8, 2020, Igor's life forever changed. The youth group from the Hackettstown church gathered to witness him try on his color blindness-correction glasses for the first time. As the sky was set ablaze with the setting sun, Igor's eyes detected the full spectrum of wavelengths from the electromagnetic radiation. Tears flowed down his cheeks, as he exclaimed, "It is so red!" and "Are these leaves really this green?"

In the time of prophet Elisha, the Syrian army's horses and chariots surrounded the city of Dothan. Paralyzed with fear, the prophet prayed that God would open his eyes to behold the chariots of fire. Like Elisha, Igor could not see the beautiful sunset—"the chariots of fire"—until his eyes were opened.

God and His fiery angel chariots are always surrounding us, and we can witness them in full grandeur if we allow Him to open our eyes.

Dear God, please open my eyes to witness You at work today! Amen.

Stephen Lee is the pastor of the Tranquility, Phillipsburg and Hackettstown churches in New Jersey.

Through it All

"For I consider that the sufferings of this present time are not worth comparing with the glory that is to be revealed to us" (Rom. 8:18, ESV).

This is one of my favorite verses in the Bible because of the comfort it has brought me. In my life, I have struggled with mental health issues. These struggles can vary from mild anxiety and discomfort to full-on breakdowns and fearing for what the future holds. Will I ever get better? Will this ever go away? How can I possibly cope with these fears? These are the questions that swarm my mind during these hopeless periods in my life.

For someone who doesn't struggle with obsessive-compulsive disorder, these thoughts and worries, as disturbing as they seem, can be shrugged off, often without a second thought. But for someone like me, they can seem unbearable and unavoidable. This verse comforts me, because Paul is basically saying, "Hey you! I know these times seem hard, and I know you may feel like giving up. But God has a plan for you, and the glory that he has firmly planted in your future is so wonderful that these bad times don't even hold a candle to it!"

This is coming from a man who was shipwrecked, thrown in prison and persecuted throughout his life. And he overcame, even when all seemed hopeless. That is comforting to me.

God loves every single person on earth. He is always in control, including the times that seem to be out of control. When all seems hopeless, He holds us in His loving hands through it all.

Thank You, God, for being such a good and loving Father. Amen.

Robert Air is a pseudonym for this member from the Spencerville church in Maryland.

More Than Enough

"And He said to me, 'My grace is sufficient for you, for My strength is made perfect in weakness'" (2 Cor. 12:9, NKJV).

Some years back, I was tasked with a responsibility of which I felt ill-prepared. The only reason I took it was because I knew that God put me there in the first place, and I didn't dare walk away!

I was scared to death to take on this task. There were important things for which I would be responsible, dealing with people that I didn't know and systems that I didn't understand. I felt like Moses when God told him to go back to Egypt and deal with Pharaoh to deliver the Israelites.

As I began to put this whole new journey daily at His feet, I began to throw all of my other things there as well. I've always trusted God, but this was in a whole new way. The more I gave Him, the more he showed me how dependent I was upon Him and how much He could do for me. As I began to acclimate to this elevated way of living, I felt wonderful as I watched God intercede for me daily. Sometimes I got comfortable and would relax a bit, then would get blindsided by something I never saw coming! In those moments, I felt I had to start all over. Me and God. But it was during these times, when I was at my worst, that He showed me how awesome He was.

When you feel you aren't good enough, smart enough or just enough, know that this is when God is getting ready to show up big time, and you'll be more than enough for whatever the situation.

Thank You, Lord, for showing up big time in my life. Amen.

Valerie W. Green is the principal of Worthington Adventist Academy in Ohio.

Accepting God's Love

"And we have known and believed the love that God has for us. God is love, and he who abides in love abides in God" (1 John 4:16, NKJV).

A lifelong Seventh-day Adventist, I periodically glossed over the fundamentals of Christianity while claiming status as a mature believer. A drive home after my junior year of college commenced my reform.

My semester had been challenging. God provided, but the limits of human strength, which I usually ignored, were now blatant. Guilt over personal imperfections flourished as I wrestled with a toxic family relationship. A visiting relative's objections to God—and my insecure response—completed my spiritual crisis prerequisites.

Driving home one afternoon, I turned on the radio and encountered a sermon explaining God's love. How basic, I thought. What more could I learn about something I had known about all my life?

Nearing home, I listened until I pulled into the garage. I turned off the radio, and, unexpectedly, started crying. Gradually, the Holy Spirit revealed why: I no longer believed in God's love.

Misconceptions about God's nature had convinced me that I was irreparably unlovable. The belief, though common, is dangerous. Not accepting "the love God has for us" means that we cannot value ourselves and others properly. We cannot discern God's direction. And we cannot, in these last days, obey out of love and not fear. "I desire a true relationship," God was saying, "let us remedy your unbelief now."

Describing the resultant growth as arduous would be an understatement. But by clinging to 1 John 4:16, and reflecting on Jesus' sacrifice—love's ultimate expression—my faith strengthened. May yours too.

Lord, mature us as we abide in Your daily, unconditional love. Amen.

Yasmin Phillip is a member of the New Market church in Virginia.

A Faithful Walk

"For we walk by faith, not by sight" (2 Cor. 5:7, NKJV).

This may look like a simple verse. It contains only eight words, but certain carefully-chosen words put together can be very powerful. "We walk by faith" means we can't get through life alone. We choose to follow God and live for Him. The earth is not all sunshine and rainbows; it's also filled with sin and mistakes. Sin is our natural instinct, and we don't always mess up on purpose. But if we do mess up, we trust that God will lead us back to the right path after getting lost in our temptations.

If we choose to live a life led by what we see, we wouldn't have hope, we wouldn't be happy and we wouldn't have a purpose. Living a life by sight makes us blind and invites death and distractions.

God told Noah to build an ark, and by faith he did. Blinded by the fact the community had never seen rain before, they did not allow God to open their eyes to see the bigger picture. Faith makes us strong—stronger than we could ever be on our own. Faith gives us hope.

Lord, when we are tempted to see life through our eyes, may we walk by faith. Amen.

Megan Shull is a freshman at Spring Valley Academy in Ohio.

My Darkest Hour

"Then Samuel took a stone and set it up between Mizpah and Shen, and called its name Ebenezer, saying, 'Thus far the Lord has helped us'" (1 Sam. 7:12, NKJV).

From age 7, this was my favorite Bible verse, never knowing how it would carry me through the darkest period of my life, when a trusted friend and colleague tried to destroy me as a pastor with false allegations.

In this dark crisis, I felt as if I was suffocating. Oxygen seemed to seep from my lungs. Moment after moment seemed to go by slower and slower. Time stood still and became an enemy. Insomnia was my new reality, as sleep fled from me. Thus, daily I became more fatigued, as my life was drained from me. There are not many things in life that are so vicious and destructive to one's emotions and well-being as the anxiety and stress within and after trauma.

Even though I sought medical and professional help and was supported by family and friends, it was God who brought me through this deep and painful valley. I clung to the promise that "thus far the Lord has helped us," and He would not forsake me now. He helped me in the past; therefore, he would help me in the present, no matter how dark it was. This imbued me with hope, in that, even if the future seemed dim, God would help me.

I can testify that God kept His Word! He helped me, and today I can help others going through similar trauma.

Father God, thank You for promising that, as You have helped me in the past, You will help me in the present and future. Amen.

Reinhardt Stander is the pastor of the Williamsport church in Maryland.

His Strength Is Perfect

"That is why, for Christ's sake, I delight in weaknesses,
in insults, in hardships, in persecutions, in difficulties.
For when I am weak, then I am strong" (2 Cor. 12:10, NIV).

The reason this verse resonates with me so much is because it reassures me that it's OK to have faults. I think that sometimes, as Christians, there is a misconception that we have to put on a brave face at all times. When I read this verse, it reminds me that we can come to Jesus just as we are. There is no need to pretend like we have life all figured out or that we don't have problems.

A few years ago, I lost someone very close to me in a car accident. It was the hardest thing I had ever experienced, and it forced me to grow up very quickly. For a long time after it happened, I felt like I had to hide my feelings. For whatever reason, I felt like I wasn't allowed to be sad.

I had never before felt such a constant need for Jesus. It was like I could hear Him calling out to me and telling me that He was there to help me. However, I had a very hard time telling Him about my situation. I didn't feel He could do anything that would help that horrible feeling go away. It was during this time that I discovered 2 Corinthians 12:10.

I discovered that it is in those moments, when it feels like the world is falling all around you, that God's strength is revealed the most. He gives us strength to meet every challenge with courage and trust.

Dear Lord, thank You for giving us strength. Thank You that we don't have to feel alone, because You are with us. Amen.

Samantha Armstrong is a 2020 graduate of Shenandoah Valley Academy in Virginia.

Just Let Go

"Therefore humble yourselves under the mighty hand of God, that He may exalt you in due time, casting all your care upon Him, for He cares for you" (1 Pet. 5:6–7, NKJV).

This verse has deeply impacted my life, especially when I turn my cares, anxieties, worries and concerns over to God. I have a reminder on my phone with this verse, and I contemplate and pray it every morning. Being reminded daily that He affectionately cares and closely watches over me helps me grasp that there is nothing that gets past His loving attention.

I am amazed how often I move forward in my own "wisdom." Could it be that I do not want to pester God? Maybe it is because I am impatient.

When I broke my ankle, I had no choice but to see a specialist who could diagnose me and offer a solution. Never having surgery before, I felt my most important need was to pray over the procedure. After my plea to God, I had peace that He would be attending my surgery—the peace that comes from letting go and laying all of my burdens at the foot of the cross.

God Almighty, our El Shaddai, it is such a relief to know that You are the only One who truly understands and meets our needs. We praise You for Your care. Amen.

Rhonda Gadway is a member of the Mount Vernon Hill church in Ohio.

'Mommy, Where's Papaw?'

"Behold, I tell you a mystery: We shall not all sleep, but we shall all be changed—in a moment, in the twinkling of an eye, at the last trumpet. For the trumpet will sound, and the dead will be raised incorruptible, and we shall be changed. For this corruptible must put on incorruption, and this mortal must put on immortality. So when this corruptible has put on incorruption, and this mortal has put on immortality, then shall be brought to pass the saying that is written: 'Death is swallowed up in victory'" (1 Cor. 15:51–54, NKJV).

For me, this is one of the greatest promises of the Bible. It breaks our hearts to see our family members pass away, our pets die and our children ask the question all parents dread: "Mommy, where is Papaw?"

As Paul helps us to understand that death is a sleep, he calls it a mystery. He announces that we will all be changed at the last trumpet. And when it sounds, those whom we have lost will live again—and forever.

God did not create humankind to eventually die. He created us to be immortal—life without an end. On that glorious day, it will be true what is written: "Death [will be] swallowed up in victory." You can count on it, because the Bible tells me so.

Dear Heavenly Father, thank You that one day soon we will all be changed in the twinkling of an eye to live with You forever. Amen.

Larry Murphy is the director of Adventist Community Services for the Mountain View Conference.

Self-Control Honors God

"He said to his men, 'The Lord forbid that I should do such a thing to my master, the Lord's anointed, or lay my hand on him; for he is the anointed of the Lord'" (1 Sam. 24:6, NIV).

To be kind to someone who treats us badly is probably the hardest thing to do. When someone hurts you, the first thing you think of is to plan out your revenge. It takes self-control to honor God by learning to "turn the other cheek."

Saul was the king of Israel, but he turned his back on God, and God chose someone else to be king. God picked David to be Israel's king while he was still a boy. This made Saul very angry. Once Saul realized that he had lost his favor with God and that David would be king, he wanted to destroy David.

Saul, who was anointed by God, was in harm's way too. Twice David had the opportunity to kill him. However, both times David chose to use self-control, sparing Saul's life and honoring him as king. David could have disobeyed God's promise and killed Saul, but he knew in his heart that it was not right.

We, too, have the opportunity to display self-control when dealing with others. We honor God by doing what is right instead of following our impulses. We must approach all of our relationships with self-control and compassion, just as David modeled in the story.

Dear Father in Heaven, please help us to learn self-control and honor You in everything we do. Help us to model Your compassion toward others. Amen.

Giselle Landgrover is an eighth-grader at Vienna Adventist Academy in Virginia.

Because He Loves Us So Much

**"Trust in the Lord with all your heart, and do not rely
on your own insight. In all your ways acknowledge Him, and
He will make straight your paths" (Prov. 3:5-6, RSV).**

Have you ever wondered what or who specifically helps us survive? In the story of Elijah and the ravens, King Ahab chases Elijah to kill him. God sends Elijah to a nearby brook, and He commands ravens to feed exhausted Elijah and provide water to quench his thirst.

When God's people wandered in the wilderness, they whined and fussed about having to walk for 40 years in the desert, but God still cared for them. Their clothes didn't wear out, and their feet did not swell. He provided manna, quail and sweet water so that they had food to eat and drink. He guided them with the cloud by day and the pillar of fire by night.

In the story of Elijah and the widow, God provided flour and oil in the middle of a drought because of her faith.

In the story of Jesus' birth, God provided salvation to all mankind because He loves us so much. Even though we are disobedient to Him, He still has those arms open, inviting everyone to come back to Him. When we think everything is about to fall apart, He is right there, giving us just what we need to survive in this world.

Father in Heaven, thank You for everything You give us to survive. Without You, we would not exist, period. Help us to trust You more. Amen.

Najely Zuniga is a seventh-grader at the Harrisburg Adventist School in Pennsylvania.

Rivers of Difficulty

"When you go through deep waters, I will be with you. When you go through rivers of difficulty, you will not drown" (Isa. 43:2, NLT).

Thoughts swirled around in my head as the cold water from the Ocoee River in Tennessee swirled around my body. *I need to breathe! How do I get out? Oh Jesus, help me. I don't want to die yet.* This whitewater rafting adventure had quickly turned from fun to frightening when our raft went up a rock, and we fell out.

As I was being swept down the river, I remember yelling to my friend that I could not swim. Suddenly, I got sucked into a whirlpool from which I could not escape on my own power. The situation looked grim, as there was no one close enough to pull me out of the rapids that are normally rated 3, but were more dangerous after the previous day's heavy rainfall. When I thought I could not hold my breath any longer, something seemed to push me from underneath, forcing my head to pop out above the surface of the surging river. Soon I was hauled to safety with a rope thrown by the staff.

What whirlpools do you feel stuck in right now? Whatever "rivers of difficulty" you are passing through, God promises in His Word that He will be with you. Even though the situation might seem grim from your viewpoint, God promises that "you will not drown." I am so glad we serve a God who holds the power over the deep waters of our souls and the difficult rivers of life. His promises never fail.

Dear God, thank You so much for promising to be with me, protecting me when I journey through deep waters and difficult rivers in my life. Amen.

Alissa Tanguay is a member of the Williamsport church in West Virginia.

Unlimited, Unmerited Love

"I am crucified with Christ: nevertheless I live; yet not I, but Christ liveth in me: and the life which I now live in the flesh I live by the faith of the Son of God, who loved me, and gave himself for me" (Gal. 2:20, KJV).

When I became a Christian, I felt that this verse was the perfect summary of my salvation experience. Before I understood my redemption in Christ, I was living under a huge burden of trying to be accepted by God. I never felt good enough for Him to accept me as a candidate for heaven. I was lonely and depressed.

Then, one day I had an awakening. The Holy Spirit activated the Word to clearly tell me that Christ died personally for me. Salvation was all His doing. I am accepted because Jesus took my sins and gave me His righteousness. Now, every day I asked for this salvation anew. Hence, I am crucified with Christ. I am no longer lonely, for I am not alone.

By His unlimited, unmerited love, Christ gave me His Spirit and made me His friend. He is faithful to hold me, keep me and love me. He is the beginning and the end—the Author and Finisher of my faith. Because He lives in me, I can overcome in His grace, for He assures my salvation— yesterday, today and forever.

Lord, thank You that You loved me, You love me today and that You will always love me. Amen.

Antoinette Franke is a member of the Mansfield church in Ohio.

Take a Stand

**"'Teacher, which is the greatest commandment in the Law?'
Jesus replied: 'Love the Lord your God with all your heart and
with all your soul and with all your mind.' This is the first and
greatest commandment. And the second is like it: 'Love your
neighbor as yourself'" (Matt. 22:36–39, NIV).**

In 2020, I performed with Takoma Academy's chorale at the Capitol Hill
church in Washington, D.C. Earlier that week, I had celebrated my 16th
birthday. But sadly, I lost a family member the next day. I walked into
church that Sabbath with intense emotions.

The sermon was on being a community, and, during the appeal, I decided
to take a stand! I took a risk because I stopped caring about other people's
opinions. My friend Elli'ette Hicks and I walked to the front of the church.
Some deacons and leaders escorted us to a room and held us with
comforting arms. We took their hands and prayed together. The prayer
brought us to tears. That powerful feeling brought me closer to God. This
experience, in a church I had never been to, changed my life.

Three years previous to this, I had resorted to extremes to please others.
This negatively affected my happiness, health and other aspects of my life.
My "take a stand" experience showed me that God's love is always with me,
and He tells me how much I'm worth—a whole lot.

I've learned through the years that loving others isn't easy, but it pays off,
and self love is necessary for me to love others. Matthew 22:36–39 has kept
me grounded in Him. These verses remind me that God loves me and wants
me to spread His love to others.

*Dear God, please help me to grow in Your love. As I share Your love with others,
may it have a positive impact in their lives, as it has in mine. Amen.*

Valerie Ganta is a sophomore at Takoma Academy in Maryland.

'In Remembrance of Me'

**"Take, eat; this is My body which is broken for you;
do this in remembrance of Me" (1 Cor. 11:24, NKJV).**

I woke up this morning with "The Lord's Last Supper" on my mind. We participate in this ceremony once a quarter, but do we really think about its meaning? Does it stimulate our remembrance of Christ?

For me, the Lord's Supper reminds me that God is the Sustainer of our lives. We are not self-sustaining; a loving God provides for us. We are dependent on Him, not just as our Creator but our Redeemer. With the inability to save ourselves, God sent His Son, Jesus Christ, to earth to die for our sins that we might be saved. We rely on Christ, the Bread of Life, to sustain us physically and spiritually.

Moreover, the Lord's Supper also reminds me about the assurance of God's forgiveness and pardon. As a result of Christ's death for me on the cross, He, my Advocate, even goes before His Father and pleads for me to be cleansed and forgiven!

Yes, my heart rejoices because the Lord's Supper sums up the totality of the Gospel, for John 3:16 says: "For God so loved the world that He gave His only begotten Son, that whoever believes in Him, should not perish but have everlasting life" (NKJV). Jesus gave us His righteousness, and His blood cleanses us of all sins. By His stripes we are healed.

Father God, thank You for loving us so much that You were willing to send Jesus to die on the cross so that we could live with You eternally. Amen.

Rosita Dee is a member of the Capital Chinese church in Maryland.

"Blessed are the peacemakers, for they will be called children of God."
MATT. 5:9, NIV

OCTOBER

Choose to Scroll

"For we do not have a High Priest who cannot sympathize with our weaknesses, but was in all points tempted as we are, yet without sin" (Heb. 4:15, NKJV).

I don't know about you, but sometimes I think it is impossible to not sin. Temptations come my way, and many times I give in to them. The thing is, when a temptation pops into my head, I tend to think I have already sinned, but nothing could be further from the truth.

For example, say I'm scrolling through Instagram and something unholy comes up in my feed. I have a choice: to keep looking at it or scroll away? In this analogy, the Instagram post is a temptation. But did I already sin if I decide to keep scrolling? No! I decided to not cherish that thought, and instead looked for something more holy.

Remember that Jesus was tempted in every way that we have been tempted, but He never once sinned! He "chose to scroll." And He has the power to help you overcome any temptation.

Ellen White says that Christ "knows by experience what are the weaknesses of humanity, what are our wants, and where lies the strength of our temptations" (*The Desire of Ages*, p. 329).

We must keep the Word of God in our hearts at all times so that we can overcome the temptations of the devil (Psalm 119:11). Whenever you are tempted, think on holy things to conquer the desire to sin.

Father, help us keep Your Word in our hearts so that we can overcome Satan's temptations! Amen.

Matthew Ullom is a junior at Blue Mountain Academy in Pennsylvania.

Giver of All

**"So Israel took his journey with all that he had,
and came to Beersheba, and offered sacrifices to
the God of his father Isaac" (Gen. 46:1, NKJV).**

This journey occurred after Joseph revealed himself to his brothers in Egypt. Jacob was living in Canaan when he heard the good news: His "dead" son was still alive! And the ruler of Egypt! As Jacob traveled to Egypt, he arrived at Beersheba, where the first thing he did was offer sacrifices to God in worship. His circumstances were changing right before his very own eyes, and he didn't take these blessings for granted. He honored the One who was working behind the scenes.

Our lives can change from doom to gloom overnight. God can arrange circumstances to give us a better life, a better education, a better job. Like Jacob, let us remember to worship the One who is worthy of our praise. Ask God to help you worship Him in all things, and give Him glory for working in our behalf.

Dear God, thank You for Your many blessings in my life. Forgive me when I forget that everything I have comes from You. Please help me to recognize You as the Giver of all. Amen.

Jose Luis Espinoza Vasquez is the pastor of the Morgantown Spanish church in West Virginia.

Fear Not

"Fear not, for I am with you; be not dismayed, for I am your God. I will strengthen you. Yes, I will help you, I will uphold you with My righteous right hand" (Isa. 41:10, NKJV).

I heard this verse many times when I was a toddler—in the Bible, in Sabbath School and on TV—but it didn't impact me until last year.

It was the summer before sixth grade, and almost every night I would wake up with fear and anxiety about the upcoming school year. In fifth grade, I didn't make very good grades, which led to problems. I made excuses, using my ADHD as a cover, but my parents knew that my condition was not that bad.

But this time, my anxiety kept me up so much that my doctor started to recommend medicine for it. But instead of taking medicine, my mom and I would pray, "Dear Jesus, please take away my fear. Put it into Your hands, and let me be comforted by You." Now, whenever I am afraid, I pray to God and ask for His help.

I love this verse because I think it was meant for me and other high-anxiety individuals who need to be reassured and comforted. It lets you know that God is there and has your back. It gives you confidence that God will hold you up.

If you have a serious medical condition, please take medicine to heal your body. But if you have a spiritual condition that needs a boost, take God to heal your soul.

Thank You, God, for always being with us and helping us. Amen.

Danielle Maloney is a seventh-grader at the Tree of Life Christian Preparatory School in Virginia.

God Cares

"Casting all your care upon Him; for He careth for you"
(1 Pet. 5:7, KJV).

When I was growing up, memory verses were a fact of life. There are still dozens of them tucked away in my head. Oftentimes, they come back to mind at moments when they are most appreciated, like today's verse.

There is no shortage of things to worry about—and most of us have a pretty long list. Our health, kids, parents, co-workers, the economy, getting older, how we look, the future, being loved and accepted, job performance, safety, diet. Did I list anything you worry about?

This verse contains both a command and a promise. The command is to cast your cares upon God. It's not a suggestion, it's not an invitation, it's not something you give consideration to as an alternative to carrying the burdens yourself. It's a command: Cast your cares. Give those worries to God to carry for you. Don't just consider it—do it.

The promise is even better: He cares for you. There are no exceptions; in every situation, He cares for you. There is no one for whom He does not care. And it's not just that He loves the whole world—it's personal: He cares for you.

This verse is especially meaningful to Adventist HealthCare, whose mission is to extend God's care through the ministry of physical, mental and spiritual healing. It tells us that God is at work to make our efforts to reflect His care effective, and that He seeks to make this work a joy, not a burden. And it reminds us that every individual we serve is a person that God cares for—that no one is ever outside of His love and grace.

God, in 1 Peter 5:7, You give us a command and promise. May we follow and believe. Amen.

Terry Forde is the president and CEO of Adventist HealthCare in Maryland.

A Message From God— Your Creator

"I will praise You, for I am fearfully and wonderfully made; marvelous are Your works, and that my soul knows very well" (Ps. 139:14, NKJV).

Dear Child,

You delight me! I love you because I made you! I crafted you as my masterpiece. Every fabric of your being was meticulously made by Me. You are beautiful and priceless, because My hands create masterpieces.

My child, you worry too much about vanity and earthly possessions, but I am coming back to make you new—to fully restore you. Therefore, why do these things matter? Let go of your worldly worries for a moment and bask in My precious presence. I created you to enjoy My peace, My joy, My love!

No matter how unsteady your emotions are right now, My love for you is constant. Because of sin, your emotions tend to blur your vision of who I made you to be and how valuable you are to Me. Read Psalm 139:14 again and again to remind yourself that I created you and am at work in your life. Do not allow your emotions or feelings to alter your perspective of who I truly am, who you truly are designed to be and what I have truly done for you.

Keep in mind that everyone is My creation. Let me continue to do the marvelous in your life by allowing Me to be your Master, Friend, Teacher, Father and Creator.

I Love You!

Your Maker and Forever Friend, God

God, thank You for the Bible—Your love letter to us. Amen.

Ava Gruia is an eighth-grader at Spring Valley Academy in Ohio.

No Need to Fear

**"For God has not given us a spirit of fear, but of power
and of love and of a sound mind" (2 Tim. 1:7, NKJV).**

As I prepared for a final exam during my senior year of college, I became overwhelmed with worry about how I would do. My degree would be in Early Childhood Education, so I sought my grandmother Helen's guidance, since she was a retired teacher. She comforted me with this Bible verse and spoke of the many times she turned to it in times of fear. It's been more than 20 years since this conversation, and I still hide these words in my heart.

Referencing this verse, the *Seventh-day Adventist Bible Commentary (SDABC)* says, "Genuine Christianity doesn't produce cowards" (vol. 7, p. 329).

I've often reminded my daughter that fear and faith cannot share space in our heart. Faith is a gift from God, and He gives it abundantly. When doubt and fear surface in our minds, it's a relief to rely on verses like 2 Timothy 1:7. God's spirit of love "will carry us through the opposition we may meet with. It will set us above the fear of man and all the hurt that man can do to us" (*SDABC*, p. 329).

In a world that is often filled with chaos and confusion, it's reassuring to know that, not only is Jesus' pattern an example of how to move through our days with power united with love, but also with the opportunity to use the good sense God gave us.

Thank You, God, for alleviating all of our fears. Amen.

Alison Jobson is the associate director of early childhood education for the Columbia Union Conference.

The Law of Attraction

"And, behold, one came and said unto Him, Good Master, what good thing shall I do, that I may have eternal life? ... Jesus said unto him, If thou wilt be perfect, go and sell that thou hast, and give to the poor, and thou shalt have treasure in heaven: and come and follow Me. But when the young man heard that saying, he went away sorrowful: for he had great possessions" (Matt. 19:16, 21–22, KJV).

Letting go of his possessions and reaching his hand to grasp what Jesus offered was too high a cost for the rich young ruler to pay for the free gift of eternal life. And while Jesus didn't tell the young man to go, He didn't beg him to stay either.

Jesus was called to do His Father's will. Whoever ministered with Him over time became an unselfish servant for the poor and needy. The influence of His life had the power to repel anyone who was not willing to give everything to live for God's glory and humanity's uplifting.

A magnet's power to attract is only as strong as its power to repel. What do you want to attract to your life? You have to be willing to repel the opposite. If you want to attract grace, you have to be OK with repelling legalism. If you want to attract excellence, you have to repel mediocrity. Many make the mistake of wanting to be liked by everybody, and run the risk of being truly valued by nobody; of trying to have everything and ending up with next to nothing.

Know what God has in store for your life. Purpose in your heart to have it at any cost. And be OK with the force your life generates to repel the opposite.

God, may I attract You and repel evil. Amen.

Anthony C. Burrell is the pastor of the New Hope church plant in West Virginia.

Never Too Young to Share

**"If I give all I possess to the poor and give over my
body to hardship that I may boast, but do not have love,
I gain nothing" (1 Cor. 13:3, NIV).**

Seven-year-old me always prayed before lunch, even though I was in a
public school. I never realized that my friends noticed. Sometimes they
would ask, "What are you doing?"

"Praying," I'd respond. "I have to thank God for my food." I remember
bits and pieces about what I told them. "Jesus is God's Son. God created
the earth and everything in it. Including you. And Jesus came to earth
as a baby, but when He got older, He died for us. Because He died, God
forgives all of the bad things we do, but only if we say sorry."

After a couple weeks, I caught my friends praying before eating. Every
now and then, one would ask if I had prayed, because sometimes I forgot.
Even though I moved schools and didn't keep in touch with them, I hope
my younger self's words made them realize that the one true God will
always care for them.

*Dear God, please help me continue to spread Your words, and be with those
who hear me. Open people's hearts so that they may come to You. Be with
me so that I may do the right things. Please help everyone in need of Your
guidance, and, if it is Your will, use me; You say that no one is too old or too
young to spread the word of God. Please help us to be strong and brave for
You. Amen.*

*Valeria Varela is an eighth-grader at the Manassas Adventist Preparatory School
in Virginia.*

The Big Picture

"Trust in the Lord with all your heart and lean not on your own understanding; in all your ways submit to Him, and He will make your paths straight" (Prov. 3:5-6, NIV).

This verse reminds me to trust in the Lord, regardless of whatever is going on in my life or the world. It points out that, although I may not understand things and/or people at times, if I acknowledge Him and continue to believe that He knows what's best for me, everything will turn out fine.

When I was younger, I was certain I would marry one of the first guys I dated. When we broke up, I was devastated and so depressed that I didn't think I could go on. I wasn't familiar with Proverbs 3:5-6 at the time, but when I learned it, I related it to this terrible time in my life. I now have an incredible husband who I would have never met had I continued to date the first guy.

When I encounter challenges in my life that don't make sense to me, I cling to this verse, knowing that I can't always see the "big picture." But God can and does. He wants what's best for me. God is like the top of a puzzle box; He sees the whole picture, while we only see the individual pieces of the puzzle.

Dear Father in Heaven, thank You for promising to "make our paths straight." Help us to submit our ways to You. Amen.

Nickie Pinnick is a member of the Beltsville church in Maryland.

Moving Experience

"Now may the God of hope fill you with all joy and peace in believing, that you may abound in hope by the power of the Holy Spirit" (Rom. 15:13, NKJV).

When I got the news that I was moving to Ohio, I was so mad at God. It was so unfair that I had to move again. I felt like I was just getting used to living in Tennessee, but now I had to pack everything up. It was so hard for me to let go of all the friends I had met.

Moving to Ohio was hard at first, but then things got easier. I started to realize that God sent me here for a purpose. If I had only trusted Him from the start, then things would've been a lot easier.

This verse helped me through this hard time in my life because it reminded me that I should always trust God. He has a plan for my future, and He knows what is best for me.

He wants us to always have faith in Him, just like He has faith in us. We should always have hope and find the good things God puts in our lives. He made us for a reason, and He wants us to spread our faith to others.

Lord, someone right now might be going through a hard time. Help them to have faith and trust in You, because You know what You're doing. Amen.

Samantha Schneider is a freshman at Spring Valley Academy in Ohio.

Let Me Tell You About Joseph

"Then Pharaoh said to Joseph, 'Since God has made all this known to you, there is no one so discerning and wise as you'" (Gen. 41:39, NIV).

I like Genesis 41:39 because it shows God's power and what He can do, especially in this abbreviated version on the story of Joseph:

Joseph lived with his father, Jacob, and 11 brothers in Canaan. Jacob made Joseph a coat of many colors, and God gave Joseph two dreams. One day, Jacob asked Joseph to take food to his brothers who were taking care of the sheep. When Joseph arrived, his brothers, except for Reuben—the oldest, and who wasn't present—sold Joseph into slavery. Later, Joseph's slave master took him to Egypt and sold him again.

Soon Joseph was put into prison for something he didn't do. With God's help, he interpreted the dreams of the king's baker and cupbearer, and those predictions came true. Two years later, Pharaoh had two dreams, and the cupbearer remembered Joseph and told the king about him.

The king sent for Joseph, who interpreted the dreams. As a result, Joseph became second-in-command in Egypt. When famine came to the land, the storehouses were opened. Joseph's brothers came to buy food. Joseph recognized them, and told them to bring their younger brother, Benjamin, when they came again. As part of the deal, Simeon was to stay in Egypt until Benjamin came. Joseph later revealed his identity and invited them to stay in Egypt. When the family arrived, Jacob was ecstatic!

Overall, this story has impacted my life by showing me the importance of forgiveness.

Thank You, God, for placing this story in the Bible. May we learn to forgive like Joseph did. Amen.

Peniel Amo-Mensah is a sixth-grader at the Roanoke Adventist Christian School in Virginia.

A Very Present Help

**"God is our refuge and strength, a very present help in trouble"
(Ps. 46:1, NKJV).**

One of the earliest memories I have of growing up in rural Jamaica is that of daily morning and evening worship. I fondly remember the songs we sang and the many verses we memorized. We listened to countless Bible stories along with personal recollections from my parents and grandparents who taught me the value of full dependence on God and that He always hears and answers our prayers. While I firmly believed these lessons and stories, I thought that answered prayers were a gift only for certain adults who enjoyed a special connection with God. As I reflect on those years, I can now say that back then I did not have an experiential relationship with God and had not personally learned to depend on Him.

As a young man, I left home to pursue an education in a Seventh-day Adventist college. After I graduated, a few years later I was happily married, and we welcomed our precious daughter, Danielle. Our little family was complete. This was the happiest time of my life, but that happiness was marred by tragedy in the death of my wife.

While in that valley—raising Danielle alone—I was constantly comforted by God's promise that He is our refuge and strength, always willing to help in troublesome times. This He demonstrated daily to me through His Word and by the people He placed in my path—family, friends, co-workers and a team of medical professionals. It is said that experience is the best teacher. Thus I learned through my experience that God truly is a very present help.

Dear Lord, whatever challenges we face today, and in our lowest moments, help us to know that You are with us. Amen.

Donovan Ross is the vice president of education for the Columbia Union Conference.

A Lot of Whys

"Never will I leave you; never will I forsake you" (Heb. 13:5, NIV).

This verse became real to me during my junior year in college. I had just come home from my student nursing clinical on April 6, 1993, when I received a call from my mother. I could hardly believe the news she told me. Daddy fell in the bathroom over the weekend; she had called 911; he was in the ICU; and later died there. As I listened, I felt as though the walls of my world came crashing down on me.

I was very close to my Dad and loved him dearly. I asked God a lot of whys. Why did Daddy have to die before I graduated from nursing school? Why would he have to miss giving me away at my wedding? Why wouldn't my future husband and children know and love him like I did? On and on, I asked the Lord.

I searched His Word for comfort, and found Hebrews 13:5. I read it over and over for reassurance from the Lord. Some days, I could almost hear His voice speaking it to me: *Never will I leave you; never will I forsake you.*

The weeks that followed were a blur. I could barely concentrate on my studies. Every evening, I needed someone to study with me because my mind would often wander. I clung to the promise of this verse in those dark days. Only by God's grace did He carry me through that difficult time. He can do the same for you.

I thank You, Lord, that You are with me when I feel alone in my problems, my pain, my grief. You promise to never leave me, and I claim that promise today. Amen.

Ellen Morgan is a member of the Vienna church in Virginia.

You Are Unique

"I will praise thee; for I am fearfully and wonderfully made: marvellous are Thy works; and that my soul knoweth right well" (Ps. 139:14, KJV).

Is there something about yourself you don't like? Maybe you have freckles, a loud laugh, curly hair or a quiet personality. I would venture to guess that we all have insecurities. We see characteristics in others we wish we could have and features we wish we could look like. The question is, why aren't we confident in who we are?

Personally, I have struggled with my confidence. In 2020, I worked at a summer camp. While there, I realized that I had a subconscious idea of what people wanted me to be—funny, outgoing, the life of the party. I struggled not being comfortable with simply being myself—a caring, relaxed, observant extroverted-introvert.

Through a co-worker's testimony, I saw I wasn't the only one who felt this way, and I didn't need to continue to hide my feelings. God made every single person different on purpose. Because of how I was uniquely made, I saw that there were people that only I could reach—my friends, classmates, co-workers and family. It's the same for you.

As Psalm 139:14 says, we are "fearfully and wonderfully made." God, our Creator, made you, and He doesn't make mistakes. He placed each freckle, composed each laugh, crafted each curl and gave you your core personality. There are people only you can reach, if you let God into your heart and ask Him to use you. He'll take you out of your comfort zone and help you do things you never thought possible.

Father God, thank You for Your unfailing love and for making each of us unique—a special treasure designed to reach others. Amen.

Summer Dekle is a senior at Blue Mountain Academy in Pennsylvania.

He Gives the Victory

"No temptation has overtaken you except such as is common to man; but God is faithful, who will not allow you to be tempted beyond what you are able, but with the temptation will also make the way of escape, that you may be able to bear it" (1 Cor. 10:13, NKJV).

Victory is won by standing on the promises of God. As I neared the end of 2016, I never would have guessed it would mark the end of some 20 years of my pornography addiction. I was in absolute darkness with almost no hope left. But Jesus always pursued me, and He found me as I looked to heaven for help. In that moment, my chains broke, and I found a way of escape. God proved His faithfulness by giving me victory.

This verse, penned by the apostle Paul, became my firm foundation in Christ. It gave me a solid assurance that the Lord would never allow me to pass through a temptation that was too difficult to endure. Many times each day, I repeated this promise that empowered me to take hold of God's hand as He strengthened me for every test, trial and temptation.

Just as I have found my freedom in Christ my Savior, His gift of salvation is free to you as well. As you look to Him for victory, you can rest in His word that affords you the strength to stand against every attack from the enemy. When you believe what God has promised, you will know that He will always provide a way for you to endure all things. Will you stand each day on His promises of victory in Jesus that lead to eternal life?

Father, may we look to Jesus for strength to overcome and daily gain the victory. Amen.

Michael Howard is a member of the Amicus church in Virginia.

'Arise and Go'

"Moses My servant is dead. Now therefore, arise, go over this Jordan, you and all this people, to the land which I am giving to them—the children of Israel" (Josh. 1:2, NKJV).

The servant of God has died. Moses, who spoke to God as a friend, has perished. The Israelites' leader, friend and loving intercessor would no longer be with them.

Even in the midst of loss or pain, God always has a plan. After Moses' death, God said to Joshua, "Now therefore, arise ..." Arise is a difficult word when living in sadness, clueless about how to confront the challenges of life. However, God invites us to trust in Him and calls us to "arise."

God continued, "... go over this Jordan, you and all this people ..." When we are struck with tragedy, we typically wait for the sadness to wane. We let ourselves grieve before resuming our responsibilities. Joshua doesn't have a long time to grieve before being called into action. Reminded of God's plan, he was given the charge to lead Israel "to the land which [God was] giving to [them]."

We may not be called to cross a literal river, but we are admonished to indeed "arise, and go over" our own personal Jordans, and to help others accomplish this too. Let us hold onto the beautiful promise found in Titus 2:13, as we wait for "the glorious appearing of our great God and Savior Jesus Christ" (NKJV).

God, may we remember that Your promises are stronger than our circumstances. Push us to "arise and go!" Amen.

Luis M. Bernedo is the pastor of Hispanic Ministries for the Parkersburg church in West Virginia.

Thankful for God's Plan

"For I know the thoughts that I think toward you, saith the Lord, thoughts of peace, and not of evil, to give you an expected end" (Jer. 29:11, KJV).

In my early twenties, I began wondering about everything I had experienced in my life. I endured verbal abuse as a child. My heart was badly broken at age 16. I was kicked out of my home at 17. I experienced a fire that claimed all my belongings at 20. What was my life's purpose?

That is when, through Jeremiah 29:11, God said: "Come to Me first, for I created you. I know where the winding paths you walk will lead. I know how to use the most heart-wrenching moments in your life to propel you to passionate, free, purposeful living. Every thought I have about you is good, never evil, to ensure your future is bright. When you come to Me first, you position yourself to receive an injection of hope each day. Seeking Me will reveal sneak peeks into the phenomenal life I have planned for you. The plans I have for you are to make of you what I expected when I conceived you in My infinite mind. I am always right here waiting for you to remember that you have someone in your corner who is, by divine providence, turning all your hardships into glory. Will you trust that My every thought about you is good?"

In response, I whispered, "Yes. I believe that You know the thoughts You think toward me, that they are thoughts of peace and not of evil, to give me an expected end. Thank You."

God, sometimes I still wonder about the events in my life, but now I know there is Someone in my corner making beauty from my ashes. Amen.

Shari A. Loveday is the children and youth pastor at the Beltsville church in Maryland.

Sabbath Peace and Monday's Miracle

**"Casting all your care upon Him, for He cares for you"
(1 Pet. 5:7, NKJV).**

It had been a difficult and long month. Rent was due, and we were running out of diapers and food. We were going crazy.

On Friday evening, after our "Sabbath Welcome" worship, I prayed, "Lord, I can't carry these worries into the Sabbath. I'm just going to give them to you! I know You will take care of us." At that moment, an amazing peace entered my heart. Our Sabbath day was a delight. So much so that when Monday came around, I was still at peace.

When Monday's mail arrived, two envelopes caught my attention. One was from my aunt Lillian, and the other from an insurance company. The envelope from my aunt—who was unaware of the financial struggle we were having—contained a check and a note saying, "I was impressed by the Lord to send this to you."

The second letter was from my wife's former employer. She had left the company more than two years earlier. Inside was a check and a letter explaining that, in reviewing their payroll records, they found a discrepancy in my wife's paychecks.

These two unexpected checks provided us with enough money to pay rent, buy diapers and food, and even make a trip to Taco Bell.

We learned two powerful lessons that weekend: Sabbath is best enjoyed when we give our burdens to God; and God takes care of our problems.

Lord, I know it is hard, but help us to cast our cares upon You! Amen.

Eli Rojas is the ministerial secretary for the Chesapeake Conference.

An Answered Prayer

"May the God of hope fill you with all joy and peace as you trust in Him, so that you may overflow with hope by the power of the Holy Spirit" (Rom. 15:13, NIV).

This verse is important to me because there was a moment in my life when I felt I was losing everything; that there was no hope. But God showed me there was hope and that I would be fine.

In 2020, my mom got into a terrible car accident. I was sick at home with bronchitis when my mom's friend called my older brother and told him that she had been in an accident. We talked with the paramedics, and they explained that it was very bad. We rushed to the hospital, and I was very upset because they wouldn't tell us anything.

They finally told us my mom had hit a semi-tractor-trailer, and her car had gone under it. At that moment, I thought my mommy was dead, so I decided to pray. I have never prayed so hard. I was so scared. I didn't know if my mommy was alive. But God gave me hope and peace. After I prayed, I was able to see her, and she only had a broken knee and a few cuts. The doctor said they didn't know how she was still alive. But I do.

No matter what happens or how hopeless it seems, you can always pray to God and ask Him for help. I thank God for everything He has done in my life. If you have faith in God, He will give you hope and power.

Dear God, please give me joy and peace when I am in trouble. Amen.

Scarlett Castillo is a seventh-grader at the Tree of Life Christian Preparatory School in Virginia.

Learning From the Past

**"For I know the plans I have for you, declares the Lord,
plans for welfare and not for evil, to give you a future and hope"
(Jer. 29:11, ESV).**

I like this Bible verse because it says God knows what will happen throughout your life, through all your troubles, hardships and times of despair. I think of these as wars between God and Satan, between your guardian angel and Satan's demons.

But just as God knows the outcome of the whole universe, you choose the outcome of your battles; whether or not you'll let something ruin your day or try to see the good that can come out of a bad situation. We've all had our times of trial. For some it may not have been as bad as others, but it's up to you whether you choose to let the demons win or let God take command.

No one is saying that there won't be any work involved. That has to be put in. You're only human, so don't beat yourself up. Take the information you can from a bad situation, and think about what you could have done differently and how you can do better in the future.

Dear God, please help us to not focus too much on the past. May we apply the lessons we've learned to help guide our future situations. Amen.

Victor Rivera is an eighth-grader at the Harrisburg Adventist School in Pennsylvania.

Help Us to Listen!

"How can you say to your brother, 'Let me take the speck out of your eye,' when all the time there is a plank in your own eye? You hypocrite, first take the plank out of your own eye, and then you will see clearly to remove the speck from your brother's eye"
(Matt. 7:4–5, NIV).

Most of us have experienced a time when we've completely underestimated someone's point of view, whether in an argument or in a situation where one lacks confidence to support themselves. I have been on both ends of the spectrum in my education and everyday life, making Matthew 7:4–5 my favorite verse.

In our attempt to be right, we refuse to hear the other side of the argument and judge others for seeing things differently than we do without even trying to understand them. What we need to realize is that sometimes the picture they see is a bit clearer than the one we do.

I consider myself to be a stubborn person. If I am right, I am right, but if I am wrong, I will bring another person into the mix to prove I am wrong. Many times, I am so quick to point out the tiny flaw in someone's logic that I don't see the plank in my own. This verse is a reminder that sometimes all I need to do is sit back and listen and accept.

Lord, grant us the wisdom to listen and understand before judging others. Amen.

Wright Makambi is a member of the Capital Chinese church in Maryland.

A Refuge in My Distress

"But as for me, I will sing of Your strength; Yes, I shall joyfully sing of Your faithfulness in the morning, for You have been my refuge and a place of refuge on the day of my distress" (Ps. 59:16, NASB).

This verse outlines the many problems, mountainous difficulties, troubling times and numerous enemies that were surrounding David on every side. David opened up his heart to the Lord, and his urgent prayer for help and deliverance poured forth unabated. This surrender of heart has also worked in my life.

At school, we have a skiing program. The most important rule is to never leave a friend alone. One time, my skiing partner, Naomi, and I decided to ski down a slope called the Mack Attack. Although I didn't want to go, she did. I couldn't let her go alone, so I accompanied her.

As we got off the ski lift and looked at the slope, we realized it was a bit different, a bit scarier, than we expected. "We got this, Naomi! Remember God's with us!" I said.

On my way down, I tried to maneuver around a large patch of ice I saw at the last moment. I slipped on the ice and started rolling down the slope. One ski fell off. Pop! Then the other. Pop! As I continued to roll, I closed my eyes and prayed, "God, please don't let me get injured. Please put Your hand over me and protect me."

God protected me that day. He was "a place of refuge on the day of my distress." He promises to protect you too.

God, please help us to understand that, through it all, You are the One who's always by our side. Amen.

Leslie DeArevalo is an eighth-grader at the Manassas Adventist Preparatory School in Virginia.

He Delivers Us

"The angel of the Lord encamps all around those who fear Him, and delivers them" (Ps. 34:7, NKJV).

This verse is so powerful because it reminds us that God is always ready to deliver us, and that we have no reason to be afraid. In my personal experience, I found Psalms 34:7 to be true.

A few years ago, my house caught on fire. My family was at church when it happened, so luckily no one was injured. One of our friends, however, was living with us at the time. She stayed home that Sabbath to watch a couple of baby birds we had found the day before.

God was definitely looking out for her, because she was on a walk with one of our dogs when the fire started. However, our two other dogs were still in the house. When my friend got home, thankfully she was able to retrieve them unscathed. Our church was far away from my house, so my family and I returned after the fireman put the fire out.

At first, I was very sad about losing my house to a fire, but looking back, I see it as a blessing. My new house is closer to my school, so now I can take extracurricular classes. If I still would've lived at my old house, I probably wouldn't have been able to take advantage of this opportunity. I guess it's true when people say that God works in mysterious ways.

Lord, help us to see the good in situations, even when they might seem bad at the time. Help us to trust You, and thank You for protecting us. Amen.

Emily Dekle is a sophomore at Blue Mountain Academy in Pennsylvania.

Prepare for the Latter Rain

**"And it shall come to pass afterward that I will pour out
My Spirit on all flesh; Your sons and your daughters shall prophesy,
your old men shall dream dreams, your young men shall see visions"
(Joel 2:28, NKJV).**

We need to understand that near the close of earth's harvest, there will be a special outpouring of spiritual grace to prepare each and every one of us for the coming of Christ.

Just like the latter rain, this added power that Christians must request is very important for the last days. Being Christians, we must allow God to do the work through us. In order for Him to do this, we must surrender our hearts. When we do this, it allows our character, recreated in the image of God, to witness to our families and community. Since we tend to get in God's way and make our own arrangements, it is important to remember that God's timing and plan for each of us is always perfect.

Today, let's remember that, during these times of sorrow in which we live, many people are watching us. As Christians, we are the family of Christ, and we must represent that family with love, mercy and grace. The more we let God do the work, the more souls will be saved at the coming of the great and awesome day of the Lord. We are unable to accomplish things on our own, but, with the power of Christ, each of us can receive eternal salvation.

*Lord, thank You for saving us by Your grace. Help us to be a blessing to others.
Amen.*

D. W. West is a student youth pastor of the Parkersburg church in West Virginia.

Perfect Timing

"For I know the plans I have for you, says the Lord. They are plans for good and not for evil, to give you a future and a hope. In those days when you pray, I will listen" (Jer. 29:11-12, TLB).

Sometimes God amazes us with how He reveals His plans. In 1978, I was almost finished with my Elementary Education major at Walla Walla College (Wash.). It was time to think about where I wanted to teach. My parents had moved back to California and wanted me to be closer to them, but I wasn't sure I wanted to move there. With graduation looming on the horizon, I needed to start seriously thinking about teaching positions.

Every year, the college sent out a book to conferences with the seniors' pictures and majors. A friend from college, who was the assistant dean at Shenandoah Valley Academy in Virginia, encouraged me to apply to the Potomac Conference.

Before I could even call, they called, as well as the Dakota Conference (N.D.), both offering me teaching positions.

What to do? When I was growing up, my father had to make a choice between two pastoral job offers. He put them in front of God and prayed, then accepted the first one to return his call. I followed his example. I prayed and then waited. Dakota Conference was supposed to call back first. Two days later, Potomac called and offered me a teaching position, which I accepted.

God has never failed to lead in my life. He knew just where I needed to be, and when.

God, we know You have plans for us. Open our hearts to follow. We trust that You will continue to lead and bless. Amen.

Dainett Bowers is the second- through fourth-grade teacher at the Manassas Adventist Preparatory School in Virginia.

Kindness Is the Best Comeback

"Do to others whatever you would like them to do to you"
(Matt. 7:12, NLT).

The golden rule. When I was younger, I interpreted this verse a bit differently than most. Whenever my sister was unkind to me, I would be mean to her in return. Then I would try to justify my behavior: "Treat others the way they treat you!"

The intended meaning of the golden rule, however, is to put yourself in someone else's shoes. How would you want to be treated if the roles were reversed? I know I'd prefer to be treated with love and respect.

First Thessalonians 5:15 has a similar concept: "See that no one pays back evil for evil, but always try to do good to each other and to all people" (NLT). When I read this verse, I automatically think about revenge. Have you ever been the victim of rude behavior and shot back something not so nice. How could the situation have ended differently? Lamentations 3:30 says to turn the other cheek and to accept the insults of an enemy. God wants us to love our enemies, even though can be difficult.

One time, David had to choose which battle to fight: one of vengeance or love. Saul, pursuing an enemy with his men, stepped into a cave to rest—the same cave David and his band inhabited. David could have easily slayed the oblivious Saul. Instead, David sliced a corner off of Saul's robe.

David had the perfect opportunity to get revenge on Saul, yet, he did no such thing. Don't strike back. Choose to fight with love, because kindness is the best comeback.

Lord, when we want to be mean to someone because they are mean to us, may we take the higher road. Amen.

Gabrielle Savoy is an eighth-grader at Richmond Academy in Virginia.

Take Root and Grow

**"The righteous shall flourish like the palm tree:
he shall grow like a cedar in Lebanon" (Ps. 92:12, KJV).**

As David poetically writes this Psalm dedicated to the Sabbath day, he uses verse 12 to instruct us on how to grow. He states that the righteous shall flourish like the palm tree. This is no ordinary palm tree; it is a date palm, known in Hebrew as "tamar." The date palm is tall and slender and stretches upward of 75 feet. This incredible tree grows amid the drought of the desert. It vigorously plunges its roots into the earth until it reaches the hidden waters beneath the surface. As a result, it is able to produce large clusters of fruit, about 100 to 200 pounds each year.

David also references the cedars of Lebanon. These noble trees shoot upward to heights of 120 feet and can be found in almost every climate region. The roots of these towering trees not only plunge deep, but they also spread wide, providing extraordinary stability that can endure even the most treacherous storms.

David is drawing from the book of nature to tell us to thrust our roots deep into the Word of God amid the spiritual drought that surrounds us to find the living waters that will enable us to grow tall and allow us to flourish and bear the fruit of the Spirit.

Let us start and end each day giving thanks to the Lord and singing praises to His name. Let us flourish like the date palm and grow like the cedars of Lebanon by sinking our roots deep and wide into the Word of God.

God, in all that we do, let us declare that the Lord is upright. Amen.

Matthew Haire is the pastor of the Mountaintop church in Maryland and the Kingwood and Morgantown churches in West Virginia.

An Unexpected Blessing

**"So shall My word be that goes forth from My mouth;
it shall not return to Me void, but it shall accomplish
what I please" (Isa. 55:11, NKJV).**

As an accountant by profession, I have often counseled my clients,
wherever appropriate, to prove God's Word when it comes to finances.
I know this also from personal experience.

Several years ago, I was visiting my former church in New York when a
call was made for donations for a special project. I debated whether to
respond, as I had only $20 in my wallet. I knew that I would need cash
to pay the tolls on my way back home to Pennsylvania. As the appeal
continued, I made the decision to respond and gave the $20 bill. I figured
I could stop at an ATM later to withdraw funds for the trip home.

After the service, my family and I drove to a hotel venue for a planned
50th birthday celebration for one of our friends. On entering the lobby,
I was greeted by a former client who had moved away from New York
several years before without paying his tax preparation fee. While
greeting me with a firm handshake, he slipped money into my hand
indicating that this was for his prior debt. It appeared that he had been
awaiting my arrival. An hour after I gave my last $20 at church, God
rewarded my faithfulness, with a 400 percent return on my investment
in His cause.

God is the CEO of my company, and I consult Him and seek His
guidance daily. Over the years since that incident occurred, I have
seen Him respond and bless in countless ways.

Lord, thank You for the ways in which You prove that Your Word is true. Amen.

Vernon A. Bramble is the lead elder of the Bucks County church in Pennsylvania.

Not Immune to Grief

**"When Jesus heard what had happened, He withdrew by
boat privately to a solitary place" (Matt. 14:13, NIV).**

Are you grieving today? This pain cuts to the core and is deeper than
just a bad day. It's bigger than a pint of ice cream or a walk around the
block that can handle. Sadly, we may feel as though we must carry these
emotions alone. It's in these times that the support of loved ones, and
even complete strangers, is so needed.

To be honest, in the back of my mind I don't think I ever pictured Jesus
grieving. Sure, there's that "Jesus wept" memory verse in Sabbath School
we as kids so desired to memorize, but why would Jesus ever be sad? He
was so closely connected to the Father that how could He possibly ever
experience that human ache? Plus, we know He was fully aware that His
time on this planet would be relatively short, and that we'd soon go to live
with Him in heaven and never ever mourn again.

It was while preparing to lead a worship some time ago that a verse I'd
read many times before caught my attention. And it still speaks to me.

In Matthew 14:12, Jesus is told that His cousin John has just been
beheaded. The idea of Jesus being immune to depth of emotion over
death melted as I read what followed. In verse 13, we see Jesus quietly
withdrawing to a solitary place to grieve. Jesus was sad enough that He
needed to be alone to deal with this loss. He wasn't immune. He grieved
deeply—just as we do.

*Jesus, remind us that You are not only with us in our grief, but that even
You grieve too. Amen.*

Chandler Riley is a member of the Triadelphia church in Maryland.

Do You Love Jesus?

"So when they had eaten breakfast, Jesus said to Simon Peter, 'Simon, son of Jonah, do you love Me more than these?' He said to Him, 'Yes, Lord; You know that I love You.' He said to him, 'Feed my lambs'" (John 21:15, NKJV).

Have you ever wondered how to love someone even after they hurt you? After the death of Jesus, some of His disciples, including Peter, went fishing. They had spent almost all night with no success. Early in the morning, an unknown man on the shore told them to throw the net on the other side. Confused, they did. At that moment, Peter immediately knew it wasn't an ordinary person; it was Jesus. He couldn't contain his excitement after seeing all the fish, and he jumped out of the boat and swam to shore to see Jesus.

There was unsettled business between them, because, prior to Jesus' death, Peter had denied him three times. After the third time, Jesus looked at Peter, and Peter knew immediately what he had done. Following, he "went out and wept bitterly" (Luke 22:62, NKJV). The love that Jesus had for Peter did not die; instead He wanted to restore Peter.

After the morning breakfast by the shore, as told in John 21, Jesus asked Peter, "Do you love Me?" Peter replied, "Yes, Lord, You know that I love You." Jesus repeated the question three times, each time breaking Peter's heart. But then Jesus went on to say two words Peter was desperately in need of: "Follow Me." Peter had been restored!

Jesus asks us today, "Do you love me more than anything else—your job, your sports team, even your family? When we tell Him, yes, like Peter did, He heals, restores and calls us to follow Him.

Lord, thank You for loving the unlovable like us. Amen.

Eddie Reyes is the pastor of the Marlinton, Lewisburg and Rainelle churches in West Virginia.

Grandmother's Legacy

"Fear not, for I have redeemed you; I have called you by your name; you are Mine" (Isa. 43:1, NKJV).

As a child, I grew up in an Orthodox family in Romania. Every Sunday, we went to church, and we kept all the Orthodox holidays. On weekends and vacations, I stayed with my grandparents, as they only lived 11 miles away.

When I was 7-years-old, my grandmother discovered the Seventh-day Adventist faith. Every Friday night, she took me with her to an Adventist neighbor's house to welcome the Sabbath. After we attended a few times, I asked her why we were worshipping on Saturday instead of Sunday. She explained to me that the Bible said God created the Sabbath for us when He created the world. We began reading the Bible together so I could learn more.

On November 13, 1993, my lovely, very faithful grandmother passed away due to renal failure. After her passing, my mother found out that she had been attending an Adventist church. She had many questions, and, together, we began attending church occasionally.

When I turned 16, we moved to the United States. For one year, my mother and I searched for an Adventist church. One day, we discovered that a church was only a few miles from our house! The very next Sabbath, my mother and I were in church.

On April 27, 2002, I gave my life to Jesus through baptism. I look forward to the second coming of my Lord Jesus, when I will see my grandmother again.

Father, thank You for calling us by name and making us Your children. Amen.

Adriana Folscher is the English/Spanish teacher at Richmond Academy in Virginia.

NOTES

"Bear with each other and forgive one another if any of you has a grievance against someone. Forgive as the Lord forgave you." COL. 3:13, NIV

NOVEMBER

A Lasting Presence

"I am with you always" (Matt. 28:20, NIV).

I am privileged to have been blessed with the best parents, and, equally, in-laws. Although they now rest in hope of the resurrection glory, their joyous memories are with me. Christ Jesus is with me, too, and all of us.

Due to my own prodigal experiments at the age of 16, I was far away from home. Dad was busy with the Lord's work, but kept a dozen prayer warriors praying for me at the conference church. Mom was overseas working on family projects so that all seven children could be educated.

On returning home, every child was present to greet her except for me. "Where is Joe?" She discovered my location in a faraway country, and visited me. It was such a joy and surprise to be with my parents again. I had just answered God's call but was resigned to be a witness where I was. And now with Dad and Mom's presence, I decided to follow God's purpose in the context of family community—friendship, oneness and partnerships.

During this unprecedented season, what Christ declared is still relevant: "I am with you always." No matter what is happening in this world, God's promise is an intimate, continual guarantee for our eternal existence through His real presence. We can share His presence continually through His Word, the Holy Spirit, our guardian angel and devotional life.

Experience with me today, the assurance, blessing, deep joy and satisfaction gained from receiving the anointing of the spoken logos by the Logos. Feel His presence, sense His power and celebrate His amazing protection. He is our Savior, Deliverer, Healer, Teacher, Judge, and is ready and waiting to give us His glorious presence.

Lord, may "I am with you always" be our daily solution in 2021 and eternity. Amen.

Joseph M. Hutchinson is the interim pastor of the Prince Emmanuel All Nations church in Maryland.

Prayer of Faith From 32,000 Feet

**"Before they call, I will answer; and while they
are yet speaking, I will hear" (Isa. 65:24, KJV).**

It was 1979, and we had just completed a year in Osaka, Japan, as student missionaries from Oakwood College (Ala.). The last stipend had been received and was just enough to get my husband, Thomas, and me home to Richmond, Va. Our plan was to see parts of the world on our return trip that we might never visit again. We would spend two days each in Taiwan and Hong Kong, connecting to a flight into Washington, D.C., with a short bus ride to Richmond. Our traveling companion, Sandra, was also returning to the United States.

Arriving in Hong Kong, we learned that all DC-10 airlines had been banned from the U.S. Our two days turned into four. Taking another airline, from 32,000 feet up we prayed that God would provide and protect. We landed in New York City at midnight with no means to take us home.

At the airport, my husband was impressed to share our dilemma with two gentlemen. They could help, but we would have to trust them. Considering our lack of funds and nonstop prayers, we decided to trust God. We were loaded on a bus with about 20 others, and taken to a motel for the night.

The men, both from Alabama, were familiar with Oakwood College. They turned out to be officers who routinely provided food and lodging for undocumented immigrants. They provided breakfast and paid our cab fare to the bus station.

We still marvel at God's mysterious and miraculous ways. He provided us with just enough money to get home.

Dear God, thank You for hearing and answering prayers in ways in which we would never think. Amen.

Alberta Jefferson is a member of the Ephesus church in Virginia.

How to Overcome Fear

"The wicked flee though no one pursues, but the righteous are as bold as a lion" (Prov. 28:1, NIV).

Think of a time when you were scared. What did you do? When I was younger, I went to a camp, and one of the activities was water tubing. Even though I was very excited to try it, I was also very scared. I was so nervous that I got butterflies in my stomach.

As I was trying to calm myself down on the water tube, the boat started moving faster and faster. I decided that the best thing was to start singing worship songs to help remember that God was looking out for me. After singing "Jesus Loves Me" three times in a row, I realized water tubing was really fun. I wasn't scared anymore, and I had one of the greatest experiences of my life. I would've missed this wonderful time if I had let fear take control.

There are many stories in the Bible that exemplify characters who dealt with overcoming fear: David fighting Goliath; Queen Esther saving her people; and Shadrach, Meshach and Abednego in the fiery furnace, to name a few.

What is something in your life that you are afraid of? What can you do to remind yourself that God is the One in control? He tells us, "'For I know the plans I have for you,' declares the Lord, 'plans to prosper you and not to harm you, plans to give you hope and a future'" (Jer. 29:11, NIV).

Dear God, thank You for giving us the assurance we need to overcome fear though prayer and love. Amen.

Hannah Johnson is a senior at Blue Mountain Academy in Pennsylvania.

My Angel at the Beach

**"The angel of the Lord encamps around those who
fear Him, and He delivers them" (Ps. 34:7, NIV).**

I was living in St. Croix, the U.S. Virgin Islands, with my wife, Marlene, and
baby daughter, Priscilla. Two of my wife's siblings, Ruven and Beth, were
visiting, and we went to the beach, which was noticeably empty.

In the afternoon, Ruven, Beth and I went into the water. Shortly after, an
undertow began to pull us out to sea. Ruven and Beth held onto their
floats and made it back to shore. I, thinking I'd be able to stand, jumped
off the float. Fear overwhelmed me as I realized the undercurrent had
dragged me close to the 1,000-foot drop, famous for its scuba diving.

I began to drown. Down and up. Back down again, and up. As my life
flashed before my eyes, I prayed, "Lord, please send someone to save
me." Understanding that maybe God had other plans, I left it in His hands.

As I was drowning, my wife and family, unable to help, saw a couple on
the beach. My wife cried out, "Save my husband!" Immediately, the man
jumped into the water to rescue me.

With my last breath of air, I shouted in faith, "Save me!"

Suddenly, someone grabbed me out of nowhere and pulled me to shore.
I began coughing up water and breathing again. My wife turned to thank
the gentleman who had rescued me.

No man. No woman. No footprints.

God had sent an angel to deliver me. He had a plan for my life. Two years
later, that plan was fulfilled in the form of my baby boy, Ricardo.

Thank You, God, for saving me time and time again. Amen.

Gerald Bacchus is a member of the New Hope church in Maryland.

Everything Happens for a Purpose

**"'For I know the plans I have for you,' declares the
Lord, 'plans to prosper you and not to harm you, plans
to give you hope and a future'" (Jer. 29:11, NIV).**

I was 2-years-old when part of my finger was cut off. My parents had a
boat, and I loved to play on it whenever my dad was working in the house.
I was playing one day, when I suddenly fell off, and my finger got stuck
in the motor. My dad rushed me to the hospital. My life hasn't been the
same since.

It has been hard growing up without part of my finger. I've gotten
bullied, and, at times, no one has liked me. But then something amazing
happened. After this accident, my parents got closer to God, and we
started going to church. It was the first church I went to, and I made true
friends—one of which became my best friend. Nobody made fun of my
finger there. They were all nice to me.

I love going to church and look forward to it because I can see all my
friends every week and because I can learn about God and get closer to
Him. Church is my happy place. In fact, getting my finger cut off was worth
it because it led my family to God.

*Dear God, thank You for thinking ahead and making plans for us. Everything
that happens is for a purpose. Your purpose. Amen.*

Sofia Segura is a sixth-grader at the Manassas Adventist Preparatory School in Virginia.

Leave It to God

"Unless the Lord builds the house, the builders labor in vain. Unless the Lord watches over the city, the guards stand watch in vain. In vain you rise early and stay up late, toiling for food to eat— for He grants sleep to those He loves" (Ps. 127:1-2, NIV).

It was my senior year. I was living in the dormitory at Mt. Vernon Academy. We had returned to our rooms after a Saturday evening program in the gymnasium. I no longer recall just what it was that was plaguing my mind. It could have been stress over a test or project in one of my classes. Perhaps there was turmoil with my girlfriend.

But whatever the cause, I do remember I was too worked up to sleep. I finally decided to pull out my Bible, opened it up in the middle and started to read. I didn't have a particular promise in mind. I was just reading, hoping to find something that would bring me peace. A message that would provide encouragement and allow me to get some needed rest.

When I got to our verse for today, I immediately knew it had the wisdom I needed. I could fret and worry, plan and work late into the night. Or I could trust God with my problem, confident of His love and care. And If I chose the latter, He would put my mind at ease and give me sleep.

I've long since forgotten the problem. But, over the years, I have frequently returned to the promise I discovered late that night in my dorm room. When new stressors threaten to rob me of peace, I am reminded it is the Lord who builds, guards and watches. And I can sleep.

Lord, today and tonight, may I rest in Your care. Amen.

Rick Remmers is the executive secretary of the Columbia Union Conference.

Say 'I Do'

"When they had finished eating, Jesus said to Simon Peter, 'Simon son of John, do you love me more than these?'"
(John 21:15, NIV).

There is a powerful truth that comes through this passage. For reasons not entirely clear, Peter had returned to fishing. In the days after the resurrection, he was an uncertain and insecure individual. What lay ahead, he didn't know. In denial and cursing Jesus, Peter utterly failed when Jesus needed him most. He may have even thought that his sin and failure eliminated the possibility of ever being used by God again.

I have felt that way more times than I can count. You may feel that way, too, that there are unforgivable sins or failures in your life. But Jesus says to both Peter and all of humanity: "You are forgiven." There is no need to hide or run. God's plan for your life still stands, as He calls to you from the shore of your life. He knocks on the door of your heart, and, when you open it, "Do you love me?" is His only question. Notice Jesus doesn't ask, "Are you sorry?" nor "Will you promise never to do that again?" All He wants to know is if you will give Him your heart, for Jesus knows that when you say, "Yes, Lord, you know that I love you," everything else will fall into place.

So close your eyes. Imagine Jesus lovingly looking deep into your eyes, as He asks you, "Do you love Me?" And may you, with humility, and even tears, respond, "Yes, Lord. I do. I do. *I do.*"

Father, forgive us for our wayward hearts, and receive the simple declaration of our love for You today. Amen.

John Kent is the pastor of the Simple Way Network church in Pennsylvania.

He Will Carry You

"Cast thy burden upon the Lord, and He shall sustain thee: He shall never suffer the righteous to be moved" (Ps. 55:22, KJV).

The day had been long. The boss was less than kind or fair, I felt. It had been so busy. I was tired and grumpy, feeling sorry for myself. Ungodly thoughts repeatedly raced through my mind, making me feel worse and worse. Have you ever experienced similar days? Or weeks?

The thought came to me, You don't have to keep making yourself miserable. There's a much better way. I replaced my negative thought with this reflection:

There aren't many days like this. You did your best.
You accomplished a lot! Don't worry about the words of another person.
God loves and treasures you.
He calls you His own.
He promises to be with you and care for you.

In *My Utmost for His Highest*, Oswald Chambers' words also comforted me: "If we will only roll back on God the burdens He has placed on us, He will take away that immense feeling of responsibility, replacing it with an awareness and understanding of Himself and His presence."

How thankful I am that we can "pile [our] troubles on God's shoulders— He'll carry [our] load, He'll help [us] out. He'll never let good people topple into ruin" (Ps. 55:22, MSG).

Dear Lord, thank You for the promise that You will sustain us. We praise You for carrying all of our burdens in Your hands. Amen.

Vicki C. Bernard is a member of the Hillcrest church in Pennsylvania.

Courage in Crisis

"Eleazar son of Dodai the Ahohite was the next of the elite Three. He was with David when the Philistines poked fun at them at Pas Dammim. When the Philistines drew up for battle, Israel retreated. But Eleazar stood his ground and killed Philistines right and left until he was exhausted—but he never let go of his sword! A big win for God that day. The army then rejoined Eleazar, but all there was left to do was the cleanup" (2 Sam 23:9–10, MSG).

Eleazar is one of my favorite heroes in the Bible. One of David's three elite warriors, Eleazar is chronicled in Scripture as a one-man army defeating the enemies of God with his sword. He courageously stood against those who would destroy the ways of God with corruption, destruction and moral decay.

I often apply his principles of warriorship to a Christian leader's responsibility and to the study and proclamation of truth. In today's society, truth, integrity, honesty, justice and basic human decency are under attack from the enemy.

Ellen White writes: "The greatest want of the world is the want of men [and women] ... who will stand for the right though the heavens fall" (*Education*, p. 57).

We can find courage from Eleazar's example and strategy: 1) He placed his faith in God—the only One who could guarantee the destruction of the army—and so should we. 2) It takes courage to stand against the enemy and relentless courage to stand for what is right. 3) Never let go of what God trained You to do.

Dear God, help us to fight injustice wherever we see it—at work, school or even in the church. Amen.

Anthony A. Medley is the senior pastor of the Emmanuel-Brinklow church in Maryland.

We Are All Connected

"But Ruth replied, 'Don't urge me to leave you or to turn back from you. Where you go I will go, and where you stay I will stay. Your people will be my people and your God my God'" (Ruth 1:16, NIV).

Ruth loved Naomi so much that she wouldn't leave her, even though Naomi told Ruth to go home.

Even though I live in two homes, it's not the houses that make them special; it's the family. People are what make up a home, not the building. The phrase "home sweet home" rings true because of family. And family doesn't always mean you are related by blood. In fact, even though my stepdad is not blood, I still love and respect him.

It is wise to have relationships with people who share your same beliefs. For instance, I enjoy spending time with my Pathfinder club because they all have the same beliefs as me.

Ruth's story has had a good influence on me. She and Naomi loved each other, even though they did not share the same blood or religion. We should be more like Ruth and treat everyone with kindness and respect, because, one way or another, we are all connected through God.

We are all His children, and like Ruth, should love other people unconditionally.

Dear God, please help us to be more like Ruth and display love to everyone we meet. Amen.

Cadence Rinehart is a sixth-grader at the Rocky Knoll Adventist School in West Virginia.

A Book in Jesus' Library

"Jesus did many other things as well. If every one of them were written down, I suppose that even the whole world would not have room for the books that would be written" (John 21:25, NIV).

When I first read this verse, I wondered, "How can the entire earth not hold enough books to list Jesus' works?" I volunteer as an assistant librarian at my church, and we have over 3,750 books. Whether missionary stories, biographies, nature lessons, Bible stories or doctrinal beliefs, all of the books ultimately point to God and what He has accomplished. If one small library can contain so much information about Jesus, think of how much a world library could contain!

Then I thought of Jesus' work of creation. Being in the solitude of the woods or the grandeur of the mountains reminds me of Jesus and how much larger He is than I can comprehend. Nature's sheer variety and complexity of minerals, plants, marine life, birds and mammals, and how they all communicate with each other never ceases to amaze me. The precision of cells and organs perfectly interacting to form a living human being testifies of a Master Designer who fashioned and cares about us. These topics would fill countless volumes.

Jesus is not only our Creator but also our Redeemer. He wants to write His law on our hearts and remove our sins. We can demonstrate a life changed by Christ working in us through the power of the Holy Spirit. We can be books in Jesus' library.

Lord, please write your character in my heart so I may be an example and a book for You. Amen.

Caleb Palmer is a member of the Centerville church in Ohio.

When Times Are Tough

"For the Holy Spirit will teach you at that time what you should say" (Luke 12:12, NIV).

This verse is important to me because it shows that God will help me when I need it. I can trust that He will help me to know what to do or say in times of trouble.

There have been many times that I have become upset over something, and I lash out at those around me. Other times, I try to get over the bad feelings myself. When I get upset, many times my Mom will come and pray with me. We ask that God can help me feel better and to help me express myself in a better way. Overall, it is very hard for me to express my feelings to others, but I can tell God everything. I almost always feel better after my Mom and I have prayed and asked for God's help. I am learning that He is there for me when I need help.

I also think Luke 12:12 means that God can give us the words to say when we try to tell people about Him. It is sometimes hard to share our faith, and we don't always know how to do it. But God can give us the words if we let Him speak through us.

Dear God, I know that times can be tough, but I also know that You will be there when we need You. Please help us to make better choices and to be careful about what we say and do. Give us the words to say to others. Amen.

Aiden Wareham is a sixth-grader at the Rocky Knoll Adventist School in West Virginia.

Never Alone

"For thy Maker is thine husband; the Lord of hosts is His name; and thy Redeemer the Holy One of Israel; the God of the whole earth shall He be called" (Isa. 54:5, KJV).

I have been a widow for many years. Although the burdens of day-to-day life are heavy, I have the assurance that God cares for me.

I discovered one of my favorite passages of Scripture after my husband's death. During a very lonely time of grief and pain, I reached out to God for strength to help me get through each day. In my devotions, I discovered this beautiful text of comfort and reassurance.

As the words of the hymn, "Does Jesus Care?" by Frank E. Graeff say:

> *Does Jesus care when I've said "goodbye"*
> *To the dearest on earth to me,*
> *And my sad heart aches*
> *Till it nearly breaks,*
> *Is it aught to Him? Does He see?*
> *Oh yes, He cares, I know He cares,*
> *His heart is touched with my grief;*
> *When the days are weary,*
> *The long night dreary,*
> *I know my Savior cares.*

God's great love for me is demonstrated in Christ's sacrifice. Extending compassion further and walking with me every day, God comforts me with the presence of His Spirit.

Lord, thank You for protecting me with angels and surrounding me with Your Spirit. With You by my side, I am not alone. Amen.

Deadra L. Griffeth is a chaplain at the Southview Medical Center for the Kettering Adventist HealthCare in Ohio.

Don't Settle

"Now to Him who is able to do far more abundantly than all that we ask or think, according to the power at work within us, to Him be glory in the church and in Christ Jesus throughout all generations, forever and ever. Amen" (Eph. 3:20–21, ESV).

We serve a limitless God who can do in us more than we could ever think or imagine. Still, despite my many experiences with the Lord, I continue to live a life governed by scarcity principles. I often don't want to risk attempting church projects beyond the local church's budget or perceived talent pool.

It reminds of an experience I had in eighth grade. My uncle, seeing that I was unmotivated to give my best effort, challenged me with a little incentive. He told me if I got straight A's in the next grading period, he would buy me a model airplane of my choice. I applied myself, and for the next three months, I became a stellar student. I proudly showed my uncle my report card. As promised, he took me to buy a model plane, but, as we walked into the store, my mind began to wonder: What if he didn't have enough money to buy the model I wanted? Worried about stretching his budget, I chose a cheaper model. As we left the store, part of me questioned what would have happened if I had picked the model I really wanted instead of settling for something cheaper. I will never know the answer to that question, but the experience stayed with me.

How often do I size the Lord down to what I think I can see or do instead of swinging for the fence?

Lord, help us to live a life of abundance in service as You dwell within us. Amen.

Kosly Joseph is the pastor of the Charlottesville and Harrisonburg churches in Virginia.

Pray and Believe

"Then Jesus looked up to heaven and said, 'Father, thank You for hearing Me. You always hear Me'"(John 11:41–42, NLT).

Have you ever felt like God doesn't hear you when you pray? I had the privilege of listening to a message at a recent women's retreat. Here are some points the speaker shared, who paraphrased the story in John 11:

Mary and Martha personally sent a messenger to Jesus, asking that He come heal Lazarus. Yet Jesus waited two days. The Bible says He loved Mary, Martha and Lazarus, but He still waited. When He finally did go, both Mary and Martha independently asked Him, "Why didn't you come? Our brother died!!"

Seeing Mary crying, Jesus' heart was so touched that He wept. He saw His friends in so much pain, and He felt their pain as well. Even though she didn't understand, Martha's faith didn't waiver, and she said, "I know that whatever You ask of God, He will do it." Then, at the moment Jesus was about to do something, Martha—with good intentions—tried to get in the way. "Lord, it will smell! Don't do that!" she cried.

When Jesus prayed to His Father, He said, "Father, thank You for hearing Me. You always hear me, but I said it out loud for the sake of all these people standing here, so that they will believe you sent me."

When life doesn't go the way you think it should, don't let your faith waiver, and don't get in God's way. God hears, and answered prayers bring glory to God!

Thank You, Father, for hearing us when we pray. May we never be discouraged by doubt, and may we always trust in Your timing. And when our prayers are answered, give us the courage to speak out and to give all the praise and glory to You! Amen.

Monica Zill is the principal at Parkersburg Adventist Academy in West Virginia.

In Every Battle

"Have I not commanded you? Be strong and of good courage; do not be afraid, nor be dismayed, for the Lord your God is with you wherever you go" (Josh. 1:9, NKJV).

God has creative ways of bringing Scripture into our minds to encourage us. This verse became a favorite of mine during an anxious period in my life.

I woke up one morning to a spinning room, so I asked my sister to take me to the hospital. As a student in the middle of my clinical pastoral education, I was accustomed to being in a hospital, but not as the patient.

I will never forget the moment the doctor shared the diagnosis with me: "You have a tumor in your brain." It was during this time of uncertainty that God shared Joshua 1 with me. It became my source of comfort.

Joshua had big shoes to fill, since his great mentor, Moses, had passed away. All of Israel was looking to him to be the next great leader. The burden and anxiety weighed on him. God encouraged Joshua with these words: "Be strong and of good courage; do not be afraid, nor be dismayed, for the Lord your God is with you wherever you go."

In my time of need, this was the message God was sharing with me; that He would be with me in this battle and every battle to come. My "tumor" ended up being an aneurysm, and God healed me after surgery.

God, in our struggles, let Your Word be our encouragement. May we believe and recognize that You are with us in every battle we face. Amen.

Mariya Marton is the pastor of the Stillwater church in Ohio.

Keep on Moving

"Let us run with patience the race that is set before us"
(Heb. 12:1, KJV).

I am not a runner, but have been married to a runner for 25 wonderful years. My wife, Malou, started running in college. About five years ago, I finally decided to join her. We have met many neighbors in our community and made friends in our town, out of state on vacation and overseas through our walking and running experience together.

While I enjoy running (most of the time), it has not been an easy ride. I have learned to keep on moving and "run with patience." I run at my own pace and do not stop. I keep on moving while Malou passes me and comes back for me, sometimes more than once. Even when she leaves me, I know she will come back for me, and we will make it home together. And I know better than to try to outrun her. All I must do is to keep on moving and enjoy the experience at my own pace. To run with patience is not to compete but to enjoy the run.

In our spiritual lives, we must keep on running, knowing that we are not alone. The One who has set the race before us is always with us. At times, we may feel that we have been passed by, but we must continue to run with patience. And when we feel that we have left the path, we must return, knowing that our Savior is not only waiting for us, but is running toward us to complete the journey together (Luke 15:20).

Dear Lord, today and always, please help me to keep on moving with patience, and help me to never stop pursuing my spiritual journey with You. Amen.

Sadrail Saint-Ulysse is the superintendent of schools for the New Jersey Conference.

For the Least of These

"Then the king will answer, 'I tell you the truth. Anything you did for any of my people here, you also did for me'" (Matt. 25:40, ICB).

In preparation for the kingdom of heaven, Jesus wants His disciples to feed, clothe and visit anyone in need. In doing so, we are blessed because we are serving Him also. Jesus explains Himself, saying that if we did this for anyone, we did it for Him. We could be missing out on serving the Lord and growing His kingdom if we ignore opportunities to help others.

This verse helps me when I am saying or doing something to or for someone. It reminds me that I want to be known for treating all people as God does and love them as He loves, for all people belong to God. I learned that we need to be watchful and pray that we don't ignore anyone or say or do anything that does not represent the character of Christ.

This verse has helped me to share kindness with others and find pleasure sharing God's Word in the opportunities that I get with friends and family. I am thankful for God's promises in the Bible that encourage me when I need help and get me through difficult times. I need to surrender to Him every day and ask Him for wisdom and forgiveness for not always putting Him and the "least of these" first in my life.

Dear God, thank You for always being there for me. Please help me to remember that in everything I do, to do it for You. Help me to see You in people in need, and show me how You want me to help them. Amen.

Nolynn Dahlberg is a seventh-grader at Tappahannock Junior Academy in Virginia.

Worrywart

"Therefore do not worry about tomorrow, for tomorrow will worry about itself. Each day has enough trouble of its own" (Matt. 6:34, NIV).

When I was younger, I struggled with anxiety about what would happen the next day. It got to the point where I could not sleep well at night. "What-ifs" would whirl around my head, like, *What if someone came into my room?* or *What if I don't wake up from my sleep?* This made me scared of the dark. I remember being so scared of what the future would hold that I could not focus on what was happening right in front of me.

One day, my mom sat me down and said I did not need to worry about the future. That my family would protect me from bad things. That God would protect me, too, and that I should talk to Him about it. Before I went to bed that night, I prayed to God about it. I went to sleep almost instantly. No bad thoughts, no thinking about the next day, nothing.

Now I am not afraid of what's going to happen tomorrow. I am still scared of the dark sometimes, but I know God has my back no matter what.

Dear Lord, thank You for being there for me and letting me talk to You anytime. Thank You for helping us face our fears. Amen.

Erica Montano-Lopez is an eighth-grader at the C. F. Richards Christian School in Virginia.

The Lord Is My Shepherd

"Thy rod and thy staff they comfort me" (Ps. 23:4, KJV).

The 23rd Psalm has given me a sense of peace and comfort throughout my spiritual journey. In fact, it was one of the first passages of Scripture I committed to memory. "Thy rod and thy staff they comfort me" has particularly been helpful, as I have sought to balance the ups and downs of life.

The rod and staff have different protective functions. The rod directs and protects the sheep, preventing them from danger. The staff, on the other hand, is used to hook the sheep to pull them out of danger. Sheep tend to lose focus and place themselves in danger because of poor eyesight and a wandering attention span. It has been a comfort to me to know that God, my Shepherd, is in constant watch, looking out for me in every situation.

As I reflect on my life, I have experienced the Good Shepherd's rod and staff on numerous occasions. Take a moment and reflect on how God has used His rod and staff in your life, and how you have experienced His wonderful blessings.

Lord, thank You that I can claim Your promise in Psalm 23:6 that "surely goodness and mercy shall follow me all the days of my life." Amen.

William T. Cox Sr., is the executive director for the Regional Conference Retirement Plan Board.

I Can't Wait for Heaven

"I thank my God upon every remembrance of you" (Phil. 1:3, NKJV).

Philippians 1:3 is my favorite Bible verse because I can relate to it. Unfortunately, many family members of mine have passed away. However, when they've passed, I have never gotten angry with God. Instead, I have thanked Him for bringing them into my life, for their wonderful personalities and for giving them a fun and joyful life.

At a young age, my great-uncle passed away from cancer. It was very sad because I was so close to him, and he loved me so much. Right before he died, he wasn't really aware of anything that was happening around him, so when my grandma would stand close to him, he would just blankly stare. But when she lifted me up over him, he would open his eyes really big and smile. I miss him so much, and can't wait to see him smile again in heaven.

My great-grandma died in November of 2019. I was very close to her. She made me laugh when I was sad, and she always made me smile. Even though she is gone, I still smile when I think about her. Right after she died, I thanked God for her wonderful life, her sweet personality and all the fun memories we made together. I can't wait to see her in heaven too.

Dear Heavenly Father, I'm thankful for everyone who is and has been a part of my life. I miss those who have passed away, but I'm looking forward to seeing them again. Be with us now. Amen.

Mya Perdue is a seventh-grader at the Roanoke Adventist Christian School in Virginia.

Jehovah-Jireh: The Lord Will Provide

"And this same God who takes care of me will supply all your needs from His glorious riches, which have been given to us in Christ Jesus" (Phil. 4:19, NLT).

Traces of this text can be easily seen in my journey with a God who consistently provides for me and my family beyond which we can ever ask or imagine. He is our Jehovah-Jireh, the Source of our provision.

At the end of my seminary experience, I was left hanging in the waiting place. With no pastoral call, not knowing what my next step would be and confined with limited resources, I kept asking God, "What's the plan?"

While waiting for an answer, I got a surprise visit from a colleague. She introduced chaplaincy to me and connected me with a colleague of hers at a Clinical Pastoral Education (CPE) Center that needed students for their summer intensive program.

I applied and was accepted, but financially could not accommodate a move to another state, tuition and living expenses. I continued my talk with God and confided in my CPE educator. As a result, I received a subsidized tuition and full-time summer accommodation. Later that year, my church family helped me enter the one-year residency program.

Today, I'm employed in chaplaincy ministry. Only God could have sent a colleague to visit me and provide for me throughout my journey.

Whatever your needs are, cast them on Jesus and trust in His plan. God's response might not be what you want, but it'll be certainly what you need.

Father, thank You for being the One who supplies all my needs. Amen.

Dale Walton is a chaplain at the Troy Hospital for the Kettering Adventist HealthCare in Ohio.

If You Resist, He Will Flee

"Therefore submit to God. Resist the devil and he will flee from you"
(James 4:7, NKJV).

If someone were to ask me what the best advice I have ever received was, I would quote this verse. I have learned that the Bible is a guide, a place I can go to learn what I need to do.

Satan is the king of lies. He left heaven with that title. And there is no doubt that if he deceived the angels, he can and will deceive us. The devil even deceived me in more ways than I can explain.

Satan made me feel guilty. He made me feel as though I was not "enough." My parents divorced when I was younger, and my dad has never been involved in my life. Satan took the grudge that I had and turned it against me. He whispered to me that I was the reason my father didn't care for me. And he made me feel unworthy of having such a loving stepdad. But when I submitted myself to God, the devil fled and I was stronger than ever.

That is why I encourage you to submit yourself to God. When you do, Satan won't find room to attack you—no matter how badly he wants you to fall—and he will flee.

Lord, help us resist Satan's traps in all circumstances. Show us Your will, even in the toughest situations. Amen.

Naomi Coreas is an eighth-grader at the Manassas Adventist Preparatory School in Virginia.

Where You Go, I'll Go

"By day the Lord went ahead of them in a pillar of cloud to guide them on their way and by night in a pillar of fire to give them light, so that they could travel by day or night" (Exod. 13:21, NIV).

I was wrestling with a difficult decision. I knew what I wanted to do, but I had no peace. As I was lying in bed weeping over my decision, a friend called me up and said, "Janesta, I was having my devotions, and God told me I should call you."

We talked for a bit, and I explained my dilemma. I had to decide whether to stay in the place and position I knew God had called me to or go to the place I really wanted to go. My friend read Exodus 13 with me. Then, he asked me a hard question: "Has the cloud moved?" As I tried to tell him that I didn't know, the still, small voice in my heart said, "You do know. We have been here before. You know the peace that you have when I am guiding you."

I thought about my life and how God had led me so many times in the past. I remembered how things had fallen into place as I followed God's leading, even when it was hard to know where we were going. He was right there guiding me, not making the decision for me, but showing me the way. And I knew what to do. I would stay where I was and wait on Him.

When the cloud moved, I had peace, and the cloud led me to a place that was beyond my dreams.

God, may we be willing to go wherever You lead. Amen.

Janesta Walker is the superintendent of education for the Chesapeake Conference.

Keep Your Eyes on the Prize

"Christ was once offered to bear the sins of many; and unto them that look for him shall he appear the second time" (Heb. 9:28, KJV).

In this Bible verse, the phrase "look for" means to "wait eagerly." The Greek translation is made up of three parts: apo (away); kara (head); and dokeo (to await). The literal meaning is very similar to a spring turkey hunter. It means to wait with the head outstretched. The prefix, apo, is a turning away from everything else, with your head raised and your eyes fixed on a single object or an object to come.

Imagine you are a turkey hunter in the woods on a beautiful spring morning. After conversing with a wild turkey gobbler you know to be the boss of the woods, you have made your last call. He has sounded off his last time and has zoomed in on your position. There is no doubt he is coming straight toward you. You've flipped off the safety and your finger is on the trigger. Barely breathing, your eye is fixed on that one spot where you are sure he will appear. Nothing can distract you, even if your wife were to suddenly appear and whisper she had just won a million dollars. You'd reply to her, "There's a gobbler! He's coming!"

This is the picture Scripture gives of God's elect who are anxiously waiting for Jesus to appear. With concentrated expectancy, their attention is completely fixed on that spot. Nothing the world has to offer can distract them. As God's elect, we must be like that spring turkey hunter, and allow nothing to distract us or break our concentration.

Lord, may we always keep our focus on You! Amen.

Richard Cutright is the pastor of the Buckhannon church in West Virginia.

Editor's Note: No turkeys were harmed in the writing of this devotional. Happy Thanksgiving!

Finding the Courage

"An honest answer is as pleasing as a kiss on the lips"
(Prov. 24:26, NCV).

I can imagine it is an exceptionally busy day for King Solomon. He calls his advisors together to ask for feedback on proposed strategic plans and initiatives which he hopes will enrich the quality of life for the people entrusted to his care. I imagine him turning to his counselors and asking for their opinion, only to see them glancing at each other in a hesitant and uncertain manner, wondering what answer he, the king, would find to be most aligned with his preferred option—not one that would ultimately expand his thinking and advance their society. Frustrated by their attempts to placate him, I then imagine King Solomon standing up, towering above the others and banging his hand on the table before demanding, "Just give me an honest answer!"

Perhaps later, in his quiet time, he journaled the proverb, "An honest answer is as pleasing as a kiss on the lips." Here I find insights that are extremely relevant for me today. May I have the courage to speak truth to power, specifically as it pertains to sensitive issues where the answer may not be the popular vote. And may I speak truth that will be refreshing, through which the wisest context for decision-making is created, such that organizations experience positive transformation and our global society is enriched.

Dear Lord, thank You for the courage to speak truth in delicate situations so that joy in our world will ever increase and goodwill toward all people will ever expand. Amen.

Cheryl Kisunzu is the provost of Washington Adventist University in Maryland.

A Willing Offering

"Now therefore, our God, we thank You and praise Your glorious name. But who am I, and who are my people, that we should be able to offer so willingly as this? For all things come from You, and of Your own we have given You" (1 Chron. 29:13-14, NKJV).

Near the end of his reign, King David assembled the people of Israel for what was one of his last public appearances. It was a praise service in which he recounted God's providence and all the preparations made for the great work of building the temple of God. More than once, the Bible records that David and Israel's leaders "offered willingly" to the Lord.

I am thankful that Scripture records David's own words of blessing in 1 Chronicles 29. To the Lord belongs the greatness, the power, the glory, the victory and the majesty, and He reminds us that "both riches and honor come from You" (verse 12). What a picture of God!

But what really speaks to me is the shift that King David makes in verse 14: "But who am I, and who are my people, that we should be able to offer so willingly as this?" David understood that any service or offering rendered to God must come from a right perspective of our relationship to Him. Here was a man who felt his own deep unworthiness. It convicted me that, regardless of position or service, there is nothing as elevating as when I fall low before God.

The latter part of verse 14 is a reminder that all I am and possess is from the Lord. And what I have given to Him is simply returning a portion of what He has given to me.

Lord, I devote my treasures and service to You today. Amen.

John Rengifo is the associate pastor of Evangelism and Discipleship for the Atholton church in Maryland.

Storms Will Come

**"He said to them, 'Why are you so afraid? Have you still no faith?'"
(Mark 4:40, ESV).**

The disciples, several of whom were experienced sailors, had been scared to death as a windstorm brought waves crashing over the side of their boat. Water filled the vessel faster than they could bail it out. Yet, Jesus slept peacefully until the disciples woke him. After calming the storm, He asked them, "Why are you so afraid? Have you still no faith?"

Peter would take this lesson to heart. In Acts 12, he endured a different kind of storm. Shackled between two guards, he slept peacefully in prison though his death was imminent.

How can one sleep in the middle of a storm? I wrestled with this idea at 3 a.m., as once again sleep alluded me. For weeks, I had been struggling with anxiety, which robbed me of peaceful rest night after night. As I prayed to God, He showed me the reason for my distress. I wanted to be in control of everything. God said: *You are not in control. I am.*

My responsibility centered around choosing to trust Him and work alongside Him. I had to trust that He knew the desires of my heart and would continue to do what was best for me in His way and at His time.

It was with this realization that a peace that had eluded me began to grow. Storms still come, and every now and then I find myself awake in the middle of the night. But I remember it is God Who is in control. I simply need to rest in Him.

Dear Lord, help me to remember that You have my life under control. I simply need to choose to have faith in You. Amen.

Michele Joseph attends the Charlottesville and Harrisonburg churches in Virginia, where her husband pastors.

Remember That Verse?

**"Thy word is a lamp unto my feet, and a light unto my path"
(Ps. 105:119, KJV).**

When I was growing up, a standard part of my week was memory verses. Some of the earliest verses I remember learning are "The Lord is my shepherd; I shall not want" (Ps. 23:1, KJV), "All things work together for good" (Rom. 8:28, KJV) and "For God so loved the world" (John 3:16, KJV).

Many of these verses have stayed with me, and they will come to mind when prompted by everyday circumstances. When thinking about this devotional book, I found my thoughts turning to those memory verses from long ago.

One was a text that reminds us that God is always with us. It was written to God's people at a time when they had many reasons to wonder what their future held: "Fear not, for I am with you," is the message of Isaiah 41:10 (NKJV). And Joshua, the leader who had wandered with Israel throughout his nomadic life, is able to confidently state, "The Lord your God will be with you wherever you go" (Josh. 1:9, NIV). There is comfort in remembering that our destiny and ultimate happiness is in God's hands.

Isaiah also reminds, "Those who hope in the Lord will renew their strength" (Isa. 40:31, NIV), affirming the great power that hope brings to our lives.

A verse that has been both a comfort and challenge to me is Micah 6:8: "He has shown you, O man, what is good; and what does the Lord require of you but to do justly, to love mercy, and to walk humbly with your God?" (NKJV).

I'm thankful for the way faith guides our daily lives. I'm thankful for these little bits of Scripture that help bring God's care and calling into focus.

O Lord, let the verses we have learned provide direction for the way we should live. Amen.

Terry Forde is the president and CEO of Adventist HealthCare in Maryland.

Leap of Faith

"He who believes in Me, as the Scripture has said, out of his heart will flow rivers of living water" (John 7:38, NKJV).

Have you ever made a decision that you were uncertain about the outcome? Yet, you took one big leap of faith in God, trusting Him to direct your path?

In February 2007, my then-family of four, made a big decision that eventually changed our lives forever. We left our loved ones in Kenya—the one place we had always known as home—to relocate to a foreign land where we knew no one, nor what the future held. We trusted in God's guidance and leading every step of the way.

During our first few weeks in the United States, we encountered trials that made us regret our decision. At times, we found ourselves questioning if God had forgotten us when we had fully surrendered ourselves to Him. My purse was stolen at a grocery store, we were robbed at gunpoint just outside our house and we almost died in a car accident that wrecked and totaled the vehicle. Witnesses couldn't believe anyone survived. But, through all of this, God was in control.

Since that time, God has blessed our lives immensely. He opened doors for my husband to continue his ministry journey. He gave us two more children—making us a family of six—and made it possible for all of them to get a Christian education.

Always commit your plans and decisions to the Lord and fully trust and obey Him. Patiently wait on His timing, and you will be amazed at what He can and will do in your life.

Father, thank You that we can always rely on You to lead the way. Amen.

Peris Apola is the administrative assistant and accounts clerk for the Columbia Union Revolving Fund in Maryland.

"Salvation is found in no one else, for there is no other name under heaven given to mankind by which we must be saved." ACTS 4:12, NIV

DECEMBER

The Real Superman

"The Son of Man came to find lost people and save them"
(Luke 19:10, ICB).

I have a bad habit of getting lost. I've been lost in grocery stores, malls, parks and even at church.

When I was 2, I climbed out of my stroller at Hershey Park to look at some flowers, and, when I turned around, my parents were gone. I don't remember what happened next, but somehow I ended up at the Lost and Found with a nice lady. Soon after that, my dad came and found me.

When I was 4, we went to Disney World, and just before the big fireworks show, we went into a souvenir shop. I spotted a Minnie Mouse hat with a crown on it that looked really cool. As her biggest fan at the time, I *had* to get my hands on it. When I turned to show my mom and sister, I couldn't find them. An employee sat with me until they came and found me.

Another time, my dad, sister and I were walking in our town. We waited a long time for the light to signal that it was our time to cross the street. Knowing it would soon change, I started walking, and didn't notice a bus heading toward me. Suddenly, my dad picked me up and carried me back to the sidewalk, just as the bus passed. Once again, my dad had rescued me.

Luke 19:10 reminds me that Jesus loves us so much that He came to save us. And when we get into trouble or when we are lost, He rescues us. He is the *real* Superman!

Dear Jesus, thank You for loving me. Thank You that You came to rescue us and save us. Amen.

Sarita Blyden is a fourth-grader at Atholton Adventist Academy in Maryland.

The Power of Peace

"Peace I leave with you; My peace I give to you. Not as the world gives do I give to you. Let not your hearts be troubled, neither let them be afraid" (John 14:27, ESV).

Why do we need peace? Better yet, why do we need God's peace, and how is God's peace better than the world's? God gives us a kind of peace that the world cannot give. A kind of peace that takes away fear. One that is stronger than the world itself.

When we are stressed or scared, we often wish for a calm feeling of peace to comfort us. Sometimes we have stressful days, and other times we have to face very hard decisions. God can take away those fears! All we have to do is ask Him.

God will give us peace so we don't have to be afraid of whatever we are dealing with. Our problems may seem big, but God is greater than those problems.

Sometimes it is very hard to feel peace with all the trials and tribulations of this earth. However, even though there is all this darkness, there is a light at the end of the tunnel. Jesus tells us in John 16:33, "I have told you these things, so that in me you may have peace. In this world, you will have trouble. But take heart! I have overcome the world" (NIV). The world may scare us, but God is the One who is ultimately in control.

Lord, thank You for being the One in control of our world. Thank You for the peace You give and the promises we can claim in Your Word. Help us to trust You in every situation. Amen.

Kaley Walls is a seventh-grader at Vienna Adventist Academy in Virginia.

My Strength and Song

"The Lord is my strength and my song, and He has become my salvation" (Ps. 118:14, NKJV).

It was late Tuesday night, and I desperately wanted to sleep as I paced around my dorm room. It was the second day of our student-led Week of Prayer, and I was scheduled to speak the next day.

I had spent the last four hours writing out my mini-sermon, and it was finally done. I was happy with the result and extremely excited to share it with my peers, but the idea of speaking in front of the entire school left me sick to my stomach. I grabbed my Bible and flipped around in the book of Psalms, trying desperately to find reassurance.

I found myself at Psalms 118 and read it once, twice, three times; first in my head, and then aloud. The words were everything I needed at that moment. The psalm promised that God is there in my moments of distress, that He hears me when I feel overwhelmed and helpless and that He is my strength.

When I stood in front of my school the following day, I was still terrified. My hands were shaking, but my voice was clear. Despite my fear, I had confidence in God and myself—in a way I had never experienced before.

I wish I could say I always turn to God in times of trouble, but I usually rely on my own strength instead of relying on the most powerful Being in the universe, forgetting to consult with Infinite Wisdom. Yet, He is always there, ready to welcome me with open arms the moment I cry out for help.

Lord, in our moments of fear and anxiety, please give us Your strength and peace. Amen.

Aubrey Benton is a 2020 graduate of Shenandoah Valley Academy in Virginia.

The Lost Wallet

"My voice shalt thou hear in the morning, O Lord; in the morning will I direct my prayer unto thee, and will look up" (Ps. 5:3, KJV).

Sabbath morning dawned bright and fair, but icily cold. It gave every appearance of imminent snow, and, sure enough, I could soon see the flurries making their unique design on my windowpane! From all accounts earlier in the week, the church service promised to be a real blessing. My husband and sons were ready to go, and all I needed was my pocketbook. A quick look inside revealed that my wallet was not in its usual place. I tried not to panic and began to search all the likely places I might have left it.

An inner voice kept telling me that I was just wasting time. I pushed it aside, but another frantic search through the house and car yielded no positive results. I decided I might have left it at the nearby high school where I taught, but a quick trip there proved fruitless. By then I was totally despondent and sure that the prayers we had offered up were not helping. Should I wallow in self-pity, remain at home and allow my family to go on to church without me? I certainly was not in the mood for praise or rejoicing. Nevertheless, I yielded to the voice of faith, not doubt. "Dear God, please see me through this situation," I whispered.

Although late, my family and I made our way to church. A wonderful sermon brought a new commitment to Christ from our firstborn. And more joyous news arrived: Two days later, my husband searched the car again and found my missing wallet!

Lord, help us to trust You through all the vicissitudes of life. Amen.

Gloriadine Bramble is a member of the Bucks County church in Pennsylvania.

Be Kind

**"A man who is kind benefits himself, but a cruel man hurts himself"
(Prov. 11:17, ESV).**

What is kindness? According to the dictionary, kindness is "a behavior of being friendly, generous, and considerate." This means that smiling at someone, holding a door for someone, helping someone with schoolwork or giving money to homeless people are acts of kindness.

Do we need kindness? Absolutely. Kindness is valued by all cultures and religions. Proverbs 11:17 says that "a man who is kind benefits himself, but a cruel man hurts himself." I agree with King Solomon. When someone is being kind to me, I feel good, and when I do something kind to others, I feel good too.

As followers of Jesus, we are to be kind to everyone, even if we don't feel like it, and even if the person is not nice or is different than us.

When David became king, he searched for anyone in Saul's house to whom he could show kindness. He found Mephibosheth, the son of Jonathan and the grandson of Saul. Mephibosheth was so afraid, thinking David would kill him! But David came to show kindness for the sake of his friend Jonathan. David gave Mephibosheth all the land that Saul owned, and Mephibosheth ate at the king's table like one of the king's sons. Now *that* is kindness.

Dear God, thank You for being "compassionate and gracious, slow to anger and abounding in lovingkindness" (Ps. 103:8, NASB). Amen.

Dale Flynn is a fifth-grader at Vienna Adventist Academy in Virginia.

God Is in Control

"'For I know the plans I have for you,' declares the Lord, 'plans to prosper you and not to harm you, plans to give you hope and a future'" (Jer. 29:11, NIV).

Throughout my life, this verse has always reminded me that God is in control. There are times when I wonder why things happen the way they do or if something in my life is the right thing for me. However, each time these doubts fill my mind, I remember that God puts everything in my life for a purpose.

When I was 13, I started attending Shenandoah Valley Academy (SVA)—a Seventh-day Adventist boarding school. Prior to this, I had attended public school and I didn't look forward to leaving home and transitioning to an Adventist private school. At first, my outlook toward SVA was very pessimistic, and I found myself asking *Why am I here?* God answered that question, and He completely changed my outlook.

At SVA, He surrounded me with caring and loving people who accepted me for who I was. God knew that I would receive a great education and develop a stronger relationship with Him. I was able to grow in my studies and in my spiritual life.

Even though I doubted at times, Jeremiah 29:11 reminded me that God always had a plan for my life. God knows what is in store for all of us, and He will lead us to success. A God so loving will never leave our side and cause us to crumble in our own doubts. Whenever we find ourselves questioning why things happen, we can know that He is in control.

Lord, thank You for the assurance that You have a perfect plan for our lives. Amen.

Josselyn Villatoro is a 2020 graduate of Shenandoah Valley Academy in Virginia.

Everything We Need

"By his divine power, God has given us everything we need for living a godly life. We have received all of this by coming to know Him, the One who called us to Himself by means of His marvelous glory and excellence" (2 Pet. 1:3, NLT).

I love this text, mostly because it is a simple proclamation of the gospel. But also because it sets the record straight in regard to the lies the serpent told in the Garden of Eden. Many people are still being convinced that God's Word is not reliable, that God uses obedience to keep good things from his people and that we do not already have everything we need to reflect the image of God.

Jesus counteracts these lies and restores the damage they have done. Jesus, Himself, is the evidence that we can trust in God's promises, that God holds nothing back from us and that, in Him, we have everything we need to realize our God-given identity and escape the power of sin.

If we feel that we do not have everything we need, we are reminded that it is not because God is not there or that He is keeping good things from us. It is only an optical illusion that our sin is greater or more powerful than what God has done for us. Satan loves to use the continued presence of sin to convince us that God has abandoned us or that we are disqualified to participate in the good things that God has given. Sin can blind us and cloud our minds, but it cannot take away our calling and election. All other thoughts that cause us to doubt this are illusions and lies.

Thank You, Lord, that our calling and election are safe and secure in Jesus.

Leah Jordache is the Bible teacher and chaplain at Spencerville Adventist Academy in Maryland.

The Vinedresser

**"I am the true vine, and My Father is the vinedresser.
Every branch in Me that does not bear fruit He takes away; and
every branch that bears fruit He prunes, that it may bear more fruit.
... Abide in Me, and I in you. As the branch cannot bear fruit of itself,
unless it abides in the vine, neither can you, unless you abide in Me"
(John 15:1-2, 4, NKJV).**

These words have brought me so much comfort over the years. When I was a junior at Southwestern Adventist University (Texas), I felt lost and not ready to face my senior year. God had not answered my prayers and desire to travel the world.

Then, a few weeks before my junior year came to a close, I walked past the Student Missions office, and felt God telling me to go inside. Mind you, it is not my nature to walk into an office and talk to strangers. But I found myself asking the director about places student missionaries had been to in the past. It did not take long to realize that God was calling me to be a missionary. I prayed and asked Him to show me how this would be possible.

That fall, I went to Chuuk, a state in the Guam-Micronesia Mission field. While serving there, I recall reading John 15, seeing God "prune" areas in my life that did not fit His plan and fulfilling a plan He had already laid out perfectly for me. Allowing the Vinedresser to prune desires that were against His plan helped me to see how much more potential I had when I placed Him at the forefront.

Thank You, God, for continuing to prune me so that I can bear fruit for You. Amen.

Tabita Martinez is the undertreasurer for the Columbia Union Conference.

Our Comforter

"Thy word is a lamp unto my feet and a light unto my path"
(Ps. 119:105, KJV).

In the movie *The Sound of Music*, Maria sings "My Favorite Things" to the von Trapp children to comfort them during a thunderstorm. She tells them that whenever she's scared or upset, she simply sings about things that bring her comfort and joy. I figure if she can sing about "raindrops on roses," then I should be able to use Scripture to do the same thing.

Set to this song's tune, this is "My Favorite Things: The Christian Version."

The Lord is my shepherd, I shall not want.
No weapon that's formed against me shall harm.
Be anxious for nothing, and in all things pray.
Trust in the Lord that He'll make a way.

He's my strong tower and He's my defense.
His angels around me, protect like a fence.
Casting my cares upon Him I know,
He died for my sins 'cause He loves me so.

All things they work together for good,
To them who love and are called by the Lord.
If God be for us, who can be against?
The battle's not ours, but it's His to win.

When the new is bad,
When the lion roars,
When I'm feeling scared,
I simply recite some of my favorite texts, and realize that God is near.

God, may Your words comfort me during times of distress. Amen.

K. L. Watkins is the principal of the Sharon Temple Adventist School in Delaware.

Beans and Rice

"And my God will meet all your needs according to the riches of His glory in Christ Jesus" (Phil. 4:19, NIV).

Many people live from paycheck to paycheck. In fact, many are one paycheck away from being homeless. I've been there before.

I had three small children living in Texas. There was no food, no job, no money and no husband. I had one cup of rice and one cup of beans, and, like the widow in the Bible, I was going to make that meal and then try to figure it out from there. She had made up her mind to die; I wasn't quite there yet, but I was very discouraged.

I was living in a town where I had no friends, church or family. My baby daughter needed milk, but I didn't have any way to get it. I felt hopeless.

So I did what I saw my parents do. I prayed. I prayed to a God that I was not sure about and really not following at the time. I wasn't sure if He would even listen to me. I asked Him to help me to know what to do and where to go. I didn't know anyone and wasn't sure where to get help.

When I finished praying, there was a knock at my front door. There stood a lady with a huge box of food. I didn't know her, and I don't remember her ever saying where she was from. She just said she felt impressed to bring me food. I was so grateful. Tears streamed down my face.

Through every difficult circumstance since that time, I've found God to be true and reliable. He's always supplied the "beans and rice."

Thank You, Lord, for taking care of all of our needs. Amen.

Lori Farr is the pastor of the Miamisburg church in Ohio.

Armed to the Teeth

"Put on the whole armor of God, that you may be able to stand against the wiles of the devil" (Eph. 6:11, NKJV).

"The term 'armed to the teeth' originated in Port Royal Jamaica in the 1600s when pirates were constantly looking for ships to loot and their guns were very primitive. As a result, pirates could shoot only once before a long reloading process. Consequently, they needed to carry a gun in each hand, and perhaps in each pocket. For extra power, they would also hold a knife between their teeth. To be 'armed to the teeth' means to carry the maximum number of weapons possible."*

Because we are in a war against the devil, we need to be "armed to the teeth." The Bible is our weapons store, our armory where we may arm ourselves for the struggle. Our loins must be gird about with truth. Our breastplate must be righteousness. Our feet must be fit with shoes of the preparation of the gospel of peace. The shield of faith must be in our hand. Our sword, the Word of God, must be in hand. Our head must be covered with the helmet of salvation. And we know where our help comes from: "[Our] help comes from the Lord" (Ps. 121:2, NKJV).

We have a General—Jesus Christ. When He died on the cross and rose on the third day, He obtained victory over the powers of death and the evil one. Jesus has never lost a battle, and He never will. He has promised us victory at the start of our battle and has given us victory at the end. So let us arm ourselves to the teeth!

Lord, may we put on the whole armor of God every day. Amen.

Kelly Strickland is an elder at the Rehoboth church in Pennsylvania.

* timesofindia.indiatimes.com/what-is-the-origin-of-the-term-armed-to-the-teeth/
articleshow/274090.cms (accessed November 19, 2020).

Light of Salvation

"Your word is a lamp to my feet, and a light to my path"
(Ps. 119:105, NKJV).

It seems as if the jungle, the mountains and rural areas are favorite destinations to send new ministers. I was no exception. My first district was in the deep forest of Nicaragua, surrounded by rushing rivers and deep lagoons. Our congregations resided in small communities nestled around these lagoons. Ninety percent of travel between them was by river, so we used an outboard motorboat to carry out pastoral work.

Although it was not advisable to sail at night in those areas, sometimes the work required it. This was the case during one of our pastoral visits. A powerful storm overtook us and darkened the route much earlier than we expected. There was no moon, no stars, no lamps or anything that could help us see in the middle of the dense and dark night.

Oh, how we needed light! At times, thunder and lightning brightened the way momentarily, enabling us to advance. Suddenly, the engine stopped. For a few seconds, we were silent and perplexed. *Why was this happening to us now?* I thought. Instantly, a powerful lightning bolt illuminated the entire sky and river, and, to our amazement, we were right in front of a sunken boat jutting out of the water.

God had delivered us from certain death. His light guided us and showed us imminent danger. In the same way, God acts in the midst of this dark world. His words act like those lightning bolts, illuminating our path to give us security and salvation.

Thank You, God, for lighting our path. Amen.

Peter M. Simpson is the coordinator of Hispanic Ministries and director of Global Mission for the Ohio Conference.

The Branch, Not the Vine

"I am the true vine, and My Father is the vinedresser"
(John 15:1, NASB).

Jesus' teaching in John 15:1 illustrates our dependence on Him: "I am the true vine," He says. How often have we tried to be the vine, but produced sour grapes—the ugly works of the flesh? We have tried to find holiness and love for others in ourselves, which we will never find. "I know that nothing good lives in me, that is, in my sinful nature" (Rom. 7:18, NIV).

Jesus, the true Vine, will produce the fruit of the Spirit as we allow Him to live in us. "I am crucified with Christ; nevertheless I live" (Gal. 2:20, KJV). Paul, who was crucified with Christ, was not the vine, vainly trying to do his best. He was the branch, whose self-confidence was broken and dependent on the Lord.

The responsibility of trying to be the vine makes us tense, predisposing us to further sin. Attempting to depend more on Him without repenting of trying to be the vine is vain. Dependence on the true Vine, and, our willingness to be the branch and not the vine, allows His salvation and blessings to be worked out through us to reach others.

Lord, may we stop trying and start depending on You. Amen.

William Peterson is the executive secretary of the Pennsylvania Conference.

God Chose You!

"But now listen, Jacob, my servant, Israel, whom I have chosen" (Isa. 44:1, NIV).

You can be the one through whom God changes the course of the world. Through the annals of time, shining examples of people were used by God for that exact purpose. David was a young shepherd when he faced Goliath. Jeremiah was about 20 years old when he accepted God's call to be His voice. Esther was a woman in a foreign land when she saved her people. Martin Luther was a young adult when he started the Protestant Reformation. God called William Miller, a 50-year-old farmer, to proclaim the Advent message to the world. Not long after, Ellen White, at the age of 17, received her first vision. They each heeded the call and obeyed the commission to shine as bright lights during periods of darkness.

Today, the same voice that spoke to Isaiah can be heard saying, "Whom shall I send? And who will go for us?" (Isa. 6:8, NIV). The Holy Spirit wants us to occupy a special place in the history of redemption.

We live in a world that carries the virus called evil: the horror of terrorism evidenced in suicide attacks, the war in the Middle East, racial tension and homicides recorded in real-time.

Today, what is desperately needed is a generation of disciples who will commit to engage in interpersonal relationships. In this way, as Seventh-day Adventist Christians, we will have a resounding and far-reaching impact on the world. We must decide to make a positive change in our circles of influence. When we do, God will work in us and through us so that the reflection of Jesus will become a daily experience on this earth.

Lord, when You call, may we answer. Amen.

Javier Moreno is the pastor of the Baltimore Spanish church in Maryland.

The Lord Is My Song

"God is my salvation, I will trust and not be afraid; for Yah, the Lord, is my strength and song" (Isa. 12:2, NKJV).

The phone rang. A voice on the other end had bad news to share with me.

"Your dad is not getting better," she said.

That sunny day turned gloomy and gray.

Prone to depression, I asked my husband, "How can I be happy when dad is suffering? How can I enjoy the sunny days when he is cooped up in a hospital and I cannot visit?"

Thankfully, there is Someone who is faithful and kind and who every morning gives me the strength to continue on my journey. He promises to carry my burdens and heavy load.

Little by little, I've learned how to smile in the midst of sorrow. My dad and I receive help and resources from many people and places. God sees all our needs and supplies them. My Strength restores my soul and energy. My Song puts a tune in my heart to rejoice in Him during stormy situations.

There will be a day when I meet my Savior, and I will thank Him face-to-face as I thank Him now.

Lord, I am not afraid of the future because You are my salvation. Thank You. Amen.

Laura Ottati-Romero is the director of Children's Ministries and the executive assistant of Multicultural Ministries for the Allegheny West Conference.

Salt on a Bird's Tail

"And [Jesus] said, Verily I say unto you, Except ye be converted, and become as little children, ye shall not enter into the kingdom of heaven" (Matt. 18:3, KJV).

When I was a boy, my grandfather used to say, "If you can put salt on a bird's tail, you can catch the bird." He would then hand us the saltshaker, and off we children went for hours of fun that brought joy and laughter to the adults watching from the porch. Needless to say, we wasted lots of salt and could never get close enough to those illusive birds.

When I was married and had children of my own, I told my wife about the grand adventure I had as a child. Like any good parent, we had to try this experiment with our own children. And like my own elders, we spent hours watching our children enjoy childhood in its purest form.

As time went by, the salt and the birds were forgotten in our minds, but not our kid's. One morning, we awoke with a sense of alarm. The kids were running through the house with excitement. It did not take long to figure out the cause of their joy. "Get the salt!" we heard our daughter exclaim. A bird had flown through an open window, and they wanted to catch it.

In that moment, we fully understood why Jesus said it takes the faith of a child to get to heaven. A child trusts and believes until the sin of the world—through experiences and hurt—destroys that trust. Only Jesus can restore our childlike faith and hope.

Heavenly Father, teach us to put our faith and trust in You. Amen.

Chris Trent is the pastor of the Grace Outreach and Grace Community churches in West Virginia.

Prayer Still Works

**"With men this is impossible, but with God all things are possible"
(Matt. 19:26, NKJV).**

"This can't be happening to me!" I said. The doctor's diagnosis hit me like a ton of bricks. I was suffering from a painful illness that was spreading aggressively. In spite of this distressing news, I remained optimistic that surgery was still an option.

Unfortunately, I awoke from that first surgery only to be confronted with more dismal news. There was nothing they could do for me! Naturally, I started to blame myself because I knew something was wrong years ago, but I ignored all the warning signs, choosing to bear the pain silently.

I prayed to God to help me to find a doctor able to handle my case. I had nearly given up when my mom called me. She was not ready to give up. As we prayed, an overwhelming sense of peace entered my heart. I did not know what God would do, but I was certain that He would do something.

Months later, we found a doctor who believed this impossible surgery was indeed possible! However, he cautioned that it was no easy task. A team of specialists had to be assembled.

When the day finally came, I felt the divine assurance that God was with me. The surgery did not go smoothly, and the doctor confessed that he thought they might lose me. But to his surprise, I survived.

My very existence is a testimony to the fact that with God all things are possible! What are you worried about today? Give it to Jesus.

God, there is nothing too hard for You. Help us to trust You with the circumstances of our lives. Amen.

Anastacia Ferguson-Bansie is the director of Women's Ministries for the Chesapeake Conference and an associate pastor of the Atholton church in Maryland.

He Will Direct Your Path

"Trust in the Lord with all thine heart; and lean not unto thine own understanding. In all thy ways acknowledge Him, and He shall direct thy paths" (Prov. 3:5–6, KJV).

Many times throughout my life, I have followed these passages, and the Lord has led me in the right path.

Several years ago, I lived in a mobile home that, unbeknownst to me, was affecting my health. I had been dealing with pneumonia for several months. One day, I saw an ad for an apartment and prayed for the Lord's leading. I was able to sell my mobile home, and I moved into the apartment. I have not had pneumonia since!

In this community, I have made a lot of friends and have been able to help many of the elderly residents. I have even been called an "angel." All credit goes to the Lord for giving me the strength to do all I can.

Lord, please be with each of us in these difficult times, and let us remember that You are still in control. Amen.

Becky Newman is a member of the Springfield First church in Ohio.

When Grace Happens

"I do believe; help me overcome my unbelief!" (Mark 9:24, NIV).

There are times when believing does not come easy for me, because too many people that I care about hurt too much to let believing come easy. People close to me get cancer and die. My friends' marriages turn into battlefields. God does not seem to do many miracles for my crowd.

But people in my little orbit are just starters. All those starving children I pray for around the world keep on dying, and the oppressed people I pray for keep getting their heads banged and their freedoms choked. I know we make many of our own miseries. I am only admitting that when I believe that God really cares, there are a lot of hurts that suggest He does not seem to care enough.

Believing sneaks into my heart when my mind says, "God, where were you when I needed you?" I'm speaking about really believing, the kind you do with your deepest self, down where your deepest feelings flow. These are the feelings that push my life toward joy or misery—feelings of the heart, the window of my being, where I am open to God.

That's when I rediscover grace. Grace happens when I feel a surge of honest joy that makes me glad to be alive in spite of valid reasons for feeling terrible. It happens when grace tells me I can be sure that my future is going to turn out better than I dare imagine. Grace gives me hope, and it happens on many layers of my life.

Please Lord, when we deeply feel that life is all wrong, help us to overcome our unbelief and really believe that your grace can make it all right. Amen.

Rob Vandeman retired from the Columbia Union Conference after nearly 50 years as a pastor and administrator.

No Limits

"'The Lord did not set His love on you nor choose you because you were more in number than any of the peoples, for you were the fewest of all peoples, but because the Lord loved you'" (Deut. 7:7-8, NASB).

When I was 7, I had been in and out of hospitals multiple times trying to find answers on how to correct severe congenital birth defects that affected my hands and feet. Now I was on a stage at a major university medical center, complete with spotlights and about 30 adults around me wearing white jackets—presumably doctors, researchers and interns. A professor got up and listed the great qualities I possessed. Good grades in school. Socially well-adjusted. Loving home. Then the show really started, at least for me.

I was asked to demonstrate how I could not tie my shoes, button my shirt, etc. The professor said, "Because of this boy's lack of key abilities, he will always need to be tended to by others." This made me furious. I refused to follow their instructions any further and ran out of the room to find my parents.

Today, I am in the middle of a second career as a pastor, and God has favored me with blessing after blessing, including a beautiful wife, children and grandchildren. And I was once a businessman, vice president and set sales records in Fortune 500 companies.

Never limit the potential of others by what you see on the surface, because our God makes big statements by getting the most from the least.

God, remind us that whether it's Jericho, Gideon or a boy's lunch, You do not need our strength but our willingness. Amen.

Roy Weeden is the district pastor of the Williamsport, Milton and Lock Haven churches in Pennsylvania.

The Mind of Christ

"Let this mind be in you, which was also in Christ Jesus" (Phil. 2:5, KJV).

What is the mind of Christ? How does God think? If we continue with this passage in Philippians, we learn that even though Jesus was God, He humbled Himself to become a man. But He didn't stop there. He didn't come as a king or some wealthy person; He became a servant.

He didn't stop there either. He humbled Himself to be subject to death on a cross—the worst and most humiliating form of punishment any human could endure. Accordingly, the mind of Christ is complete and utter selflessness and humility.

Because of His selfless sacrifice, we learn that Christ was exalted above every name. And "that at the name of Jesus every knee should bow" (Phil. 2:10, KJV).

Contrast this with Lucifer, who said, "I will ascend into heaven, I will exalt my throne above the stars of God. ... I will be like the most High" (Isa. 14:13–14, KJV). Lucifer wanted everything, including the worship of all living creatures. Pride ruled his heart. And what will happen to him? "Yet thou shalt be brought down to hell" (Isa. 14:15, KJV). Lucifer was unwilling to give up pride and selfishness, and he will suffer the consequences.

Am I willing to give up my own desires, selfishness and pride and follow Christ? God promises that "it is God which worketh in you both to will and to do of His good pleasure" (Phil. 2:13, KJV). So God will give us the victory, then give us the reward at the end, just for allowing Him to do His will in us.

Father, thank You that You give us victory through Jesus. May we have His selfless mind. Amen.

Perry Heinrich is an elder and the treasurer of the Linthicum church in Maryland.

Closer Than Before

"Trust in the Lord with all your heart, and lean not on your own understanding; in all your ways acknowledge Him, and He shall direct your paths" (Prov. 3:5–6, NKJV).

The book was *How People Grow*, by Drs. Henry Cloud and John Townsend. I had been courageously absorbing its wisdom for several weeks. Eventually, though, I had to stop and address a painful realization: I'm nowhere near the emotionally healthy adult I should be.

I knew it was unwise to wallow in such self-criticism. Emotional maturity can be altered by many factors, and emotional abuse during one's formative years is no small one. I needed to tread carefully, and slowly heal the wounds that had altered everything from friendships to the bedrock of my identity. Still, I could not shake the feeling that I was behind in my progress.

It was time to revisit Proverbs 3:5–6. I had reflected on this passage many times concerning my career aspirations; but now, a different application surfaced. I could no longer lean on my own understanding of myself. God could see my progress report much better than me. Clinging to His understanding of me was key to enduring the winding paths of growth.

We all may encounter self-doubts, whether via a thought-provoking book or another experience. But instead of focusing on our incomplete areas of healing, it is imperative that we continue accepting what God is accomplishing in and for us. We may still not be where we should be, but thank God we can be closer than before.

Father, You have instructed us to replace our finite understanding with trust in Your infinite discernment. Help us to do so! Remove the power of sin and brokenness over our lives as we abide in Your gift of restoration. Amen.

Yasmin Phillip is a member of the New Market church in Virginia.

I've Got the Joy!

"Then he said to them, 'Go your way, eat the fat, drink the sweet, and send portions to those for whom nothing is prepared; for this day is holy to our Lord. Do not sorrow, for the joy of the Lord is your strength'" (Neh. 8:10, NKJV).

"The joy of the Lord is your strength." What a wonderful promise God has given us. Unfortunately, there is a great misunderstanding that we have to straighten out to understand God's gift correctly. We need to dispel the idea that joy is not dependent upon the situations and circumstances of life. A survey of the context of joy in the Bible reveals that it is very much dependent upon life situations. What's important for us to recognize is that the joy God promises us is not just any joy: it is a joy that is "of the Spirit," or, as Nehemiah called it, the "joy of the Lord."

This is the joy, that, when set before Christ, caused Him to endure the cross, despising the shame. This is the joy Christians have that enables them to face various trials with a spirit of rejoicing. This is the joy that remains, regardless of outside circumstances, a joy that no one and nothing can take away, a joy that will grow and flourish until your entire life is full of it.

This joy—like all joy—is dependent upon circumstance. What makes this joy special is that it is only dependent on the active, interested, loving presence of Jesus—the very One who has promised, "I will never leave you nor forsake you" (Heb. 13:5, NKJV).

Father, thank You for the joy Your presence provides. Help me to abide in Your joy today and every day. Amen.

Jon K. Clayburn is the pastor of the Meridian Road, New Castle and Shenango Valley churches in Pennsylvania.

Look for the Miracles

"I would have lost heart, unless I had believed that I would see the goodness of the Lord in the land of the living" (Ps. 27:13, NKJV).

Have you noticed that in the difficult times we're living in, there have also been many miracles? For example, during the coronavirus pandemic, a young husband and father from New Jersey was on a ventilator, and doctors prepared his family for the worst. His sister sent out a desperate plea for prayer, people everywhere interceded for him, and, against all odds, he recovered. "God defies science!" she later testified, "He performed a miracle for my brother!"

The Bible recounts many miracles. Miracles happened when there was someone in need, in trouble, or in crisis. When our world was in crisis, Jesus came to earth to save us. Our Miracle came wrapped in swaddling clothing and spent His first nights in a stable. During His ministry, Jesus fed a hungry crowd with just two fish and five loaves of bread. He healed the sick, the blind, the lame and calmed the storms. In each situation, Jesus defied the odds and expectations and brought healing, restoration and peace. His miracles made doubters believe, set captives free and saved sinners.

At a well, Jesus met a woman who was lost and empty, and transformed her life and the lives of the people in her town. When Jesus transforms our lives, that's the greatest of all miracles.

Troubles won't last always, but when they come—and many will in these last days—look for the miracles and the opportunities to witness the work of our God. He is able, and He is mighty to save!

Dear God, thank You for the miracles—evidence of Your goodness and grace. Amen.

Celeste Ryan Blyden is the vice president for Strategic Communication and Public Relations for the Columbia Union Conference, and editor and publisher of the Visitor magazine.

The Best Gift

"One person gives freely, yet gains even more; another withholds unduly, but comes to poverty. A generous person will prosper; whoever refreshes others will be refreshed" (Prov. 11:24-25, NIV).

For me, Christmas has always been a time of immense gratitude for all that God has done in my life. However, amid the wonderful festivities and excitement—glimmering lights, delicious food and gifts wrapped with bows—it's easy to forget that for some, these displays are a further reminder of what they don't have.

Some of these folks live in our communities, go to our schools and work in our organizations. Some of them wake up, put on a badge and go to work—just like we do. One day, I was chatting with a staff member at one of our hospitals who shared the plight of her colleagues struggling to put food on the table and pay bills, let alone spend money on anything extra. It touched my heart and was a startling reminder that outward appearances can be deceiving.

When Jesus came to this earth as a baby more than 2,000 years ago, each of us were given a remarkable gift—the promise of forgiveness and the hope of eternal life. The "glad tidings and great joy" that Jesus brought, and the gifts He gives, transcend economic barriers and earthly status. When it comes to God's love, we're all on the same level. One way we can reflect His love to our communities is to give graciously and continuously, just like He does for us.

This Christmas, I pray that God will open our eyes and hearts to see the needs of those around us and remind us that giving isn't seasonal.

God, You have given so much to us. May we be Christlike and give freely to others. Amen.

Fred Manchur is the CEO of Kettering Adventist HealthCare in Ohio.

The One

"I am the way, the truth, and the life. No one comes to the Father except through Me" (John 14:6, NKJV).

Growing up in a loving Muslim home—led by my generous, strong, industrious mother—was a tremendous blessing to me. A commitment to the five pillars of Islam provided a foundation upon which I developed a reverence for an omnipresent, omniscient and omnipotent God.

However, that foundation also left me seeking more. In spite of my questions and misgivings, I persisted in my desire to walk with God unreservedly. I wanted to know truth—even if it made me uncomfortable. One day, while at my university campus job, I lowered my head onto the desk and prayed, "God, please show me truth. No matter how you direct me, I just want to know truth."

Through books, people, music and study helps, God was preparing my heart and mind to be confronted by a powerful claim by Jesus: "I am the way, the truth, and the life. No one comes to the Father except through Me." I was struck by the absolute nature of this statement. I was struck by its simplicity. I grappled with it, nonetheless. Jesus was not *A* way, but *The* way—*The One*. The more I learned about the exceptional beauty and overwhelming love and character of this God, the less I could deny His claim. I became convinced of Christ's sovereignty.

My life changed completely. I had found Truth! The peace, joy and strength of choosing to walk in His way, rest in His truth and experience and anticipate His abundant life is daily encouragement for the world-ravaged soul.

God, may we walk, rest, abide and trust in the love and care of the One who is the way, the truth and the life. Amen.

Naeemah Shakir Phillip is a member of the New Market church in Virginia.

Hold On to the Rock

"My soul clings to You; Your right hand upholds me" (Ps. 63:8, NASB).

An item on my bucket list is to climb the Sydney Harbour Bridge in Australia. Adventurers who cross the structure for a 360-degree view of the waterfront city must wear a special suit that straps them to a railing. Gale winds at the summit can reach 55 miles per hour, enough force to rip a roof off a building.

Securing people to a structure for safety harkens back to ancient Greek literature. In Homer's epic *Odyssey*, the hero Odysseus' ship passes by Sirens, monsters disguised as beautiful women who sing enchanting melodies and lure sailors to their deaths. Odysseus demands to be strapped to the mast so he can hear the music but not be enticed by the Sirens.

The secular world sings a special "Siren" song to each of us that can shipwreck our faith. We all struggle with something—alcohol, sex, drugs, pornography, other vices and issues—that distracts us from our Creator. I have often clutched at food for comfort when I should have clung to God. The pleasures that evil provides seem highly entertaining in the moment. As the end of time grows closer, the devil goes about like a roaring lion seeking to devour us, just as the Sirens sought to devour Odysseus. He pinpoints our weaknesses and desires and targets us with gale-force temptations to lure us away from God to our downfall.

When we spend time in God's Word and prayer, we shore up our harnesses to a Rock that will hold us steady when temptation blows in.

Protector God, we have no power in our own strength to resist the temptations that buffet us from all sides. Help us to cling to You and uphold us when our strength fails. Amen.

Connie Kuykendall is a member of the Far West End church in Virginia.

Crucified With Christ

"I am crucified with Christ: nevertheless I live; yet not I, but Christ liveth in me: and the life which I now live in the flesh I live by the faith of the Son of God, who loved me, and gave Himself for me" (Gal. 2:20, KJV).

This text comes alive as I reflect on my past and present Christian experience. Paul experienced many challenges in sharing the gospel (2 Cor. 11:24–30). Although not suffering physically like Paul, I gave up my military career to serve Christ. My plan was to retire after two decades and go on to another career and then retire from within the public sector of the same field of service. I could have had two pensions and been financially set for life. At the time, I thought I was really living Galatians 2:20. That was nearly 29 years ago.

But God had other plans. I got married and had four wonderful children, followed by six grandchildren. I have been involved in a pastoral role for 18 years, five as a part-time pastor/construction worker, and the last 13 full time in West Virginia.

I realize there was, and is, more crucifying that needs to be done in my life. And I am thankful that I can choose to place myself in Jesus' hands each day and be crucified with Him. The pain of this life, although present at times, is so much easier to deal with than His pain on Calvary for me.

I also realize that whatever I go through in my flesh is because Jesus is allowing me to experience challenges for my best good. He wants me to someday be like Him (1 John 3:2).

God, thank You for leading my life. May I be crucified daily with Christ. Amen.

James Volpe is the pastor of the Beckley and Bluefield churches in West Virginia.

'Not That State'

"A man's heart plans his way, but the Lord directs his steps"
(Prov. 16:9, NKJV).

Years ago, I started college in Alabama. The degree I chose forced me to transfer to a sister school in California for nine months. An East Coast native, I told God that I would never end up this far away from home again.

A few years later, I was working in Massachusetts, feeling quite at home. My then girlfriend was in graduate school in Maryland. The only way we could plan for our future together, without disrupting what she had started, was to transfer to a school in California. I couldn't believe that I was willing to return to the place that had me homesick.

As they say, man plans, and God laughs. Much like Moses who left Egypt, thinking he would live out his life in Midian, I had never thought that I would see that land ever again. Moses reluctantly went to Egypt; with much prayer, we decided that transferring to California was the right move for us too. We got married, and, one month later, moved across the country.

That move produced five fruitful years, which springboarded our careers and strengthened our faith. We left the state with a positive new outlook and plans to make regular visits. If I had remained stubborn about what I thought I knew about that location, my professional and spiritual growth would not have flourished. I had to admit that God knew best.

Lord, help us to always remember that when we think we know where to go, You ultimately have a better destination in mind. Amen.

Spendy Pierre-Louis is a member of the First Church of Montclair in New Jersey.

Metamorphosis

"All of us who ... can see and reflect the glory of the Lord. And the Lord ... makes us more and more like Him as we are changed into His glorious image" (2 Cor. 3:18, NLT).

Have you witnessed a butterfly leaving its chrysalis? The cycle goes from a tiny egg to a caterpillar moving around and eating leaves, followed by the chrysalis phase, where other changes take place. Finally, the adult butterfly emerges from its cocoon. Scientists call this process metamorphosis, meaning transformation—a significant change in looks and character.

The Bible also tell us about a "spiritual metamorphosis." *Metamorphoô*, a verb not a noun, appears four times in the King James Version, translated twice as "transfigured" and one time each as "transformed" and "changed."

Jesus was transfigured before His disciples (Matthew 17:2; Mark 9:2). His divinity shined through His humanity! We are admonished: "Don't copy the behavior and customs of this world, but let God transform you into a new person by changing the way you think" (Rom. 12:2, NLT). This is a divine command. Our role is passive by allowing God to transform us.

Finally, we can attain this spiritual metamorphosis by beholding Jesus through His Word, as is written in 2 Corinthians 3:18.

Ellen White says, "It is a law both of the intellectual and the spiritual nature that by beholding we become changed" (*The Great Controversy*, p. 555).

In another one of her writings, she says, "Through close study and earnest contemplation of the character of Christ, His image is reflected in our own lives" (*From the Heart*, p. 321).

God, let us behold Jesus! Amen.

Preston G. Monterrey-Clark is the district pastor of the Chambersburg, Needmore and Waynesboro churches in Pennsylvania.

Waiting and Anticipating!

"But I do not want you to be ignorant, brethren, concerning those who have fallen asleep. ... For if we believe that Jesus died and rose again, even so God will bring with Him those who sleep in Jesus. For this we say to you by the word of the Lord, that we who are alive and remain until the coming of the Lord will by no means precede those who are asleep. For the Lord Himself will descend from heaven with a shout, with the voice of an archangel, and with the trumpet of God. And the dead in Christ will rise first. Then we who are alive and remain shall be caught up together with them in the clouds to meet the Lord in the air. And thus we shall always be with the Lord. Therefore comfort one another with these words" (1 Thess. 4:13–18, NKJV).

This passage tells me that at Jesus' second coming, our Lord will awake the righteous dead, and, together with the righteous living, take them up to heaven with Him. This culminating moment will not be a quiet one. It will be extremely loud, with angels shouting and blasting their trumpets. All in heaven and on earth will hear and know that Jesus reigns on high!

I am anticipating that wonderful day! Aren't you?

God, I pray for Jesus' soon return, and that I, my loved ones and all who are willing to accept Him will be ready to leave this earth when we hear the shout! Amen.

Elsie Poorbaugh is a member of the Indiana church in Pennsylvania.